SMALL WARS

SMALL WARS

An Insider's Guide to Resolving Faith Community Conflicts

Darrell Puls

CASCADE *Books* • Eugene, Oregon

SMALL WARS

An Insider's Guide to Resolving Faith Community Conflicts

Cascade Books
An Imprint of Wipf and Stock Publishers
199 W. 8th Ave., Suite 3
Eugene, OR 97401

www.wipfandstock.com

PAPERBACK ISBN: 979-8-3852-4611-3
HARDCOVER ISBN: 979-8-3852-4612-0
EBOOK ISBN: 979-8-3852-4613-7

Cataloguing-in-Publication data:

Names: Puls, Darrell, author.

Title: Small wars : an insider's guide to resolving faith community conflicts / Darrell Puls.

Description: Eugene, OR: Cascade Books, 2026 | Includes bibliographical references.

Identifiers: ISBN 979-8-3852-4611-3 (paperback) | ISBN 979-8-3852-4612-0 (hardcover) | ISBN 979-8-3852-4613-7 (ebook)

Subjects: LCSH: Church controversies. | Change—Religious aspects—Christianity. | Conflict management—Religious aspects—Christianity.

Classification: BV652.9 P78 2026 (print) | BV652.9 (ebook)

Contents

Prelude 1

1 Small Town, Big Fight 5

2 The Challenge of Church Conflict 17

3 Personal Preparation: The Naming of Parts 28

4 Ignition: From Votive Candles to Flamethrowers 42

5 The Wounded Healer 59

6 In the Beginning . . . Practicalities 67

7 Afflicted: When the Pastor Is the Problem 74

8 What Do You Do with a Moral Failure? 90

9 The Hidden Challenges of Leader Transitions 99

10 Easing Transitions: Succession Planning 108

11 Distinctive Characteristics of Faith Community Disputes 119

12 The Big Tent 133

13 Facilitating Change 140

14 Forgiveness and Reconciliation 156

15 Forgiveness Examined: Turning 163

16 Forgiveness: Remembering 175

17 Forgiveness: Understanding 190

18 Forgiveness: Healing 210

19 Ending with A New Beginning 218

Appendix 1 The Tasks of the Transition Process 221

References 227

Prelude

THIS BOOK IS THE result of almost fifty years of working directly with human conflicts in the form of divorces, lawsuits, internal organizational fights, and battles between organizations. Venues have included families, schools, colleges, unions, medical practice, medical schools, hospitals, luxury hotels, the nuclear industry, and religious and secular organizations. Roles have included consultant, mediator, facilitator, negotiator, advocate, and interventionist. I have concentrated on faith community conflicts since 1998.

This is what I have learned.

Most books on church or faith community conflicts focus on the "identified problem" and expend the rest of their energy on the "solution." For example, an author may declare the problem to be poor communication and the solution as deep listening. Fair enough. Both are almost always part of the problem and part of a solution. But . . . there is always more going on than is visible to the casual observer. The most common practice is conflict management, where the goal is a settlement agreement that parties "can live with," meaning a balanced but continuing tension is written into a settlement agreement. Conflict management is occasionally replaced by conflict resolution, where the foundations of the fight are resolved and injured relationships are reconciled.

The word *settled* and the concept of settlement are problems in themselves. Both the word and concept are borrowed from law practice and labor relations. Both cases refer to a lawsuit's negotiated conclusion (settlement), contract negotiation, or grievance procedure. In conflict management, a settlement means finding a way around the heart of the conflict without resolving the emotional mess at the center. Left untouched are the emotional and relational wounds that will continue to fester and erupt at inopportune times.

We must go deeper. The goal in conflict interventions must be reconciliation, that is, the restoration of ruptured relationships. If the church is to be the light of the world, it must be healthy and free of infection.

The optimists among us argue that conflict can be used to sharpen the mission of the church and cement relationships. True enough, but we tend to approach conflict as a negative to be ended as soon and painlessly as possible. Conflict is threatening because we know it can go off in any direction without warning, and so we approach it with fear and hesitation. It is uncomfortable, and we prefer comfort. If you have ever been the focus of accusations, you know the defensive rage and crushing desperation for vindication. Now, increase your negative emotions to include the hundreds of people affected directly and peripherally by toxic fights in an afflicted faith community, and you will find a flowing cataract of venom.

The most efficient way of seriously damaging or destroying any organization is from the inside. In my experience, churches are particularly vulnerable to internal conflicts. The reasons are relatively simple to understand: we expect our faith communities to be havens of peace, acceptance, and tranquility in the middle of a hostile world. We expect our churches to be quiet havens away from the tumult of secular strife. But what we expect and what we find are too often opposites. We somehow expect our churches to be "different" in an undefined sense from what we expect from our other communities.

I have not seen or heard of a conflict that did not result in damaged relationships. But . . . it is possible to repair the damage and heal the ruptured relationships. Unfortunately, very few pastors or lay leaders understand the dynamics they face and usually have little to no training in conflict resolution. This book is my attempt to change this reality by redirecting anger and pain into a healing force. In that sense, it is written for everyone interested in conflict resolution in general and keeping their church healthy.

Every conflict is unique, with complexities and subtleties that must be considered when finding an intervention process. What is effective in one situation may be ineffective in another, meaning it is essential to have multiple approaches available. There are no panaceas or fixed, sequential steps that can be applied successfully in every situation. However, there are universal undercurrents in these conflicts that, once found and understood, will give the reader effective and adaptable options that most people know little about.

As I said at the outset, most books on church conflict argue for a single approach to analyze conflict dynamics and devise interventions. They promote family systems theory, altering communication patterns, active listening, guided dialogues, etc. All of these are useful, but I liken the single-avenue approach to a dessert disaster years ago. My aunt had brought a homemade lemon meringue pie to an extended family dinner. It was beautiful . . . but she had forgotten to add the sugar. The pie was inedible. Pushing the food analogy further, every conflict I have worked with was like a complex stew made with varying ingredients, spices, textures, and cooking styles, resulting in a wide variety of flavors.

This book attempts to create a more holistic approach to resolving faith community fights. It tries to fill in the blanks that other approaches do not acknowledge, thus giving anyone who attempts to intervene a larger selection of tested and effective resolution models.

While much of this book will focus on faith communities, the principles and practices it describes almost universally apply to any organizational fight. The reader should choose the most useful processes based on the situation, experience, and comfort level. Even if you never find yourself standing in the middle of a church fight, what you learn here will be useful at work and at home.

This book is intended for anyone interested in peacemaking. Some sections are highly detailed, while others are more generalized. The detailed sections serve as road maps to specific destinations and include the detours, roadblocks, and other challenges we may face on the path to peace. These are useful in unfamiliar territory, such as leading a group from anger and pain to forgiveness and freedom. The more generalized sections are intended to familiarize the reader with the underlying dynamics of group conflicts and how they may be resolved.

Surprisingly, almost anyone can become a practical peacemaker without expensive, specialized training. Even introverts like me! More on that in chapter 1.

I hope and pray that every reader will find what they need in these pages to understand the dynamics of faith community conflicts and use what they find to become safe guides to peace.

1

Small Town, Big Fight

Blessed are the peacemakers, for they shall be called the children of God.

JESUS OF NAZARETH (MATTHEW 5:9)

IT WAS LATE WINTER when I received a call from a denominational leader I had worked for previously. He asked me to travel from my home in Washington State to Indiana to mediate a church conflict. Intrigued, I asked for details.

A small church in rural northern Indiana was disintegrating. Pastor Pete had alienated his elders and many church members through his increasingly dictatorial ways. Over time, the board members became increasingly irritated by his high-handed ways, and board meetings became increasingly contentious. He expected the Board of Elders to approve whatever he brought to them without meaningful input or even discussion. Then they learned that he had given his sister $7,000 from the pastor's discretionary fund to help pay her bills. Jim, the board president, confronted Pastor Pete, and tempers flared. Jim roared, "That money is for church members, not your sister, who lives in Michigan!" Pastor Pete countered by arguing that the word "discretionary" meant he was the sole judge of who the money went to. In other words, he could use it however he wished, and they could not challenge him.

Pastor Pete was smug, and the board members were furious.

There had been a slow downward spiral in church attendance and financial support. Over time, the congregation had dwindled by about 25 percent under Pastor Pete, and the finances had become severely stretched. Pastor Pete blamed the losses on everything and everyone but himself, as he considered himself a superior speaker and teacher, and a gift to this small church.

The elders disagreed. They might be farmers, but they were intelligent men. They had been reluctant to go to the congregation with their concerns as they wanted to appear supportive. Now, they were hampered as Pastor Pete had rejected their every suggestion. Instead, Pete declared himself as "God's anointed" and would follow God's lead, not theirs. The church was meant to be a theocracy, not a democracy, and they were bound to follow him as God's personal representative, not vice versa.

However, Pastor Pete presented the board with his resignation and announced that he would retire one year from the current date. The board members conferred among themselves and saw an opportunity. They accepted his resignation on the spot, effective immediately.

Pastor Pete fought back, but the elders were adamant—he was no longer on the payroll and needed to clean out his office. He did before they could change the locks—and took decades of church birth, baptism, marriage, and death records with him. He would give them back, he said, when they paid him $60,000 in early retirement pay. The elders refused and threatened to file criminal charges for theft against him for taking the church records. A few days later, the entire elder board was served with summonses in a lawsuit against the church as a whole and each elder individually for unlawful and retaliatory severance of employment—even though Indiana is a "right to hire" state where employers do not need reasons to fire employees unless a written contract is in place that requires some form of due process. That was not the case here.

The elders responded by calling the police and filing criminal charges for theft of church property and possession of the stolen property.

My friend said that both sides had agreed to mediation and sheepishly asked if I would be the mediator for this hot mess, with the denomination paying my fees and expenses. I agreed and flew east even though both sides' attorneys told me this matter would never be settled short of a trial before a jury. I had spoken privately at length with the elders and Pastor Pete and had a different idea.

We met on a gray Saturday morning in the neutral ground of the town library meeting room. Three angry elders were present to represent the church, and Pastor Pete represented himself with his wife and a "witness" also present. The lawyers had agreed it would be best if they were not there.

Pastor Pete immediately tried to ingratiate himself with me by declaring how wonderful it was that a man of my godliness and vast experience would come to this little town in Indiana to help them. He was sure that this could be settled quickly under my wise guidance. I noticed that his wife kept her eyes averted and sat motionless. She reminded me of a cornered mouse frozen before a cat. Pastor Pete answered when I asked her a few questions. The witness seemed bored and uninterested.

Pastor Pete declared that he would settle everything for $75,000, withdrawal of the criminal charges, and a letter describing his sterling record of service to the church to be read to the entire congregation. The board's response was simple and short: "No!"

A short time later, I split the parties and met with each side privately to avoid further escalation of tempers.

The board members were livid at Pete's demands. He knew that they did not have $75,000, they fumed. What little money they did have had gone into paying attorney fees to defend against Pete's ridiculous lawsuit. They were adamant: he would not get a penny, and there was no way they would ever write a letter of praise for him, especially since he had recently started a new church and lured away a third of the remaining congregants. Thanks to Pastor Pete, the church was now on the brink of collapse.

Pastor Pete seemed genuinely surprised when I told him this news a few minutes later. He had assumed the church attorney was working for free! However, he still wanted the money and letter of recommendation.

It took a few hours and several trips back and forth between them, but a settlement agreement was reached, written, and signed late in the afternoon. A board member wrote a personal check to Pete for $500, and they wrote a tepid letter of recommendation. Pastor Pete retrieved the church records from his car and turned them over. The lawsuit and criminal charges were to be withdrawn "with prejudice," meaning they could not be refiled. Neither side was interested in reconciling their relationships.

My phone rang the following day as I drove to the airport for a commuter flight to Chicago. It was Pastor Pete's attorney. He could hardly believe that a settlement had been reached and wanted to know how I had managed to find it. He wanted to hire me as the mediator for another lawsuit with much more at stake. I was flattered but politely declined while suggesting that there were excellent mediators in the area.

I admit that this example is unusual with its lawsuits and criminal charges, but it also shows the lengths people sometimes go to force their interests—even "church people." And it certainly was interesting.

I love conflict—as long as it's not mine! I have immersed myself in organizational conflicts since 1976. My early roles included union contract negotiator, arbitration advocate, community mediator, and grievance investigator. The functions morphed over time until I was in private practice as an organizational conflict analyst, interventionist, trainer, and conference speaker. Some of my clients were high-tech corporations, schools and colleges, nurses and physicians, medical schools, luxury hotels, religious denominations, and individual churches.

My heart, though, is with faith communities, regardless of denomination.

Every organization, religious or secular, will experience internal conflicts. No organization is exempt, not even community conflict resolution programs (I once was asked to intervene in a battle between staff and volunteer mediators in a community dispute resolution center). There will be conflicts between employees, managers, professional staff, boards, administrators, and members. The results of these conflicts include lost productivity, increased use of sick leave, higher job turnover rates, higher employee replacement costs, and even sabotage, altogether costing billions of dollars every year.

Having experienced so many secular and faith community conflicts, I am comfortable saying that church conflicts are distinct from those of secular organizations. They are more relational, do more long-lasting psychological and spiritual damage, and sometimes damage the church so severely that it disintegrates. No church is immune. A church in southwest Michigan that had thrived for over 100 years closed its doors a few years ago after several attempts at mediating an internal fight did not resolve their issues.

These conflicts are much more common than most people realize. Research done over more than twenty years found that one in five churches was experiencing internal conflict at any given time.[1]

1. The 14,000-congregation "Faith Communities Today" (FACT) study in 2015 found that 75 percent of congregations have experienced conflict in the past, 20 percent at any one time. Sixty percent of congregations had some kind of conflict during the past five years. A 2001 Hartford Institute study discovered that 79 percent had a conflict in the past five years. The National Congregation Study of 2007 found that 40 percent of congregations had conflict over a four-year period. In 1996, *The Lutheran* magazine shared that between 40 to 50 percent of ELCA congregations reported serious internal

Private corporations often have written action plans for conflict eruptions. Churches, in general, do not. Churches also tend to mismanage conflict at far higher rates than private corporations and with fewer resources. Pastors, staff, and leaders are generally unequipped to guide a church through internal clashes. In many cases, the conflict will not grow to destructive levels, but in many others, the conflict will threaten the very existence of the church. Research findings show a 75 percent chance that your church is in danger of being among those experiencing corrosive conflict in the next five years.[2] When conflicts grow beyond the irritation stage and move into open positional fighting, the results are uniformly grim: lost members, split congregations, vanishing revenues, broken spirituality, and even complete destruction.

Our churches and various faith communities like to think that they are somehow immune, but we are alike even in our denial of the realities in which we exist. As Gregg Ten Elshof writes, "In self-deception, I am both the deceived and the deceiver."[3] North American churches, corporations, businesses, and even charitable non-profits exist in a hostile competitive environment. While the circumstances of church fights are like those found in corporate meltdowns, and the root causes and human dynamics are mostly the same, the results tend to be more severe in faith communities.

Churches habitually ignore the first flames of conflict as the first line of defense. It may be that the minister is so charismatic that people ignore her crumbling feet of clay. Or the congregation may have been told it is unique and believes it, which makes them somehow feel immune from the ways and wiles of those who foment trouble at every turn—faith communities tend to attract the mentally unstable, and with good reason. "[H]igher levels of religiousness have been associated with greater feelings of empowerment and self-efficacy among patients with serious mental illness."[4] Pastors in multiple denominations have told me they have little to no training in coping with conflict dynamics or behaviors—few seminaries teach it. Those who did may eliminate much of their coursework. The seminary where I earned my doctoral degree has drastically cut the program and now offers only one graduate-level course in conflict management.

---

conflict.

2. Dudley, "Conflict."

3. Ten Elshof, *I Told Me So*, 25.

4. Pargament and Lomax, "Understanding and Addressing Religion."

Sometimes, a minister may be so bloated with self-pride that they evoke an aura of invincibility, spiritual and otherwise. I recall the minister of a large church heatedly lecturing me on how a congregation such as his, which he described as totally committed to living as a Christ-centered, close-knit community, would never have a serious conflict. He said with great authority that they were too mature, loving, and dedicated to carrying the gospel message to the community to engage in such childish behaviors. That was something that happened elsewhere because the minister was not correctly leading. While he did not say it, his message was clear: they had not had serious conflict in this church because of his leadership; therefore, they would not have serious strife for as long as he was their pastor.

Well, he was wrong. A major fight broke out in less than a year, and he quickly became the focal point. Within a few months, broken and bitter, he resigned. The congregation split and then disintegrated. The church campus was eventually sold to the local school district and renovated into an alternative high school.

The American "ideal" of individuals as independent free agents casts a shadow over the reality that we are all interdependent and rely on each other for almost everything, even our survival. The idea of independent free agency conflicts with our interdependence in how we think and act toward one another. I would go so far as to call it a blissful delusion.

The apostle Paul coined the term "body of Christ" 2,000 years ago, and he was more exact than he might have realized. The Christian church is the body of Christ, and all the churches within it are its various parts. According to recent research, any organization, including faith communities, can take on the characteristics of sentient, aware entities: living, thinking, and reactive beings.[5] People are the cells of the body and need each other to survive, let alone thrive in a hostile environment. Unfortunately, the American "ideal" of the independent individual fights against the reality of interdependence. Severing that connection, or refusing to engage it in the first place, results in organizational isolation and eventual stagnation and death. C. Otto Scharmer makes a compelling case for "presencing."

> Central to Theory U is the concept of "Presencing," a term coined by Scharmer that combines "presence" and "sensing." Inspired by theater, Presencing invites leaders to embody their

5. Scharmer, *Theory U.*

> future selves, anticipating and shaping emerging futures rather than reacting to past events. The power of presencing lies in its ability to help us access a deeper source of wisdom and creativity. By suspending our habitual ways of thinking and being, we can tap into our authentic selves and connect with the emerging future. This, in turn, allows us to develop innovative solutions that align with the needs of our communities and the world. [6]

Congregational leaders can easily learn how conflicts start and how quickly they can escalate from flickering flames to an inferno. I find it tragic that my services are needed anywhere, but I have been in places where hatred and anger have replaced peace and support. I have seen the pain and personal suffering of those within them and the damage these fights cause at all levels. I have been sprayed with the vitriol of fury and revenge disguised under the banners of righteous anger and cleansing of the church. I have sat with broken pastors as they wept away the last vestiges of ministries that had started with promise and hope. I have slogged through the stinking trenches of hidden motives and vicious attacks where people who once called each other brother or sister and friend now look to hurt each other through any means available. And I have cried with others and alone over the pain and trouble we inflict on each other. The gospel message of forgiveness and grace takes the biggest hit, for we readily and publicly sacrifice it on the altar of self-righteous anger.

Being a peacemaker is not a title or position so much as it is a way of life. I did not seek it out; instead, it relentlessly called me out of the secular, corporate world. Though not nearly enough of us, others like me search for invisible pockets of hatred under thin veneers of rationality, high-sounding words, and even Scripture. A peacemaker's goal is to help those trapped within the toxic pool of contempt release their fear and pain into the healing embrace of forgiveness, mercy, and reconciliation.

The solutions to secular organizational conflicts are more straightforward to name, analyze, and implement than those for church conflicts. While not diminishing the destructiveness of workplace fights, I feel safe in saying that faith community conflicts cause more difficult-to-repair damage and wounds that are deeper and slower to heal than workplace fights. I believe that church conflicts do far more damage to the people in them than the conflicts they experience at work.

Everyone who has worked in any size of secular organization for more than a few months has experienced the intrigues, power plays, and

6. Global Leaders Institute, "Unlocking Leadership Potential."

office politics that are constantly working. We expect it. We do not expect it in our churches, but it is there.

There are proven and reliable ways to help wounded faith communities sort through the wreckage and find a new start with the same people who were there before the fight and were enemies throughout. The peacemaker becomes a conduit for the Holy Spirit to bring them back together.

A large part of the challenge is this reality: Whether naïve or not, we do not expect to find the same levels of intrigue, deception, manipulation, unforgiveness, and verbal violence in our churches as we do at work and in the larger community. We come to our faith communities with firmly held expectations of peace, love, benevolence, transparency, and forgiveness. We tend to ignore tension when we find it, writing it off as a misinterpretation of better motives, or we quickly run to another church. In other words, we expect our churches to be havens of harmony. They often are when all is well, but they shed the mantle of peace when conflicts escalate beyond a certain point; they then put on a cloak of distrust, anger, and retribution. It seems so out of place at first that we deny what we are experiencing, but there comes a point where it crosses over from the clash of contrary expectations to the stark reality of hot words and cold-blooded attacks.[7] Various groups form as the conflict spreads through the congregation, to the confusion of those who are not in one of them. They begin to experience what in psychology is called cognitive dissonance, which is the mental and emotional confusion we experience when what happens is the opposite of what we expect.

The beginnings of conflict are often barely visible and are triggered by small things. The following story is true.

THE SHRUB

Maryann planted a memorial shrub at First Church shortly after her husband of forty-three years, John, died of cancer. She faithfully watered and pruned the shrub herself for many years. Eventually, though, she became too frail to continue looking after it. She wrote a letter to the church board asking that someone else take over her duties. She intended for someone who had known and cared for John to be appointed. Instead, the board wrote back that the responsibilities would be given to

7. Scott-Kakures, "Unsettling Questions."

the custodian. Maryann intensely disliked the custodian because he was a semi-recovered alcoholic who had been drunk on duty and had chopped down some other shrubs. After all, they were in his way when mowing the lawn. Maryann protested but was told by an elder that the church did not have the resources for someone else to do the work.

Maryann and John had been chartering members of First Church when it was founded forty years before and she still had many friends in the small congregation. She went to them, and they joined her in protest to the elder board. They followed the correct procedures and addressed the board politely. Still, the board somewhat angrily rejected their arguments, which were interpreted as demands (correctly) and a power display designed to force them to change their minds (also correct). What was not obvious was that one board member and two of Maryann's supporters had been increasingly hostile toward one another over a bad business deal. No one saw the underlying emotional dynamics igniting an unquenchable fire that would eventually consume them all.

Maryann changed her tactics and circulated, then presented a petition to recall the entire board. The primary people pushing Maryann were the same two in a business conflict with Clarence, a board member. They saw this as an opportunity to even the score and get rid of Clarence, so already, the conflict had grown and taken on new, external grievances. The congregation began taking sides between "poor, sweet Maryann" and those "righteous men unfairly under attack"—and whom Maryann's supporters (primarily women) termed "boorish, insensitive pigs."

Where was the minister in all this? Unfortunately, they had called as their pastor a scholarly and shy "Mr. Rogers"-type personality who avoided all conflicts and was conspicuous by his absence in this situation. He asked everyone to pray but had no clue how to get angry people talking to each other civilly. Since the minister would not lead, others stepped into the ring. More old grievances were added, the fight grew in intensity, and people began heading for the exits.

The conflict became more chaotic as it intensified and new issues were added. The congregation began to split into hostile camps and splinter into subgroups, but not all were visible. Each identifiable group claimed the scriptural high ground by selectively choosing Bible verses with little regard to their context and quoting them to advance why they were holy and right while their opponents were misguided and wrong. Eventually, they started describing each other in guarded terms of evil. As the conflict grew, the congregation splintered even more, and claims of righteousness defending against evil became more strident and widely applied. The stream of those leaving grew from a trickle into a flood, resulting in a drastic reduction of funds. With the church now in financial crisis, they called the denomination, which called me.

Since the church was close to home, I hand-picked a team of peacemakers to work with me. I had trained them all so each person knew their role in the intervention. We were there the following weekend.

The greeting was not encouraging. Some were friendly, but many were suspicious and engaged with us tentatively to learn what our "agenda" might be. We expected to be wooed and manipulated as the various factions tried to win us over to their points of view and to declare their perspective "right" and all others "wrong." Still, the outright hostility from some was unexpected. I now know that these reactions are normal and self-protective. Rumors were circulating that we were being paid under the table by a significant donor to ensure certain outcomes. While this was false, it also reflected their fear of unknown outsiders, of being judged, and of having little to no control any longer.

We began with a plenary session with everyone in the same room to assure them of our neutrality and explain the process we would use. My team members watched the body language of those in attendance as I spoke. What they saw could have been more encouraging. Though not said, the message from many was that they had given up on finding a reasonable and acceptable settlement and instead were focused on winning it all. In contrast, others had abdicated any sense of responsibility and took part more out of curiosity than any expectation of resolution and reconciliation.

We split them into five mixed groups. Each team member would lead a group discussion to learn what they were fighting about before moving on to a much deeper conversation about their pain, sadness, frustration, and emotional and physical symptoms. This process is intense and emotionally exhausting, but nothing can happen without it, as their pain and misery are the entry points to relational healing.

Three groups were described to us during first contact: two were hostile to each other, and one was neutral. We discovered two more that were far more dangerous. The first newly discovered group ran like a submarine, invisible but carefully hunting vulnerable members. Using internet masking services, they would fire off anonymous emails full of innuendo and accusations, to which their victim could not respond as the senders covered their identities and there was no return address. The second and more dangerous group was not as careful. It came out accidentally that there was a private, password-protected internet forum where selected people would discuss others in the congregation in derogatory and even brutal terms. The people who had set up the forum had neglected one crucial thing: they did not disguise the names of the participants. Then somebody leaked the password. The rage of seeing one's name slandered found a convenient target: the people who wrote them. The attacks were open, swift, and vicious. We were fortunate to de-escalate the situation from pending violence to smoldering rage.

This was when it became clear that this small congregation had passed the point of no return. Except for a small minority, they were not interested in coming together to let us help them sort through their differences. With destruction seeming inevitable, some groups decided to ensure that all would perish. They succeeded. The minister left, the board resigned, and giving stopped—and First Church is now a combination bed and breakfast and wedding venue.

By the time it ended, few people remembered what triggered the brawl. It seems ridiculous that such a minor issue as the care of a memorial shrub could start this deadly fight. Well, it wasn't a minor issue for Maryann. To the board, it was a matter of finances, getting the job done, and authority. To Maryann, it was about the memory of and respect for her John and the fear that what meant so much to her would mean nothing to the custodian. In short, the shrub, though having little extrinsic value, held tremendous intrinsic worth in what it stood for—a living reminder of the man who was the love of Maryann's life.

In other words, the fight was not about a shrub. It was about memory, practicality, revenge, and respect.

What do congregations fight over? Anything, if by fighting over something you mean what they say the fight is about. We will call that the "identified problem." It comes from the same concept used in mental health interventions: the "identified patient" is the one in the family whom the others insist is the problem, but the actual patient is the family itself as it operates in its dysfunction. Church fights I have worked with were said to originate in who selected the napkins for the Sunday school picnic, the color and pattern of new carpet, the color of paint in the fellowship hall, power struggles between boards of deacons and elders, an elder's wife passed over for Sunday school superintendent, the length of the minister's vacation, the minister's benefits package, a minister who did not want to live in the church-owned parsonage, how a facilities expansion contract was awarded, changes in the style of music, the content and style of preaching—and money, such as how the minister used the minister's discretionary fund (noted at the beginning of this chapter). Other church fights had similar triggers.

But . . . none of the identified issues were at the core of any of the problems. They may be what the fight circles, but the reality in any conflict quickly changes from the identified problem to how the participants hurt, betray, and disrespect each other through their interactions. What may have started as a tense conversation escalates over time into insults, yelling, and threats. As people feel less heard and respected, they respond with ever-increasing intensity. The battles often have little to no connection to what they argue over. Right or wrong, every fight was about their indignation at how they felt they were disrespected.

When our first attempts to resolve a disagreement fail, and we feel denigrated, or we believe the problem is a significant issue while others do not, we tend to speak a bit louder and enunciate more clearly. As the exchange goes on, voices continue to get louder and louder. The turning point is often when someone is accused of having hidden motives or is grabbing for the power to dictate. When boiled down to their essence, and though there are always other elements, the fights were about power, respect, trust, betrayal, and hurt feelings.

This book is designed to provide the reader with practical and tested models to assess the level of a conflict, select the most effective tools, and make an effective intervention if that is what they choose to do. It does not stop where most books on faith community conflict interventions stop, which is the formal, written settlement agreement. Why? The fight is not over until the wounds are healed through authentic forgiveness and reconciliation, which is something conventional conflict management practices rarely approach.

One last thing before we get into the fray. Many people ask me how I can go into these situations and deal with such intense anger and pain without being overwhelmed. The answer is deceptively simple: It's not my fight. I have no stake in the outcome. Their emotions do not become mine. The peacemaker stands for the message of hope and guides them out of the quagmire and back onto the high moral ground. Our job is not to judge or "pin the sin" on anyone, for there is enough sin to go around. Our job is to embody the good news of the gospel message of unity, forgiveness, and reconciliation.

2

The Challenge of Church Conflict

Peace is not the absence of conflict;
it is the ability to handle conflict peacefully.

~Ronald Reagan

In the New Testament Gospel of John, we find Jesus praying these words: "Sanctify them in the truth; your word is truth. As you have sent me into the world, so I have sent them into the world . . . The glory you have given me I have given them, *so that they may be one as we are one.*" (John 17:17, 18, 22 NIV)

Jesus prayed for unity in the fledgling church he was leaving behind, for he knew the hostile landscape it would face and how easily we are seduced by power and prestige. Christians are called to be of one heart, and the church is called to be the body of Christ, a living, sentient being where all are connected in the flow of life. That is not to say we must always agree, but we must adopt ways to disagree agreeably. Sometimes these disagreements have turned into wars. In America, the first major split was between northern Baptists and southern Baptists over slavery and led to the Civil War. The church has splintered into thousands of pieces, with each piece seeing itself as superior to the others. And we have added a relatively new source of church conflicts that is as destructive to the gospel as a cobra's bite is to human flesh.

It is the Christian nationalist movement. "Christian Nationalism's singular goal is to combine religious and political power, which scholars agree likely results in 'religiously motivated genocide.' As Christian nationalism gains power, the elimination of liberal democracy and violence toward opposing groups will likely increase."[1] While claiming to follow Christ, its ideology reverses what Jesus commanded: We're number one (forget your neighbor), close the borders, lie continuously, refuse access to medical care, take away food assistance from the hungry, ignore the poor. . . and create an authoritarian rule in place of messy democracy.

The movement is based on the belief that America was ordained by God as a Christian nation, but Christians are being shut out of the political arena. It has effectively used tried-and-true tactics of shaping the argument by attacking: We are holy and right because we believe in the Bible and follow Jesus, and those who oppose us are satanic. The primary goal is to impose their beliefs on the entire country, all in the name of Jesus.

Under the command to love your neighbor every bit as much as you love yourself, Jesus told his followers to feed the hungry, care for the sick, give to all who ask, visit those in jail, welcome the foreigner as a member of your own family, clothe the naked—the Christian nationalist agenda includes closing the borders, deporting the foreigners, taking away food aid, eliminating social and medical support programs, controlling colleges and universities, censorship, and so on, all in the name of Jesus. The result? Churches are erupting in emotional, take-no-prisoners fights, or quietly acquiescing in much the same way as churches surrendered to Nazi "theology" in Germany.

I am not a fatalist, but I was trained as a police hostage negotiator in the mid-1990s, and there is bad news for the peacemaker: You cannot negotiate with someone whose only goal is to take control by sweeping all others away.[2] Christian nationalist intentions are not negotiable.

But what can we do with disagreements that aren't intractable? Often, even in these situations, we don't disagree agreeably—we disagree sharply, belittle the opinions of others, and find ourselves in conflict with friends. They resist and verbally push back harder than they felt pushed. It's a revolving thing that lives on anger and escalates with each exchange. In frustration, we seek out friends and, knowingly or not, enlist them in our defense. So does the other side. Before long, we will have groups facing off against each other. We do not want blame, so we point at others

1. White Jr., "Theology of Control."

2. See Puls, "Should We Negotiate with Terrorists—A Counterpoint." See also Saiya and Manchanda, "Christian Nationalism and Violence"; and Graves-Fitzsimmons and Siddiqi, "Christian Nationalism."

and try to blame them while hiding the dirt staining our hands. That is how conflict grows. As we will see, everyone is part of it.

Enter the peacemaker (Matt 7:9).

Peacemaking is my calling and passion. Few things call me more strongly than a congregation in pain.

Church conflicts are not new. In the New Testament book of Acts, chapter 6, we read of complaints that Greek widows were not being included in food distribution. The problem was resolved by choosing seven men, including several from the complaining group, to oversee the distribution. In addition, most of the apostle Paul's letters to the churches deal with internal arguments and conflicts. When two or more are gathered, they will eventually argue.

Conflicts in religious settings always raise questions of morality, right and wrong, and injury that must be healed. In almost every situation, each side in the conflict tries to claim the moral high ground of being "right," usually by accentuating its virtues while disparaging the opposition. How the injuries from these conflicts are addressed can take many forms. In most cases, the underlying issues at the very core of the conflict are not what the participants name or fight about. The seeds of injury are found in disrespect, personal affronts, and broken trust.

Locating the poisoned seeds takes hard work and time, something I have discovered that few ministers or congregations have the skills or patience to do. Among the highest-ranked complaints of pastors against their seminaries and training organizations is that they did not receive any training in conflict management beyond prayer or a book to read. Consequently, they are no better equipped to effectively guide their conflicted congregants to a peaceful resolution than someone from off the street. In fact, it's getting worse:

- In 2015, just 27 percent of pastors said they wished they'd been better prepared to handle conflict. In 2020, that number shot up to 40 percent.
- In 2015, 20 percent of pastors wished they were better prepared to delegate and train others. In 2020, 41 percent said the same.
- In 2015, 16 percent of pastors wished they were better prepared to navigate church politics. By 2020, 36 percent of pastors said the same.[3]

3. Barna Research, "What Pastors Wish."

Like everywhere else in our short-attention-span society, we look to the most superficial fixes and hope for the best. Then, we create more rules, policies, and procedures rather than generate meaningful communication, and the acclaimed Golden Rule gathers dust on a closet shelf. As Helen Simonson writes in *Major Pettigrew's Last Stand*, "Only sometimes when we pick and choose among the rules, we discover later that we have set aside something precious in the process."[4] She has a point. The more we rely on rules, the less we listen to one another; the result is that we find ourselves in places where rules govern everything, no one communicates, and relationships are fragile because they are not built on solid foundations of trust and open communication.

Most churches are legally incorporated entities. State laws require them to file articles of incorporation and bylaws, and they almost always have more policies and procedures. Yet relatively few have written conflict resolution policies or procedures, and even fewer have documented church discipline procedures that they use. Most churches also want to be recognized by the Internal Revenue Service as nonprofit charitable organizations. In that case, they must follow the rules of the IRS, but those rules tend to focus on conflicts of interest for board members and not conflict itself. Not following their own officially adopted policies and processes when the need arises places the church in legal jeopardy. Or, much worse, the leaders make up new policies and procedures on the fly when conflict erupts, which also leaves them open for lawsuits. That said, adopting policies and procedures is a necessary part of the fiduciary responsibilities of all organizational leaders. Though doing so will not prevent conflict or bring healing, it will usually protect the organization and the leaders against lawsuits if they follow what they adopted.

Faith community conflicts have many of the same characteristics as secular organizational conflicts, but there are also significant differences. If we do not recognize these differences, we engage in conflict management rather than conflict resolution.

The primary difference is that church conflicts are intensely relational and cannot be contained by rules; work conflicts are relational to a much lesser extent and can be controlled by rule enforcement and discipline practices.

I have a confession to make. We who work in conflict situations have suffered from a lack of imagination by practicing conflict management

4. Simonson, *Major Pettigrew's Last Stand*, 181.

rather than conflict resolution. The differences are huge. First, conflict prevention is possible in most situations through proper training and the creation of proactive conflict-sensing and reaction mechanisms. Preventing conflict has little to do with policies or procedures; it arises from creating a culture of open communication, listening, caring, and gentle restoration. Interpersonal conflict is an affair of the heart, where rules and procedures are affairs of the head. Saint Benedict reportedly said, "Listen carefully . . . and incline the ear of your heart." It is good advice. "God speaks through everything. The Word is constantly expressing Itself through creation and history. The Word can be heard in human events and through human voices. Every event carries a deeper meaning if we can tune our ears to hear it."[5]

Second, "managed" conflict is the attempt through various means to contain the conflict; we often make the faulty leap of logic that in containing it, the conflict will burn itself out without causing significant damage. Not so. Contained or managed conflict is still alive and active, with buried hotspots ready to erupt again and again with minimal provocation. Conflict resolution is a more profound process that looks to stop the fighting and heal the participants' wounds. It is the difference between the lack of war and true peace.

We must learn to communicate in ever-deepening dialogue that examines the facts and pain, fear, and dis-ease underneath each argument and point of resistance. We must then reach into those same hopes, fears, and pain to bring them into a healing light. In this respect, the peacemaker is an empathic listener and healer.

Another role of the peacemaker is to create a controlled and safe space in which to open the floodgates of pent-up fear, frustration, depression, and other toxic feelings the people have been holding inside and allow them to wash over everyone instead of pushing them back down. We don't like discomfort, and this is uncomfortable, but it is a necessary bridge over the toxic river of anger they have created. This is essential when helping former combatants reach forgiveness and reconciliation. If peacemakers remember that none of this is about them, they will not be caught up in the intense emotions of the moment. In this sense, peacemakers are pressure relief valves on boilers that are about to explode.

The peacemaker stands for justice, but not in the conventional sense of judging and passing sentences. There is a reason we rarely speak of

5. Hicks, "Benedictine Spirituality III."

justice in tender and sweet terms. Justice in our culture has become a punishment and the infliction of even more pain on those we pronounce guilty. As our lock-'em-up society has discovered, this punishment does not heal and instead has turned our prisons into graduate-level crime universities. As we shall see, true justice is a shape-shifter and always unique to the specific conflict and its people. Justice that heals is inseparable from mercy, but the forms justice and mercy take when paired are creative and unpredictable.

The next issue facing the reader arises not from qualifications but desire and motivation. Why are you reading this book? What do you want to come out of your reading? Do you want to do this work? Is it intellectual curiosity and the idea of such a great challenge, or are you helplessly drawn to it like a moth is drawn to the flame, knowing you may be consumed? What pulls you towards the flame? Are you called to become a peacemaker? Peacemaking can be a consuming calling. Properly taken, it will burn off the rubbish and petty desires we pursue as signs of success. Still, the intensity of the fire also tempers the sword, making it sharp but flexible and able to cut quickly through the root ball of fear, desire, and loneliness while acknowledging and restoring wounded relationships. It can leave you breathless and exhausted, but it can also rejuvenate you to walk into the fire repeatedly, each time without harm. People will pour out their deepest fears and wounds to you and onto you, for they will see in you the compassion of the original Peacemaker and know that you stand for hope and healing.

I believe that almost anyone can do what I do. You do not have to be particularly smart or well-educated. It is a process of "becoming" that includes a sense of adventure, positivity—and the humility of a shepherd.

I used to believe and argue that people doing this work needed extensive background training and experience and that their knowledge of group dynamics and mastery of technique were most important. The first reaction of almost every conflict management professional to the qualifications question is that you must first be a trained and certified mediator. In general, that means forty to eighty contact hours in a formal training setting where you learn the theories of mediation and then practice them under the supervision of experienced mediators before you are granted the certificate of completion. It can also cost thousands of dollars. To be "certified" as a mediator requires completing an added period where you co-mediate several actual cases with more experienced mediators. Eventually, there is an exam, and you are certified. Only then can you be trained to intervene in large group conflicts. That is the argument, anyway.

No longer. The first and most important qualification is humility. Who are you that you should walk into this bitter place, declare that you are there to lead them to safety and that you are qualified to do it? The argument for extensive training requirements falls apart when we realize that many of the procedures and techniques used in mediation are designed for only a few people at a time. At the same time, the peacemaker may face a hundred or more thoroughly angry and disillusioned people. The questioning techniques taught in mediation courses are helpful, but the procedures generally are not. The most valuable skills are more of a gift package: humility, listening deeply, empathizing, and asking the right questions.

Some will argue that you need broad training in organizational psychology and the dynamics of organizational conflict to work with faith community fights. That would include game theory, conflict psychology, family dynamics, the psychology of identity, communications theory and practice, and so on. These are all valuable, but to focus on one or two or think that an intensive training course qualifies you for this work is a mistake. Very little classroom training emphasizing theory can prepare you for the reality of standing in front of a room full of angry and skeptical people. No matter how much hype the training uses in advertising, all training can do is give you valuable tools. I once participated in a week-long intensive course in New Mexico that supposedly qualified me to work with conflicted groups of up to 10,000 people. Nope! It was all theory without application. I learned far more from the people I was with than from the course.

Experience in leading and running meetings where issues are debated is much more valuable than mediation training at this level. If you have done this, you probably know you do not need to have "the answer." The people involved have the answers—they need some help finding them. The peacemaker is not "neutral" in the sense that the term is used in mediation; instead, it describes what you will be doing: easing ever deeper into conversations between people who have hurt each other and bringing them back together as a functioning, integrated whole by guiding them in creating their solutions. You seek a covenant, not a settlement agreement—because a settlement agreement will not resolve the results of conflict. It can't.

Settlement agreements come out of law practice as an end to litigation. They are designed to end the lawsuit but not the war that started it and certainly not to heal the wounds inflicted during battle. With its settlement agreements, mediation is often sold as a panacea that fully resolves disputes. It does not, and it cannot. As an experienced mediator and trainer, I can say with assurance that mediation is a valuable and helpful process that ends litigation and often can fully resolve some issues—but not those with strong emotions attached.

Mediation is advertised as a fair and equal process where every party is heard, and a neutral mediator helps them find common ground where they can settle their differences with a written agreement. The participants may even leave feeling good. But, if you already are a mediator, you might want to try something I started in the late 1990s and continue today. A few months after a case is settled, contact the parties and ask them how they feel about the entire process, including the opposing people. Watch their eyes and faces. Anger, pain, or sadness will flash almost every time. When I discovered this, I probed further and realized that they were still hurt and angry at how they were treated by the "system," even several years later. That system included me, and I had not helped them find what they needed most: genuine but undefended acknowledgment of what happened, people taking ownership of what they did, pledges to change for the better, and seeking forgiveness (apology). They truly wanted and needed to feel respected as human beings and healed from the conflict.

This may seem insignificant in litigation, but it often is a critical tool that can break the hardest stalemate into pieces. A friend was fired from his job in the nuclear industry and filed a federal lawsuit against the employer for whistleblower retaliation. It took a few years, but a settlement agreement was finally reached where the former employer admitted nothing but paid him about one million dollars plus attorney fees to settle the matter. He told me he did not want their money; he wanted an apology and would have dropped his lawsuit altogether if one was offered. Instead, he went away with a million dollars soaking in a cup of bitterness.

Unfortunately, many church conflict interventionists have adopted the legal system's model of negotiated settlement agreements as the most efficient way of ending conflict. It is efficient, but it is not biblical, and it does not resolve the antagonism. Nowhere in the Bible will you find the term *settlement agreement*. Look all you want, but it does not exist there.

Settlement agreements may be efficient in terms of time and money. Still, they are ineffective in resolving the underlying issues fueling the fight, which fall into respect, acceptance, trust, fair play, and a continuum of justice and mercy. Mostly, the parties want their relationships to be healed, which is something settlement agreements cannot even approach. They may create behavioral protocols for the future to rebuild trust, but settlement agreements cannot heal the wounds of family strife. In my experience, churches and other faith-based organizations tend to degrade and disintegrate over time if a conflict ends with only a settlement agreement. Faith communities are based on relationships with God and each other, and wounded relationships do not heal until the opponents find their way to healthy forgiveness and reconciliation.

This outline defines the role of the peacemaker more than anything else. Taking on these mantles is a significant commitment and responsibility, but not as difficult as it may appear.

This manual has three parts: Preparation, the Wounded Healer, and Intervention. In each section, I will focus on churches rather than secular organizations whose dynamics are fundamentally different. The Preparation section describes the underlying forces and factors behind the conflict and offers various means of finding and identifying them, giving way to several resolution pathways. Preparation is linear and moves from the earliest contact through final interventions and follow-up. The Wounded Healer helps the peacemaker prepare physically, emotionally, and spiritually for intervention. Lastly, I will describe an actual intervention process where everything comes together. The three parts are integrated. Done well, they create a seamless process that moves logically and rationally, increasing power and flexibility as it progresses. This process goes beyond a settlement agreement, in which traditional mediation ends. In addressing the British people at the end of the aerial Battle of Britain, Winston Churchill said, "This is not the end. This is not even the beginning of the end. But it is, perhaps, the end of the beginning."[6] As you will see, a settlement agreement is only the end of the beginning.

As in medicine, the first rule is do not harm! Doing this work poorly or without due care and caution can leave congregants in worse condition than before you walked in the door. You will likely succeed if you answer this responsibility with humility and trepidation. If you are at this point saying to yourself, "Hey, I can do this—it sounds interesting!"

6. Churchill, "We Shall Fight on the Beaches."

I respectfully suggest you reconsider your motivations and perhaps try something else. Why? This is not about you or your satisfaction! It is about allowing the process and the Holy Spirit to work through you to bring about the miracles of resolution, forgiveness, and reconciliation. The peacemaker is the conduit, not the source.

Everything in this manual has been field-tested and used multiple times in actual organizational conflicts. While there is room for themes and variations, I think you will see that staying with the process as outlined is the most effective way of moving conflicted people from active hostility to reconciliation.

Peacemaking is a time-honored role and calling, but it is not easy. The peacemaker's job is to uncover painful and embarrassing truth—but gently. Unfortunately, the truth threatens some; they would rather kick it under the rug and pretend it never happened. Others take it personally and are so exposed by the process that they actively oppose the peacemaker to cover their responsibility. Sometimes, none of us understand. Sometimes, the people you are trying to help will turn on you out of frustration and pain. Benedictine monk and author Richard Rohr writes, "Before the truth sets you free, it tends to make you miserable."[7] It takes both courage and humility to walk into a room where there are dozens of angry people and declare to them that you are there to restore peace. They may focus on you, but remember, it is not about you! You are a representative of a holy God, and you are there to help them confront the truth of what happened, what they did to each other, and how much pain they are in, and then lead them back into the sunlight through forgiveness and reconciliation.

What qualities, then, must you have? Humility—it's not about you. Deep and empathic listening creates a safe space for people to express their deepest hopes, fears, and frustrations. Compassion. The ability to gently ask hard questions. Hope. The most essential quality is this: the ability to get out of the way and let the process work. As I already said, you are just the conduit.

You must be committed: a chicken contributes, and a pig is committed to a ham and egg breakfast. They have lost their way and are stranded in a cold and miserable place. They look to you to lead them into the warm light of day and freedom.

7. Rohr, *Falling Upward*, 73.

THE PRAYER OF ST. FRANCIS

Lord, make me an instrument of your peace,
Where there is hatred, let me sow love;
Where there is injury, pardon;
Where there is doubt, faith;
Where there is despair, hope;
Where there is darkness, light;
Where there is sadness, joy;
O Divine Master, grant that I may not so much seek to be consoled as to console;
To be understood as to understand;
To be loved as to love.
For it is in giving that we receive;
It is in pardoning that we are pardoned;
And it is in dying that we are born to eternal life.

3

Personal Preparation: The Naming of Parts

People like to say that the conflict is between good and evil.
The real conflict is between truth and lies.

~Don Miguel Ruiz

In late April 1967, I reported to Fort Bliss in El Paso, Texas, for Army basic combat training. Being eighteen years old and fresh out of high school, I had little idea of the life-changing experiences I would have. During those eleven weeks, I learned I could push myself far beyond my imagined limitations. I gained a sense of self-discipline that would go with me for the rest of my life. Surprisingly, the army brought out leadership qualities I did not know I had. I even learned to disassemble and then reassemble my M-14 rifle with my eyes closed, a skill that might save my life in combat. And I became proficient in a new language: the army's language.

Every object, process, and profession has its private language and names for its parts. Conflict analysis and intervention are no different. Each part has its name and definition.

I use various terms to describe the phenomenon of conflict throughout this book, so we must speak the same language and attach the same meanings to specific words. While you may know the terms already, some may be new to you, and I may use them differently than you are accustomed to.

WORKING DEFINITIONS

Conflict—Conflict exists whenever differing values, beliefs, assumptions, or norms are promoted in increasing opposition.[1] *Webster's Third International Dictionary* has this definition, among others: "An emotional state characterized by indecision, uncertainty and tension resulting from incompatible inner needs or drives . . ." In this sense, the word *conflict* is broadly defined. A more succinct way of putting it was said by a friend: "Conflict is two or more opposing solutions trying to occupy the same space."

Congregation—A voluntary group of people, generally self-identified and somewhat fluid in numbers, gathered for religious worship.

Arbitration—A quasi-legal proceeding where a trained and qualified neutral person considers the parties' presentations of their dispute and then makes a ruling regarding the rights and responsibilities of each party. The arbitrator's decision is usually final and binding and is often enforceable by the court system. The standards of proof are reduced from those found in the court system but still exist.

Mediation—A neutral person creates an informal process and a safe environment where parties can meet to discuss and resolve conflicts to reach an acceptable agreement. Any agreements are designed by and owned by the parties. The mediator makes no judgments or substantive decisions, staying with process issues.

Facilitation—A person acceptable to the parties (not necessarily neutral in outlook) uses their communication and meeting organization skills to create a process, a meeting format, and a safe environment for the parties to discuss their concerns and consider options for deciding or solving a problem. The design or plan of action (as well as the outcome) appears as the group works on the situation or problem. Facilitator decisions about the right intervention strategies and/or tools are fluid and driven by the nature of the interaction rather than by a set of intended outcomes.

Intervention—An outside professional is engaged to name and analyze the problem and create a process to resolve it. The typical intervention process will pressure all participants to help them understand the scope of their participation and their mutual self-inflicted woundedness and use their desire for peace and resolution to help them create

1. University of Reading, "Values, Beliefs and Attitudes."

a lasting solution that restores relationships and strengthens the entire community.

Community—There are many dry definitions of community, but faith communities are expected to resemble the church in Acts. M. Scott Peck was a distinguished Christian psychiatrist and offers the following definition: "The true spirit of community is the spirit of peace . . . How will we know we are in a community? It is a needless question. When a group enters the community, there is a dramatic change in spirit. And the new spirit is almost palpable. There is no mistaking it. No one who has experienced it need never ask again 'How will we know we are a community?'"[2]

Suppose we are going to use the word meaningfully. In that case, we must restrict it to individuals who have learned how to communicate honestly with each other, whose relationships go deeper than their masks of competence, and who have developed some significant commitment to support each other in all facets of life, from rejoicing to mourning.

Peacemaker—Anyone who intervenes in conflict at any level to ease tensions and restore healthy relationships through active listening, gently challenging assumptions, and guiding the participants into confronting themselves, the damage, grief, and emotional pain that resulted, and use their woundedness to move them towards authentic forgiveness and reconciliation. The intentional peacemaker uses multiple techniques from several disciplines to encourage internal interpersonal and organizational change.

Standing between emotionally invested, conflicted people reveals a problem: We don't like to be in the middle of conflict! It disrupts our emotional stability by introducing things about others and ourselves that we do not want to confront, and we become convenient targets. A friend said, "When you stand in the middle of the road, you get hit from both directions."

What's Your Conflict Style?

My mother was a wonderful woman, but she fervently believed any conflict would disappear if she ignored it. When conflict erupted, she would do everything she could to avoid it. We all react instantly and unthinkingly to the perceived threat of conflict through deeply ingrained beliefs

2. Peck, *Different Drum*, 74.

and habits. Many avoid it when and where possible, while others may deny it exists even though others angrily confront them, and still others immediately begin enlisting others to support them.[3] We are nothing if not complex human beings, and how we react to conflict is learned as young children. We found our way out of trouble by crying, apologizing, blaming, smiling, and changing the subject. We try several responses until we settle on one or two as our primary defenses. We then carry these beliefs and behaviors through our teen years, where they are refined, and finally take them into adulthood. By then, these beliefs and behaviors are automatic and subconscious responses to the threats presented by interpersonal fights.

The most important thing for any would-be interventionist to know is not how group conflicts work but how individuals, including ourselves, react in the throes of those conflicts. As I have said, I have adopted the premise that these are their conflicts, not mine, so I will not become emotionally entangled. But I have discovered it is not that easy. I must constantly guard against the emotional pitfalls that call me into them.

Conflict Management Styles

Kenneth Thomas and Ralph Kilmann[4] measured how each person responds to conflict by creating an axis of assertiveness and cooperativeness with five overlapping conflict styles: competing, collaborating, compromising, avoiding, and accommodating. Each of these styles is beneficial in some situations and destructive in others. Thomas and Kilmann argue that we tend to enter our favored response modes when we feel threatened and that the shift is both unconscious and instantaneous, an assessment that fits my experience. I have used their instrument in training mediators for more than twenty-five years and find it useful in helping the trainees understand their conflict reactions and behaviors. The reason is simple enough: we must know how we react to conflict to neutralize the tendency to respond defensively, overuse a specific style, or use that style under the wrong circumstances. More than twenty million people have used this instrument; it is available online for a nominal fee.

Here are Thomas and Kilmann's five basic patterns of conflict reactions in more detail.

3. Karpmann, "New Drama Triangles."
4. Karpmann and Kilmann, "Conflict Mode Instrument."

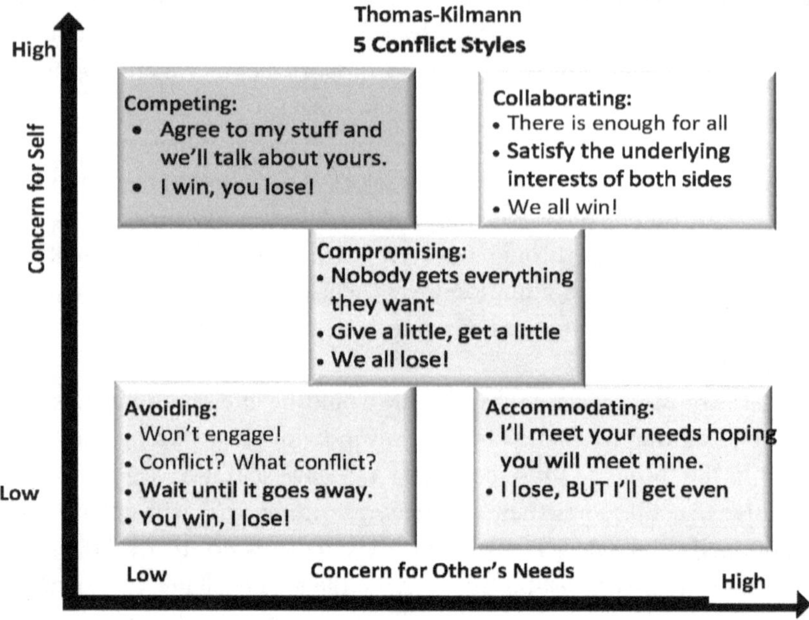

Each approach has two dimensions: 1) the extent to which a person satisfies their personal goals and interests by forcing (assertiveness), and 2) the extent to which a person attempts to maintain/improve the relationship and satisfy the other persons' goals/interests (cooperativeness).

Each style is helpful in some situations and not valuable for others. The most influential individuals and groups move towards maximizing assertiveness and cooperativeness, which is identified as collaboration.

Competing

I win, you lose; what part of that do you not understand? Competing comes from a person at war who is aggressive, assertive, demanding, usually charming and articulate, and will strive to win at any cost. They mean business and take no prisoners, with a my-way-or-the-highway approach that says "I'll try it if I can get away with it." Competitors are relentless, even in the presence of wiser minds. Their goal is to win, which translates as you lose. Their basic philosophy is one of famine, meaning there is not enough for everyone, and they will get the lion's share. Win-lose.

Avoiding

You win; I will not engage. Avoiding can be seen in those who sincerely don't want to know about the debate—they become quiet or leave the room (physically or emotionally), ignore the problem, deny it exists, and lean on others around them to resolve the situation. They are kind, sincere, and afraid—they sit in the back and commit to nothing, preferring to think it is all someone else's responsibility. Their basic philosophy is one of nonengagement while hoping that something is left when the dust clears. Avoiders are deeply uncomfortable with conflict and will hide emotionally and even physically. They generally will let themselves be exploited by others in the hope of being accepted, reinforcing their mistrust of others. Lose/win.

Accommodating

The phrase "It's nice to be important, but more important to be nice" describes accommodators. They tend to flatter, appease, and go along with "whatever." They will sacrifice their needs to please others, even when others are not appreciative. They latch on to stronger people, tag along, agree with everything (often loudly), and like to be part of the mob. In trying to please everyone, they please no one, including themselves. Accommodators have difficulty engaging in any discussion and lack commitment—they don't know how to decide and don't know what they want. However, accommodators make wonderful hosts as they are focused on the needs of others in the hope of reciprocity. They will subordinate their own needs for emotional connection to making others happy. The result is increasing frustration that may erupt into an outburst of anger. Lose/Win.

Compromising

Compromisers "give to get" and believe conflicts can be resolved through a this-for-that, transactional attitude. The concessions, compromises, and agreements must be "balanced" so neither party gets most of the negotiated items. They usually hold back on big-ticket items to use as bargaining levers later—they enjoy the debate and, as in a game of poker, will try to draw out the other person before laying their hand on the table. They often seem willing to take different positions, depending on what's at stake, and seem open, then closed; everyone gets a little of what they want, but nobody gets everything they want. Their basic philosophy is to share what little we have. Relationships tend to be transactional, where the most critical thing is equity through sharing because "nobody can get everything they want." Lose/Lose.

Collaborating

Collaborating focuses on the underlying individual and organizational unmet needs and looks to meet them. Called "interests," these are fundamental but intangible human needs such as recognition, acceptance, respect, safety, and so on. Peacemakers trying to meet these needs operate from a belief system of abundance where there is enough for everyone. The most important question is, "Why is this important to you?" Negotiations are fluid in fulfilling the mutual underlying interests of all parties. This can be successful more often than most people think. Win/Win.[5]

All these styles are somewhat unstable, and people tend to move between them seamlessly. It is no contest when someone with a competing/forcing style is confronted with an avoider; the avoider will surrender almost at once but come at you like a tiger when feeling cornered. Likewise, sparks will fly when two or more competitors face off, each believing there can be only one winner, and that one is them!

None of these approaches to conflict is simply right or wrong; their utility and effectiveness depend on the situation. We each deal with the world according to our needs and abilities. We all enter a dispute armed with whatever tools we have and use them according to how we think that style will get us what we need.

We must be aware of our instinctive methods of dealing with strife. Know them, use them, and be able to set them aside when necessary. For instance, my first gut reaction is to avoid and run away from conflict. I learned it from my mother. If avoiding it does not work, I will compete—I become determined to win, meaning you must lose. Both styles compete

5. Fisher and Ury, *Getting to Yes.*

for supremacy, but only one will prevail—until it no longer works, and I switch styles again. Knowing how I react has been a tremendous help in countering negative reactions and how I intentionally employ them when appropriate.

For example, sometimes, I choose not to respond to a provocation because I believe it will escalate the situation. If their position is vital to them but not to me, I will accommodate by agreeing—but will try to obtain a concession as the agreement price. In other words, these styles can be helpful when used intentionally.

We can use our knowledge of conflict styles to nuance, appreciate, hear, and openly accept each other's styles and harmonize with each person's confusing, alien, or maddening (to us, anyway) take on the world as they know it. Realizing that it is usually just an automatic reaction when threatened makes it much easier to deal with. Also, accepting their style only means you understand it, not that you agree with what they propose.

Innies and Outies

Another factor to explore is your tendency towards introversion or extroversion. This is relevant because of how they channel our engagement with those in conflict. I call myself a "highly trained extrovert," which means I am introverted but have a lot of training and experience in addressing large audiences. The result is that I am often mistaken for being an extrovert, and people become confused when I turn down social invitations. I engage with the parties with full-on extroversion, but it costs me energy. By the end of the day, I want nothing more than a good book and a quiet dinner alone. I know the price I will pay doing an intervention, so I place clear protective boundaries around myself.

Extroverts, by contrast, tend to be the life of the party. Nothing is wrong with that, but it becomes an obstacle when tied to a strong need to be liked, and you face off with antagonists during the intervention. The temptation may be to please everyone (one of my weaknesses, but we'll get to that), which can sidetrack any efforts to bring them together. Once again, the key here is never to forget that this is not about you; any attempt to make it about you is usually a diversion born of fear and frustration.

Let me share an example of how introversion and extroversion act out in real life. I trained a company's management and union negotiations teams to help them create a better, more functional working relationship. All went well until they were in contract negotiations, with me as the facilitator. At one point, they agreed to separate for a thirty-minute working caucus and then come back together to explore possible solutions to the problem. The management team was ready in twenty minutes and waited patiently for the union team. After forty-five minutes, I entered the union team meeting room and discovered they had hardly begun working on the problem. They had spent the first forty minutes socializing, while the management team did virtually no socializing and got to their work simultaneously. Both sides complained, with unionists complaining about being hurried and management complaining about a lack of respect for their time. I should have caught this earlier: the union negotiations team comprised seven gregarious extroverts, while the management team had seven studious introverts. The extroverts could not function without socializing first, while the introverts focused on solving the problem and did almost no socializing. We finally agreed—the union team would only socialize for the first five minutes of any working caucus, and the management team would give them ten minutes more than they thought necessary. It worked!

Beyond personality types, what drives you? Why you want to do this would be the natural question, but this goes deeper: Are you driven towards this, or is it something to be tolerated as part of the job? There is a difference.

During the late winter of 1983, I spent a whole week at a new—and mostly empty—hotel near the Knoxville, Tennessee airport, earning a stress management trainer certification. The instructor, a well-respected psychologist and author, had us focus on our personal needs by introducing us to the subconscious drives for validation and acceptance that fuel our efforts, mainly when we come into conflict. The reason was simple enough: like conflict styles, our subconscious drives are learned as children and constitute magical thinking that says if we can do ________, we will be worthy of love and acceptance. In other words, it seems we have bought into the lie of conditional love based on what we do rather than on who we are as children of God.

It was more than a bit disconcerting when he explained how these deeply held beliefs compel us to repeatedly attempt the impossible to feel worthy of others loving us. He used incredibly correct and resonating illustrations that I thought he was talking about me! He then used a series of questions to help us figure out our primary and secondary "drivers" and their relative strengths within us. Each driver is a subconscious compulsion to act in specific ways when under the stress of conflict.

Which of the following do you instantly resonate with when conflict erupts?

1. Be strong.
2. Be perfect.
3. Try harder.
4. Please others.
5. Hurry up.[6]

We all have elements of each but in varying degrees of intensity. The strongest are the ones we instantly use without forethought when we feel threatened, and they tend to pair up with our conflict styles. We learned them as very young children, and they worked well for us as we figured out how to navigate the relational landscape. They may have worked as young children, but now they create internal stress because, as adults, we know intuitively that they are all impossible to achieve. We keep using them anyway.

Let's look at how they play out at the subconscious level where they operate.

Try Harder

"If I just try harder, I'll be OK." The underlying belief is that you can achieve anything if you try hard enough, or you would have succeeded had you just tried harder. The problem is that you can always try harder no matter how hard you have already tried and still not achieve your goals. This automatically creates inner tension, frustration, and failure. The expectation for others is the same: If we *all* try harder, we can get there. Unfortunately, trying harder implies redoing the same things that have already failed but with greater determination.

6. Kahler, "Drivers."

Please Others

"If I just please everyone, I'll be OK." Being liked is paramount, so vast amounts of energy are spent convincing people to like you and approve of what you do and who you are. You feel responsible for how others feel and go out of your way to make them happy. In doing this, your needs for approval often are unmet because you are so busy pleasing everyone else that you have never learned to say "no" and mean it! You become anxious and even depressed upon learning that some people don't like you despite your efforts. As a people-pleaser, you expect everyone else to also be a people-pleaser. An assistant epitomized this idea shortly after I hired her many years ago. She firmly believed that being nice would solve all the world's problems and placed a small plaque on her desk that read, "It's nice to be important, but it's more important to be nice!"

Be Perfect

"If I can just be perfect, I'll be OK." I must claim ownership of this one as well. The Be Perfect personality constantly strives for perfection but is equally focused on imperfections in oneself. You must be the best, and everything you do must be perfect. You are deeply embarrassed when you see something that you presented as your best work and find a flaw in it—and you always find a flaw—and focus on that! You have difficulty accepting compliments and will put yourself down when praised. You like to use big words and tend to "cover all the bases" when answering a question, meaning you say more than is needed or wanted. You give out much information "to be perfectly clear," which means you are an expert. You expect others to be the same, but it drives you buggy when they are.

Hurry Up

"If I just go faster, I'll be OK." You do things fast but are often late, and many projects you start are never finished. You tend to speak rapidly, fidget when others talk, and doodle, tap your fingers, or play with small objects when bored. You get bored quickly when meetings do not go fast enough, so you always watch the clock. The problem is that no matter how fast you are going, you believe that you must always go faster! Unfortunately, you are facing the Red Queen's dilemma from Alice in Wonderland:

> "Well, in our country," said Alice, still panting a little, "you'd generally get to somewhere else—if you run very fast for a long time, as we've been doing."
> "A slow sort of country!" said the Queen. "Now, here, you see, it takes all the running you can do, to keep in the same place. If you want to get somewhere else, you must run at least twice as fast as that!"[7]

. . . And you expect everyone else to do the same.

Be Strong

"If I just hide my feelings, I'll be OK." You believe showing how you feel shows weakness and vulnerability, meaning you are open to injury. You tend not to show much excitement, meaning you may show an emotional range of A to B. Winston Churchill was known for his quiet, unemotional delivery of bad news and may be one of your heroes. Who can deny that flat, matter-of-fact tone when he said, "We shall defend our Island, whatever the cost may be, we shall fight on the beaches, we shall fight on the landing grounds, we shall fight in the fields and in the streets, we shall fight in the hills; we shall never surrender . . ."[8] Like Churchill, you tend to deny the reality of stress or pain: "I'm fine! Leave me alone!" You may believe being blunt in conversation or confrontation is the best way. Annnnnd, you expect everyone else to respond in the same way!

Are you seeing a pattern here? Each belief/driver is impossible to achieve and leads to frustration and increased stress. We place the impossible on others when we expect the same of them, which always leads to disappointment. You can reverse each driver by permitting yourself to be imperfect and even to fail, to slow down and savor your surroundings, to accept the reality that not everyone will think you are terrific, to stop being the people-pleasing doormat, and to be real by acknowledging that you are human like the rest of us, and others can help you.

Again, it helps to know what your drivers are when an intervention begins to go sideways and you are tempted to let your primary drivers take over. I venture to say that we all must rein in occasionally when our subconscious drivers feel threatened. Keeping an interested and caring demeanor when directly attacked by someone frustrated and angry

7. Carroll, *Through the Looking Glass*, 42.
8. Churchill, "We Shall Fight on the Beaches."

is challenging. You are the logical target; some will believe you are not doing enough; some will see you as too nosy, and others will challenge your credibility and ability. It's all normal defensive behavior and is not about you!

The key to success is not in defending what you are doing but in curiosity to ask why they are reacting as they are. What is going on in this person? Why is she so frustrated that she must attack you and your motives? A simple statement followed by a question such as this can reveal her needs and how to meet them: "I can see that this is important to you and that you are upset. Can you tell me what you are upset about and suggest how to fix it?" This does three things: 1) it affirms her feelings as legitimate, 2) it seeks deeper understanding to find and explain her internal reactions, and 3) it enlists her as part of the solution.

We return to the fundamental question: why do you want to do this work? It is not fun, nor is it easy. It is a calling where you commit yourself to work with this conflicted faith community. But it can also bring exceptional levels of satisfaction when things go right.

An independent Lutheran church called me to assess their situation and provide options. During the interview, it became clear that the senior pastor was the problem. He insisted on controlling every detail of worship, even when he was not in the pulpit. He would go through staff desks at night (no locks), leaving just enough evidence for the staffer to know he was there. They said he lurked in the shadows and spied on everyone. He was also convinced that the staff, including the associate pastor, were plotting against him. He would treat everyone well in public and then scream threats at them in private.

The board of elders was bewildered by it all. They struggled to understand what was happening. They finally agreed to give the senior pastor a choice: 1) he could retire with a huge celebration, or 2) they would file formal charges against him with the congregation. He chose to retire but refused to come to his retirement party.

We reconvened a few weeks later to pray for renewal and forgiveness. I ran the Crucible process with them (described in detail in chapters 7–11). The atmosphere in the room changed while we shared communion. A weight was lifted as the Holy Spirit filled the room with its presence. It is now ten years later, and all is well.

Each of us reacts to conflict differently, and how we respond depends on the amount of personal threat we feel. In sudden confrontations, we tend to prepare for combat or try to run and hide. Beyond that, though, we also have subconscious but predictable conflict engagement styles, and we shift between them as the situation warrants. Often, habitual responses direct our actions, even though what we do may be counterproductive. Our challenge is to become aware of our styles and use them appropriately.

We must also look deeply into ourselves to locate why this work may be attractive. It is too easy to become about us rather than the people who asked us to help.

4

Ignition: From Votive Candles to Flamethrowers

Conflict is inevitable, but combat is optional.

~Max Lucado

Though it may seem that way to a casual observer, conflicts never "just happen" and, like wars, never explode out of nowhere. They always have a context, and there are warning signs. Each conflict's context is unique, but each also tends to follow a predictable pattern of action and response as it grows from spark to wildfire.

An ancient wisdom book says, "As iron sharpens iron, so one person sharpens another" (Prov 27:17). True enough, but what it does not say is equally valid: sparks fly in the sharpening process. All it takes is for a flying spark to land in dry kindling to start a fire. Many of these fights begin innocently enough. People become irritated with one another over minor slights, real or imagined. Irritation builds with the addition of more incidents, and grudges are formed. As people feel increasingly disrespected and disregarded, resentment increases, and the conflict grows, even though it is still invisible to others. Like brushing against poison ivy leaves, the first steps toward war are often unnoticed. The poison works against your skin and a rash begins with only a slight itch that you absentmindedly scratch and forget. As the rash spreads, you know that scratching it will only increase the problem, but it feels so good to scratch. You momentarily forget that scratching only makes it worse, and scratch again. The itch keeps returning, and the more you scratch, the worse it gets until large sections of your skin are inflamed and blistered, and you are in real pain.

Internal church and faith community conflicts tend to follow this pattern. They begin when tiny, hidden seeds of anger, envy, and bitterness find good soil and germinate. Soon, they take root and begin to grow. Like the proverbial mustard seed, they start tiny but can grow and intensify. Eventually, like fire, what was a puff of smoke may become an all-consuming conflagration.

Conflicts escalate in predictable ways, and several escalation models chart their course. I prefer one by German conflict expert Friedrich Glasl as it is more detailed and nuanced than the others. The sequence has many signs that point to the crossing points between stages. Even so, the crossing points from one level to the next are always blurred.

The following is a synopsis of what is presented in Glasl's *Confronting Conflict*, which itself is the English translation of a more extensive work.[1]

Stage 1: Hardening

As noted, conflict can be defined as two opposing ideas competing to solve the same problem. The first stage develops when a low-level disagreement resists resolution efforts, and frustration takes hold. As irritation grows, the same viewpoints tend to be repeated more forcefully. The problem and its tension remain, leading to irritation. Repeated failed efforts to resolve the issue by advancing the same opposing viewpoints bring confusion and suspicion. As frustration increases, the problem becomes more clearly identified and fixed, and flexible proposals (standpoints) on how the problem "should" be handled are advanced. These standpoints tend to be incompatible with each other and can quickly begin to morph into simplified "this or that" choices. As proponents add energy to supporting their proposals, they are increasingly seen as irreconcilable. Eventually, they are cast as irreconcilable opposites known as polarities. The proponents then push them as "either/or" propositions. As efforts to mediate or resolve the issues fail, complex problems become overly simplified. Even though we may know intuitively that there are

1. Glasl, *Confronting Conflict*, 83–103.

other choices and avenues for resolution, the matter is increasingly reduced to a simple, even simplistic, choice.

Frustration continues to increase as proposals are opposed. Feeling the need for more substantial support, more people are pulled into the discussion to argue about one or two proposals. This is known as "triangulation."[2] Its goal is to increase pressure against the opposition. Both sides do this, so the number of people in the fray tends to multiply quickly. Increasing the number of people within the conflict circle also increases the number of issues they want to argue, which expands the conflict by increasing its complexity and the difficulty in resolving it.

Some people switch sides easily and often in the early stages of a conflict, but then single voices begin to unite to support or oppose specific standpoints. Emotions are now a driving force, and the intensity of emotional involvement dictates the "heat level" of what has transitioned into a smoldering fire.

Over time, each group tends to solidify specific and unique standpoints and eventually become identifiable factions increasingly intent on winning. As the groups gradually become more defined, their interactions slowly become more hostile and resistant to arguments from the "other side." As this occurs, boundaries and walls around each group begin to limit new members from joining, as the group will allow only those who share the same interpretation of the issue. This creates group filters for interpreting new information but also tends to screen out inconvenient disparities—and the people who hold them.

As tensions increase, opposing groups progressively begin to undercut each other though sarcasm and innuendo, e.g., "They don't know what they are talking about." Or: "They just want to control things." Negative information about the opposition is given great significance, while positive information is ignored or does not register. This is known as confirmation bias.[3] As time passes, the groups begin to emphasize their differences and lose sight of their similarities. It is common for groups that agree on 90 percent or more of their issues to lose sight of this reality and focus solely on the 5 to 10 percent where they disagree.

As the conflict persists, interactions between the groups become increasingly disheartening, with both sides feeling that their efforts are in vain. Despite viewing each other as obstinate and irrational, the

2. Karpmann, "New Drama Triangles."

3. "5.8 Biases and Errors."

individuals involved remain committed to finding a resolution. However, as their attempts prove futile, a collective belief solidifies that the "others" are unwilling to compromise and are insincere in their negotiation efforts. This belief justifies the decision to halt further negotiations until certain conditions are met.

A silent set of habitual behaviors falls into place when dealing with the opposition. Each side (there may be several "sides" by now) begins to look for ulterior motives in the "others" as an explanation as to why this conflict is so resistant to "our common sense." Unfortunately, the commonsense argument is an idealized belief of what is accepted knowledge across boundaries, but without testing to see if the belief is accurate. There is also a gradual and complex process of inclusion and exclusion, forming fluid boundaries that define who can and cannot join the group. The issues at the center of the dispute now have clarity and become more entrenched against opposing settlement proposals. Even so, a neutral third party or even some within the opposing groups may cross self-imposed barriers to settle the matter.

Suppose the attempts at resolution fail, or one or more parties/groups lose faith in the possibility of solving the problems through straight and fair discussion. In that case, manipulation replaces argument, and the conflict slips into Stage 2.

Stage 2: Debates and Diatribes

Each side now sees its counterpart as not amenable or receptive to their "well-reasoned" arguments. As a result, reason is not entirely abandoned, but it begins to be replaced by more forceful and emotional arguments, such as personal attacks or aggressive language, as the parties become less inclined to listen to each other in civil conversation. The resulting discussions develop into verbal confrontations, and more emotional energy is invested in convincing the other party of the superiority of one's own argument over the less reasonable arguments they have been offered.

The parties look for more forceful ways of pushing through their standpoints. They increasingly lock themselves into inflexible positions, which creates a growing tension. The issues are simplified and re-formed by each side into more powerful—but less accurate—bullet points that favor the party offering them. All parties tend to exaggerate the drawbacks or weaknesses in opposition arguments while emphasizing the benefits of their proposed solutions. The sides begin to ignore internal inadequacies and inconsistencies. As the rhetoric intensifies, each side defines its settlement ideas as good and righteous and the opponent's proposals as ill-considered and even foolish (but not evil—yet!). Strategies are designed to pressure the opposition from outside sources and peel away anyone on the inside who is not entirely sold on the value of the positions taken.

Rather than giving in when outside pressure is applied, their resolve to support their positions increases. As this strategy proves less than compelling, the situation expands from well-defined issues into a more generalized but also more ambiguous rephrasing. But another problem arises: the addition of ambiguity requires rejecting arguments they have previously offered as superior.

The concept of "face" is now involved, adding a personal dimension to the argument. Face is the positive social value a person claims for himself in each situation. Face is a matter of self-pride and is critical to the individual's sense of social standing. Losing face by admitting error is too much, as doing so lowers the individual and group's social status. As a counter to losing face, increasing energy is diverted into projecting a façade of strength, decisiveness, and superior skill. Any vestiges of weakness, insecurity, or incompetence must be banished. Increasingly, the internal thinking of each group becomes one of, "We can't back down now without a major concession from the other side."[4]

The concept of saving face may be more intense in religious settings, where right and wrong are emphasized more than in society. As a result, our churches have adopted a culture of politeness where harsh words or strong objections should not be expressed. As with other speech conventions, politeness can be weaponized[5] and leads to a compliance-driven atmosphere rather than an attitude of integrity.[6] As the intensity of the fight increases, people are often forced to threaten action to embarrass or otherwise "take away face" from their opponent. The goal is to gain concessions without using these tactics, but the willingness to use them strengthens with every failed interaction.

Debate outcomes between the groups place leader reputations on the line. As agreement seems increasingly distant and hard to reach, each blames the other. A primary goal at this point is winning over the opponents and convincing those not yet involved in the fight to choose sides,

4. Goffman, "On Face-Work," 217.

5. Pearson and Lee, "Politeness Phenomena," 149.

6. Verhezen, "Giving Voice in a Culture of Silence," 187.

leaving a smaller middle ground. Nobody wants to accept the blame, so they point back at the other side, e.g., "If they had just listened to reason and not attacked us in this way, we still could have worked with them. They have destroyed our trust, and we doubt that they are sincere in finding an agreement." The intent in blaming is to plant doubt in opposition supporters with the hope of turning them against each other.

For example, Charlie has been the influential treasurer for more than a decade and has declared his support of one of the groups and its positions. An easy and common way of degrading Charlie's influence is through rumor and innuendo, such as, "I like Charlie, but I wonder . . . There have been some discrepancies in his treasurer's report. I'm not saying he's stealing, but . . ." The poisoned seed is planted.

A significant shift occurs when the parties begin to assert the negative, even disastrous, consequences of following their opponent's proposed course. The fight is no longer about efficiency, time, or cost. In much the same manner as the focus changed in Maryann's narrative, the focus shifts to value issues such as trust, fair play, honesty, commitment, etc. The intent is to spotlight the opponent's positions as absurd and not worth consideration. Linkages begin to appear, tying the central issue to prominent value considerations. This makes the argument more emotionally powerful and pulls in more people willing to "fight for the cause."

When the initial attacks in a debate prove ineffective, the parties often resort to "authorities"—highly respected individuals, court decisions, or Scripture—to lend credibility to their standpoints. This strategy involves describing the opposition's positions as "extreme," a tactic designed to undermine their views and their supporters. The goal is to coerce the opposition into accepting what is claimed as a "reasonable compromise" but is a disguised demand for surrender.

These tactical tricks are designed to keep the opponent emotionally off balance and gain the upper hand. The center of gravity in verbal skirmishes quickly shifts from rational arguments to moral issues and emotional harm, especially if the rational arguments were a cover for a belief that concession will compromise honor.

Suspicion and distrust now dominate every exchange between them. Words no longer mean what they seem but contain veiled meanings and unspoken consequences. In the words of Humpty Dumpty to Alice,

> "When I use a word," Humpty Dumpty said, in rather a scornful tone, "it means just what I choose it to mean—neither more nor less."

> "The question is," said Alice, "whether you can make words mean so many different things."
> "The question is," said Humpty Dumpty, "which is to be master—that's all."[7]

Each side is now strategically using words to gain mastery over the others. Conversations between the parties and any documents they might exchange take on hidden meanings, requiring careful scrutiny as each side looks to gain an advantage at the other's expense and not to be tricked by skillfully manipulated data. All statements and actions are given added significance. Each side must project an image of solidarity and strength. Neither side shies away from confrontation, and their standpoints become more solid, unyielding—and radical.

At this point, civil discourse gives way to more passionate debates. If one side gains an advantage, the other side quickly devises a plan to "compensate," meaning get even by undercutting the opposition. Surprisingly, the parties are still partly committed to shared goals and interests, which provides a glimmer of hope during increasing competition. However, a sense of insecurity and loss of control is blossoming, which is compensated for by cultivating an image of strength and righteousness. The "other" is no longer accepted as a worthy person. Built-up tensions are often discharged in outbursts in ways they would not normally behave. While this serves as a pressure relief valve, it does not involve serious problem-solving.

When any party feels that further talking is useless and starts acting without warning the other side, the conflict has reached Stage 3.

Stage 3: Actions, Not Words

There is a profound shift in how each side sees the other at Stage 3. Before, they viewed each other as generally on the same team but could not find a common solution. Perceptions shifted to seeing each other as having different purposes altogether, which means they compete for limited resources. Each side is understood to have two agendas—one open, and one hidden. Shared interests and the prospect of resuming cooperation recede into the background as a competitive win/lose mentality takes over where the victors vanquish the losers without obliterating them—yet. Chivalrous reacceptance is offered if they only admit the error of their

7. Carroll, *Through the Looking Glass*, 57.

ways and repent—meaning surrender. Since talking has not worked, the parties shift their attention to actions.

The sense of being blocked by each other becomes paramount, and knowing they still need each other—though they are no longer sure why—is perplexing. As tensions grow, so does the sense of becoming independent antagonists towards each other. To save face, the opposers are the antagonists, while "we" are the voice of moderation and civility. Regardless of how they see themselves, both sides increasingly deny their mutual dependencies and break away in an attempt at unilateral independence.

While there is still some interest in intergroup cooperation, louder and stronger voices declare their independence and a need to block the other side from reaching its goals through pre-emptive, unilateral action.

The goal of a first strike is to force the opponent to yield, but yielding is weakness and unacceptable. Problem-solving communication devolves into positions of dominance against subservience, e.g., "We will agree to discuss your proposal after you have agreed to our proposal." This type of ultimatum is understood as the only rational course in response to irrational propositions from the other. Trust between the parties is lowered to marginal but remains in small measure because many still want to believe the "others" are honorable people, even while abandoning that belief. Once abandoned, the most logical direction is action rather than communication, which speeds up the escalation process. However, some informal back communication channels may continue to function to seek some manner of accord.

Within each party, the pressure to conform to common attitudes and interpretations increases as complex issues are reduced to party lines that all must adhere to. Group members must also conform in lockstep to show their strength and resolve to present a forceful and united front. A dramatic change in perception overshadows everything: opponents are now recast as enemies and even as less than fully human. This allows for more simplistic, even jingoistic, responses to any comebacks other than capitulation.

Images, attitudes, and interpretations now tend to be reduced to the simplest common denominator. What once may have been a nuanced approach is now presented in terms of this or that, of black or white, meaning one must choose between them. Any remaining middle ground is unsafe, and few dare to enter it. This tends to tighten the group's inner cohesion against outside threats. All groups (there are likely several by this point) stand in staunch opposition to each other. However, "back door" attempts can still be made between them to see if they can merge two or more groups to gain more power. If this is successful, coalitions that may or may not last for the duration of the conflict are formed. The premise behind this is the adage, "The enemy of my enemy is my friend."

The factions develop strong feelings of unity and shared predicament while under siege, further reducing their ability to relate to opposing concerns and perspectives. Communication between the opponents has all but ceased, limiting their options to appealing to outside sources or higher authorities. Any proposals made are characterized as "take it or leave it."

Scripture is the ultimate authority in faith communities and is increasingly used to support every position, regardless of what that position is. This is commonly called "prooftexting," meaning that a single verse or small section of holy writ is intentionally quoted out of context to gain the upper hand. By taking verses out of context and even warping them to say something they do not, the parties appeal to the ultimate higher authority, God, as their vicar, and they characterize themselves as mere conveyors of God's message and will.

Assumptions about possible motives and hidden strategies may now develop unchecked. Rumors fly and become more readily accepted than previously—what was earlier dismissed becomes increasingly believable. Limiting honest face-to-face communication further increases feelings of being blocked. The parties start to see themselves as held captive by external forces they cannot control and often cannot identify. That being the case, they will likely deny responsibility for events they initiated.

The threshold to Stage 4 occurs when the opposing groups increase veiled attacks on their counterpart's social reputation, general attitude, position, and relationship to others. "Deniable punishment behavior," also known as "plausible deniability," is a characteristic sign of slipping into Stage 4.[8] The parties know that their accusations are, at best, grossly exaggerated, if not outright lies, but this new lowering of moral barriers is accepted as necessary to defeat a now well-defined, morally bankrupt, and dangerous enemy.

8. Cox and Devine, "Stereotyping."

Stage 4: Images and Coalitions

The issues are replaced by winning or losing in Stage 4. Legendary football coach Vince Lombardi's maxim becomes their truth: "Winning is not everything; it's the only thing!" Truth is diminished as clandestine and anonymous attacks are made against individuals, particularly opposition leaders. The targeted people suddenly find themselves under attack day and night from multiple directions. Defending one's reputation becomes a significant concern. With these individual attacks comes a reduction in the number and even the importance of the issues, replaced at the forefront by personalities and power plays. Strategizing and planning what can be done to defeat the opposition rises to the highest status.[9]

Each party develops highly fixed stereotypical and simplified negative images of the others, and individual stories are swallowed by the group narrative, resulting in a larger and more powerful group image and the beginnings of a mob mentality. The group narrative becomes stronger, more heroic, and self-glorifying while, at the same time, it denigrates and lowers the view of the opposition groups. Contradictory facts that challenge the negative image are usually discarded (sort of like "fake news").

Belonging to the opposing group is tied to having specific innate, negative characteristics (unreliable, incompetent, power-hungry, devious, dishonest, perverted). In contrast, members of one's own group are granted the mantles of intellectual and moral superiority. With that shift, open attacks on the fundamental moral integrity of the "other" begin to appear, arguing why the "enemy" should be denied fair treatment because of immoral—or amoral—beliefs and behaviors.

Each group has overlaid negative images on the opposition that become screens through which they see each other and prevent them from seeing each opponent's true complexity and individuality. Instead, they are demoted to a mostly faceless "other." Of course, no side accepts the image of themselves as presented by the other side—such images are vehemently rejected and are understood as an added deception and insult from the opposition. Believe it or not, the parties may try to get the "other" to agree that this is how they are! The effort is futile, and the parties now have difficulty mentioning any positive qualities of the other party. The other side is uneducable—they are stupid, brutish, and unable to change.

9. Pearson, "Power and Politeness," 75.

New and sinister behavioral and motivational stereotypes begin to work on the people within each group. If they are going to be seen as being a certain way, they may as well act in ways that reinforce the image, which, in effect, abandons their claim to moral high ground. However, they rationalize that their bad behavior is merely a defensive reaction to their counterparts' actions and intentions and do not feel responsible for further escalation of the conflict. In an Orwellian reversal, offensive action is understood as defensive.

While the generally accepted rules of engagement may still be followed in public for propaganda purposes, commonly held rules of civility have been undermined to the point where sabotage is considered fair play. Opportunities to get away with unfriendly acts are increasingly used for that purpose. A typical form is "deniable punishment behavior."[10] The counterpart is provoked, insulted, and criticized, openly or covertly, but in forms that do not infringe on etiquette. One person told me they "weaponize their compliments so well that only the insulted party realizes that they have been insulted." This is often done through insinuation, ambiguous comments, irony, and body language, but if challenged, the perpetrator can flatly deny that this was what was intended. One of the more egregious examples of this is the question, "When did you stop beating your wife?"

Retaliation is likely to follow. The problem with retaliation is this: each retaliatory act tends to be a bit more serious than the act provoking it. This is how we warn others to cease because we are more powerful and are willing to use that power to hurt them more deeply than they can hurt us.

Bystanders must commit—they are no longer allowed to sit and watch. The middle ground is gone, and neutrality is no longer tolerated; you are either with or against us. Since the battle lines are now so clearly drawn, attacks focused on gaining the upper hand and attempts to convince the other side to capitulate are largely abandoned. Force now comes to the forefront, and the causes of the conflict are no longer understood as incompatible standpoints but rooted in the evil character of those on the other side.

Attacks on reasonableness increase dramatically. If anyone's honor is repeatedly offended, particularly in public and by deliberate action (as interpreted by the receiving party), the conflict will likely slip into Stage 5.

10. Pearson, "Power and Politeness."

Stage 5: Attacks on Face

The transition to Stage 5 is dramatic. The concept of "face" is suddenly crucial as it signifies a person's basic status in a community of people, and that status is under attack. If regarded as a respectable citizen, they have an intact "face" and are entitled to fair treatment and respect. "Face" is hurt by public events, not private gossip or individual opinions. The goal of attacking "face" is to publicly humiliate the targeted person and destroy any base of power they may have.[11]

Attacks on face lead the parties to believe that they have finally seen through the mask of the other and discovered an immoral evil lurking there. The transformation is radical. It is not an expansion of the old, biased image but an entirely new construct accepted as a sudden insight into the very nature of the counterpart. With the loss of face, the whole conflict and its history are now reinterpreted: one side feels that the other side has followed an immoral, undermining strategy from the outset, and any constructive moves from the opposition are understood as nothing more than camouflage for their true intentions.

The fight is now narrowed to right and wrong, good and evil. One side stands for the forces of goodness and light, while the other is evil, destructive, and even embodying moral corruption. A tangible sign of Stage 5 is that some feel nauseated in the presence of the other.

The issues that triggered the fight have all but disappeared—the fight now centers on deeply held values of right and wrong. This transformation vastly increases the role of negative expectations and suspicion. All seemingly constructive moves by the opposing party are now interpreted as deception, and subsequent adverse incidents are seen as proof of the true nature of the other. Building mutual trust is now both problematic and complicated, and the gestures demanded from each side to the other to start rebuilding are intentionally humiliating. One side may demand a public apology from the other, knowing how humiliating that will be. The other sees the proposed apology as a sign of weakness and public failure, leading to further status damage. As a result, demeaning the other side may be seen as the only option for gaining the moral upper hand—even though morality is often abandoned in the process. The focus becomes gaining the upper hand by pushing the other down into an indefensible moral position more than it is to regain the moral high ground.

11. Goffman, "On Face-Work."

Incidents leading to loss of face are followed by concerted attempts to regain the advantage by attacking the intentions and morality of the other. Bystanders flee the arena, leading to further isolation and a sense of foreboding. The conflict escalates into Stage 6 when the parties issue humiliating ultimatums and strategic threats.

Stage 6: Strategies of Threats

Since no other way seems open, the conflicted parties resort to threats to force each other in the desired direction. These are no longer the deniable punishment tactics of Stage 4. Strategic threats are active and open to push the opponents into conceding.

Strategic threats are clear, unequivocal, and firm. They are also dangerous for the party, making them unable to retreat from what they have threatened without losing credibility. The final stage of threats comes in the form of ultimatums that require a "this or that" decision, both repulsive.[12]

One unintended consequence of committing to forceful action is that the parties increasingly lose control over events. Their actions and rhetoric have placed them into immovable and increasingly untenable positions.

Their sense of the situation now becomes increasingly out of touch with reality. The threatening party sees only his own demands and regards the threat as a necessary deterrent to block the counterpart from using violence. Each expects the other to yield to the pressure, but also see the devastating consequences of acquiescing and rallies to issue a more powerful counter-threat.

The conflict is now highly complex, challenging to grasp, and almost impossible to control. The parties introduce time pressure on each other through artificial deadlines that limit their ability to weigh the consequences in a turbulent and chaotic situation. Instead, both parties try to exert control by demanding that their issues be dealt with precisely as they define them—ours are uplifting, reasonable, and beneficial. At the same time, theirs are immoral, unworthy, and even feral. To their combined chagrin, keeping credibility intact now depends on the ability to carry out the threat, an escalation they had not planned for.

12. Glasl, *Confronting Conflict*, 99.

A party may severely limit its ability to de-escalate by publicly binding itself to carry out its threatened actions. The other sees this as proof of aggression and seeks effective countermeasures. By following this course, the parties severely restrict their freedom to choose different avenues to the point where they are frozen in their positions. Backing down now is understood as humiliating and destroying their cause.

If the stress worsens, the parties may begin disintegrating into smaller units acting autonomously. When this happens, binding agreements between the main actors may not even stop the destruction. When the parties actively seek to harm the other side's reaction potential by acting first, the conflict moves to Stage 7. It is a pre-emptive strike designed to disable the enemy and force a surrender.

Note: Stage 6 is often the last stage where interventions may be successful.

The final three stages of this escalation model come quickly.

Stage 7: Limited Destructive Blows

The threats of Stage 6 are designed to undermine the basic sense of security of the "enemy." In Stage 7, any remaining doubt that the threats will be carried out is banished—but group cohesion begins to disintegrate. Sensing others abandoning "the cause," the need to preserve oneself easily overrides the cause. A choice must be made between personal survival or ultimate warfare. Personal survival becomes the primary concern. It is no longer possible to see a solution that includes their counterpart, and it is increasingly difficult to see a future with any of the other factions.

For those who commit to the final stages of the fight, opponents can now be written off as heretics beyond redemption; the "enemy" is now seen simply as a subhuman impairment to be eradicated by whatever means. Attacks are in the open and are no longer deniable—or denied. Retaliation, more potent than its provocation, may become accepted as the only means of personal survival. With this new phenomenon, all pretense of civility is abandoned. The only remaining option is to destroy the enemy.

The ability to calculate consequences becomes increasingly skewed: losses to one side are gains to the other, even though they give no tangible benefit to anyone. Significant losses become acceptable if the opponent loses even more. Malice may become a powerful motive.

The smoldering fire from the opening disagreements is now a roaring and barely contained blast furnace. There comes a point where the desire for self-preservation begins to move through the combatants, and they begin to peel off toward safer ground. For those who continue, the objectives are narrowed to securing survival by neutralizing or destroying the opposition's support base.

There is no longer any meaningful communication between the combatants, furthering their isolation and increasing paranoia. Each party is now concerned only with its survival. Ethical norms are ignored. This is war, and standard rules no longer apply.

At this stage, things take another dramatic turn: the parties recognize that winning is no longer possible. It is a lose-lose struggle, and more people head for the exits. For those who remain, surviving with less damage than their counterparts suffer becomes the primary goal as the "issues" they fought for so fervently are forgotten. At this point, few could even tell you what those issues were.[13] Attacks designed to shatter the enemy and destroy his vital systems signal the move to Stage 8.

Stage 8: Fragmentation

The attacks intensify and are designed to destroy the counterpart's power. Each group may try to fragment "enemy groups" into ineffective splinters to destroy their decision-making capabilities. As a result, the system keeping the counterpart whole is attacked, as are the system's negotiators, representatives, leaders, and underlying principles. Strong punitive countermeasures are now employed without weighing the facts of any individual incident. Truth no longer has merit.

The narratives that held the warring groups together disintegrate with the realization that the battle cannot be won. What had been coherent strategies and highly disciplined groups are now lost as the former allies splinter into factions that fight each other. The enemy must still be destroyed, but survival has center stage. The threshold to Stage 9 is reached when self-preservation is abandoned. When this happens, there are no longer restraints on further destructiveness. The fight is beyond salvage, let alone resolution.[14]

13. Glasl, *Confronting Conflict,* 102.
14. Glasl, *Confronting Conflict,* 102–3.

Stage 9: Together Into the Abyss

In this last stage of conflict escalation, the drive to even preserve oneself is abandoned in the need to annihilate the enemy. The enemy shall be destroyed even though it means self-destruction. This is the scorched earth policy Adolf Hitler adopted at the end of World War II. All bridges are burned, and there is no return. A total war of destruction without scruples or remorse is waged. There are no innocent victims, only "collateral damage." The only concern in this race into the abyss is to ensure the enemy will go over the edge with you—but preferably first. The mentality is one of waking up in jail and telling your cellmate, "Yeah, I'm pretty beat up, but you should see the other guy!"

Fortunately, few organizational conflicts will reach Stages 8 and 9. The most notable ones include Jim Jones and the suicide of the 900 members of his People's Temple and David Koresh and the Branch Davidians in Waco, Texas. Congregations tend to fracture long before that level of intensity is reached, causing a church split. Sometimes, those who leave will start another church, but most of the time, they will scatter as individuals and families and be absorbed into other congregations.

The most common levels of conflict at which they begin looking for outside help are stages 5 and 6. Resolving the conflict at Stage 7 is possible but also extremely difficult, as the emotional levels of engagement are intense and narrowly focused, morphing into a winner-takes-all proposition. According to Glasl, Level 7 is also the last stage where a settlement agreement is possible. Levels 8 and 9 concentrate on eradicating the enemy or going over the brink of mutual destruction together.

Amazingly, these internal wars can escalate to the final stages and still be invisible to the casual observer. I have run into it where people in total consternation asked, "What happened? Who was fighting? Why?" In one instance, the senior minister was being forced into retirement. The battle raged quietly for over two years, and a third of the congregation left, but the average member had no knowledge of the conflict. They may have wondered why the minister's sermons were suddenly and thunderously focused on Satan being loose in the congregation and why so many people disappeared, but very few questions were asked. It is now almost two decades later, and the core of the remaining members who were in the fight—and remain—have not experienced forgiveness and healing from each other. No leader, from the new minister on down, publicly and directly addressed the fight or its lingering consequences.

Is it possible to escape in these end stages? Glasl offers some sobering advice:

> Against this background of this archetypal image I always describe the escalation as a downward movement, into the underworld and baser nature of individual people and groups. As the escalation progresses, the link with the Light personality is increasingly lost. Each action provokes negative powers in the subconscious of the opposing party. Reactions occur that are no longer controlled by the Ego or the Higher Self. Therefore, the way out of escalation is always a confrontation with one's own alien, darker sides.[15]

How group conflicts escalate is charted and predictable. Each response to a provocation is likely to be stronger than the provocation itself and is intended to act as a warning to the other side of future responses if provoked again. These conflicts become more emotional and less rational as they escalate through the stages. There is usually a pause at Stage 6 as the parties sort through the wreckage, knowing they are near the precipice, and hesitate there. If no one intervenes, the conflict intensity can accelerate quickly into scorched earth warfare and even mutual annihilation.

15. Glasl, *Confronting Conflict*, 106.

5

The Wounded Healer

Nobody escapes being wounded. We are all wounded people, whether physically, emotionally, mentally, or spiritually. The main question is not "How can we hide our wounds?" so we don't have to be embarrassed but "How can we put our woundedness in the service of others?" When our wounds cease to be a source of shame and become a source of healing, we have become wounded healers.

~Henri Nouwen

Several years ago, I was at a church where the entire staff was ready to quit. I interviewed more than twenty people, from the custodian to the lead pastor, and patterns of misunderstanding, distrust, and deceit emerged. I understood the depth of their pain and uncertainty. I was deeply impressed with their resilience and equally repelled by their pettiness. I knew what the conflict was about on the surface. More importantly, I knew what was happening in the dark waters beneath this broken and sinking place. As I read my notes, I recognized and acknowledged their pain—and was caught up in it. Henri Nouwen put it well: "Your service will not be perceived as authentic unless it comes from a heart wounded by the suffering about which we speak."[1] I did not want to feel so deeply, but compassion overwhelmed the emotional wall I had built. I had to feel what they felt to be authentic, so I dropped my defenses and let it wash over me.

1. Nouwen, *Wounded Healer*, 4.

The rawness of their emotions got to me. I sensed it would be easy to influence the elders into accepting my conclusions and recommendations, but that was not my job. I was to present them with my findings and their options. The decisions were theirs to make.

I needed to confront myself honestly and change, for they had not called me to lead as a champion. I needed to be a servant peacemaker.

We all have triggers that detonate strong emotions when pulled. The problem is that left unattended, they act as biases, silently influencing how we proceed.

We all have emotional scars and open wounds near the surface that influence how we think and act. They "bias" my thinking at such a low intensity that I am unaware of their influence. To be effective in this calling, I must know my biases, acknowledge that they are active, and counter them. It is humbling to realize I am my worst enemy and must protect these people from me.

All it sometimes takes is a phrase someone says to resurrect a buried memory of a difficult time in the past. Once that memory is reawakened, I cannot quickly put it out of my mind. It sits at the edge of consciousness and influences my thinking and judgment. Some would argue that I should stand back and let someone unaffected by previous incidents do this work—but no one is unaffected. I concluded that only a wounded healer can penetrate the angry darkness. Instead of withdrawing, I must consciously build a wall between my biases and what I am doing.

Conflict is always stressful for those within it and those called to help. Though your desire may be to push forward and hasten the healing, it is always wise to slow down before offering solutions. Your solutions are not needed here. *Their* solutions can be healing. You may not recognize that you are in a very delicate place for yourself and the people looking to you for help. You are a wounded healer, and in your woundedness lurks the temptation to find your healing through them.

You will not find your healing here.

"Physician, heal yourself!" (Luke 4:23) is a warning to the healer to turn inward, away from others, to find and isolate what infects us. We must find and bind our wounds but not heal them. We must do this to protect the congregation from our woundedness.

You cannot do this work without being deeply affected. It gets to you, no matter what defenses you have learned to raise or what barriers you have erected to insulate yourself from the pain, anger, and fear surrounding you. No one is impervious to this emotional onslaught, nor could someone who does not feel what they feel do this work effectively. I was a wounded healer dragging my baggage behind me when I walked in the door, and now I am even more deeply wounded, and my baggage train is even heavier.

Every peacemaker is a wounded healer. We know the bitterness of conflict, the terrible pain of knowing friends are now enemies, and the brittle fear of being lost in the middle of familiar people and places. Only wounded healers can genuinely understand and appreciate the pain, misery, uncertainty, and betrayal that they will encounter in conflict-wounded congregations. It will wound us more if we are called upon to lead this final process. We must embrace the wounding, all of it, for in embracing our woundedness, compassion wells forth. We can reach out more tenderly, hold others more assuredly, and quietly guide them to the restoration of souls and relationships.

We all build protective walls to prevent others from getting too close, fearing more emotional and spiritual injury. The walls keep them at arm's length and leave us choosing to whom we will open the barriers and reveal our true selves. Unfortunately, we can also become hard and unyielding and develop sharp edges that serve not just to protect us but unwittingly push others away. Becoming a truly compassionate and wise guide means embracing our woundedness and doing the same things we advocate for them: going deep inside, finding our pain, and bringing it out into the light of day as something not to be feared. We must feel our woundedness in all its intensity so that we see it as the refiner's fire it is. When we know what awaits, we can walk past its trap. In finding our wounds along with theirs, we also see a new paradox: we are wounded even deeper, and in the new wounding, we find the way open to lead them home safely. I cannot explain how it works; I can only say that this is how it works for me.

We must strive to become more open and vulnerable as we allow God to change us into true peacemakers. If we are scrupulously honest with ourselves, we know we have been in the same hole they are in now. We must accept ourselves as the weak and wounded creatures that we are, full of mistakes and missteps and needing forgiveness. This transparency to others and ourselves produces a genuine winsomeness that those who look to us for help see and feel; they are more comfortable and trusting.

Empathy is also unsettling. We feel their pain, and in feeling, we absorb its essence, which becomes ours. It scars us in small ways. We cannot eradicate it by ourselves any more than we can remove melted butter from a piece of toast. Their conflict has become ours, but in ways we often do not recognize or acknowledge. We resonate with their experience, if not the circumstances, for their experience is also our own, even if in a different form.

Our biases push us towards solutions based on our desires and dreams about how things should be. In hoping for a specific outcome, a hidden temptation insinuates itself to nudge the direction of the process rather than allowing it to work on its own. In nudging, we become conduits of our wishes and woundedness in place of theirs—we must not go there. Instead, we must be open conduits for God to work through us.

GETTING OUT OF GOD'S WAY

It is right and good that we want to help others heal. Allowing them to sense our caring and see our transparency encourages trust to grow so they can seek the light of hope. Sensing our woundedness, they know we will understand when they describe their pain and sorrow. We must then get out of God's way so that they can find his path to reconciliation. We must not inject our solutions; otherwise, we rob them of the fullness and miracle of their healing and may inject the seeds of future discord. We know how we want them to heal, but only God knows how they must heal. We can open the door and invite them through, but that is all—we do not know what is best. The outcome must be theirs and their God's; we are only their guides.

No peacemaker is entirely neutral. Our biases shape us in ways we may seldom see, damaging our ability to help our clients get where they need to go. Our partialities often drive us to find solutions that might be right for us but not for them. It is a normal tendency, but it must be resisted!

Find your biases by examining what issues and behaviors irritate you and how you label people. By labeling, I place someone into a box that fits my notions of what they do, who they are, and how they should be. It locks a chain around them and "niches" them, keeping me from more deeply examining why they are that way—and how I am like them. Labeling dehumanizes, taking away both my humanity and theirs. I caution everyone who travels here that you are tap-dancing on quicksand—you will sink unnoticed until you are trapped if you do not identify and allow your biases and accumulated pain to be blocked off as you work through the process. You will feel them intimately but from a distance. There must be an impenetrable wall between your biases and the people entrusting themselves to you.

Am I contradicting myself? No. We must look deeply into our anger, fears, and resentments and find from whence they come. Otherwise, we may build our barriers in the wrong places. Only after this deep probing can we create the correct barriers to keep our biases out of their healing.

However, carefully examining biases requires confronting our need to repent and change. Steps 4, 6, and 7 of most twelve-step groups speak directly to this: "4. Made a searching and fearless moral inventory of ourselves; 6. [We] were entirely ready to have God remove all these character defects; and 7. Humbly asked Him to remove our shortcomings."[2] How elegantly straightforward. Twelve-step practitioners understand that they are their own worst enemies. So are we.

I have come to believe that evil usually approaches us in the appearance of good will and honorable intentions. If true, the most effective way to sabotage others' healing is through us rather than in direct and obvious opposition. We cannot afford to allow our good intentions to become weapons of further destruction!

The answer is in prayer, but not in the same type of prayer we often hear.

A cartoon says it perfectly. The minister is speaking from the pulpit: "Tonight, let's see if we can testify without bragging, give prayer requests without gossiping, and pray without preaching, okay?" Much prayer from the pulpit is preaching in disguise, and most private prayer is either pleading for God to change something in our lives or telling God what to do. We pray for patience rather than for opportunities to grow patience. We pray for courage rather than for opportunities to be courageous.

We need something more profound.

The apostle John wrote that another man named John (the Baptizer) recognized the hard truth that he was in the way of something far greater unless he did something to change the equation. "That joy is mine, and it is now complete. He must become greater; I must become less" (John 3:29b–30). Each of us can be a roadblock; hence, we must remove ourselves as impediments. We, too, must be diminished if God is to have full reign within the wounded souls of this congregation. Trying to help

2. Alcoholics Anonymous, *12 Steps.*

a congregation heal while full of ourselves is as futile as pushing a river back upstream.

INTO THE BIG EMPTY

A full bottle cannot be filled. It must be empty before it can be filled. And so must we. Holy emptiness comes through contemplative prayer, something few understand or practice. Even after several years of practicing, I still feel like a novice. I am learning, and this is what I have learned.

Contemplative prayer does not demand that God listen to us but instead listens for the still, small voice of God. It does not cry out but sighs within. We must be quiet to hear that voice and comprehend it for what it is. We must shut down the constant clamor that fills our minds and replace it with mindful stillness. We must shut out the tapes playing repeatedly about all that we have learned and must do. We must surrender our fear of failure and slow our hearts as they race with anxiety. We cannot hear when our minds are screaming. We must become less.

Hebrew Scripture clearly illustrates my point.

> The LORD said, "Go out and stand on the mountain in the presence of the LORD, for the LORD is about to pass by." Then a great and powerful wind tore the mountains apart and shattered the rocks before the LORD, but the LORD was not in the wind. After the wind, there was an earthquake, but the LORD was not in the earthquake. After the earthquake came a fire, but the LORD was not in the fire. And after the fire came a gentle whisper.—1 Kings 19:11–12.

The voice of God was in the whisper.

The one constant in praying/meditating like this is the silence of listening and waiting. We will never find God's voice in the tumult of our emotions.

Contemplative prayer is paradoxical as it takes us to places we have not thought of going to and may not wish to go to. It leads us. It presumes that we do not have answers, which goes against our natural desire to tell God what we want him to do: "Lord, please bring forgiveness and reconciliation to this congregation." As contradictory as it may seem in a section about woundedness, forgiveness, and reconciliation, God may not want them to have any of these, at least not at this point, and for reasons we cannot know.

By asking God what the people need rather than assuming we know what they need and by being open and unimpeded in hearing the answer, we allow God to direct us. We will not help our wounded flock get to where God wants them if we rely on what we know—we must rely on what God knows: "Trust in the LORD with all your heart and lean not on your own understanding; in all your ways submit to him, and he will make your paths straight" (Prov 3: 5–6). What a profound truth!

Peacemakers live for the cathartic moments, the breakthroughs in understanding, but this is misdirection. We seek small beginnings, hidden treasures, and seemingly lost things. Jesus spoke of the subtle beginnings of faith, not grandiose explosions. Franciscan monk Richard Rohr calls these word pictures of mustard seeds, lost pennies, and tiny amounts of yeast mixed through flour "transformative images" because they are the exact reverse of how we want God to behave.

Getting there and becoming open to God's voice means adopting a child's stance, which Rohr calls a "beginner's mind." Rohr says that getting there as an adult is like planting a seed: Hard soil and a hard soul will thwart everything. Having a mindset where we come first is nothing more than rocks and thorns—and a waste of seeds.[3]

I learned that I need a concentrated time of meditation and prayer to clear my thoughts and biases and get my ego out of the way before beginning the following practices. I need to spend several hours, perhaps an entire day, alone—no cell phone. No tablet. No email. No books. No one to talk to. No fishing pole. Just me. This is a kind of "vision quest," a time of transformation, and I must allow God to do the work. I must not skip it or cut it short.

Find a comfortable place where you will not be disturbed by distractions. You are preparing for transformation. We must go into the desert alone. No feedback. No data. Into the Big Empty. You go in as who you are but will come out as someone else.

Search your heart for those you have not forgiven. Confess it to God. Find the pain that goes with it and release it. Let your anger go and forgive. Now, open your mind to allow the Holy Spirit to fill it, open the drain, and let your pain and prejudices flow out. Consciously release them, dismiss your normal thoughts, and focus on experiencing God and not thinking or wondering about God but experiencing God. God is not in your thoughts or your wondering but is the reality behind everything.

3. Rohr, *Everything Belongs*, 32–33.

In our noisy world, we can learn from the ancient prophet Elijah. Elijah experienced an earthquake, howling winds, and a roaring fire on the Mountain of the Lord. Each of these was misdirection, just as the world's noise is misdirection for the peacemaker. The voice of the Lord is to be found in silence, for it is a still, small voice.

Perhaps you can use a way of centering by reducing the scope of your focus. Narrow the beam. A wonderful mentor taught me this simple meditation technique, and I repeat it very slowly to shut down my mind and begin to focus on becoming empty and so open that only God can fill me. I find it in Psalm 46:

Be still, and know that I am God.

Be still, and know that I am.

Be still, and know.

Be still.

Be.

And now, this simple prayer: "Holy One, please show me how I can best help these people."

Listen.

Then, wounded healer, go and heal.

Additional Resource: I find the meditations of Fr. Richard Rohr to be beneficial in centering my mind on the needs of others.[4]

4. See Rohr, "2022 Daily Meditations."

6

In the Beginning . . . Practicalities

Discord and division become no Christian. For wolves to worry the lambs is no wonder, but for one lamb to worry another, this is unnatural and monstrous.

~Thomas Brooks

Peacemakers worldwide have discovered a general reality: Faith communities tend to wait until the damage of internal conflict is deep and endangering the entire enterprise before calling on outsiders for help. When they do call, it is out of desperation. They are in crisis, their future is threatened, they are humiliated that they need help, and they do not know what to do.

The process starts small but expands to include more and more people as it progresses. There are two avenues of approach: 1) the professional peacemaker and 2) lay peacemakers.

This is how it generally works for a professional peacemaker.

INITIAL CONTACT

Members of the governing board or one of the ministers usually make initial contact by either telephone or email. Typically, their story will be too short to give enough information, so be prepared to ask questions, such as:

- How long has the congregation existed?
- How many typically attend your religious services?
- Has that number been increasing, staying static, or decreasing?
- What is the financial impact of the conflict?
- Have people left because of the conflict?
- Is the conflict in the open or within specific groups?
- When did the conflict start?
- What are the roots of the problem?
- What are the main points of contention?
- Have threats of any kind been made? If so, what are they?
- Who are the main participants?
- Are you authorized to contact me? If so, by whom?

Internal peacemakers likely already know the answers or can get them quickly.

The next step is to set up and conduct a telephone interview with governing board representatives. They will want to know who you are and why you are qualified to do this work, including your experience and training.

a) Have an up-to-date curriculum vitae ready to submit.
b) Be ready to explain the process you would use if retained.
c) Be ready to offer a scope of work agreement that includes all contracted conditions, timelines, costs, and fees.

Before you agree to work with any conflict, you must first have absolute clarity on what is expected of you and what you expect of them. These questions must be answered in clear and certain terms:

Who are you working for? My practice is that I work for the governing board, whatever its form, as that is where the legal operating authority generally lies. This may not always be the case, depending on the governance structure. This authority may instead lie with the denomination or even the minister.

Who decides when contradictory instructions are given? This happens more frequently than one might think!

What are the timelines? (They usually are in a state of great urgency, but urgency on their part does not necessarily create an emergency on your part.)

Is a written report expected? My practice is always to issue a written report with recommendations for immediate changes and follow-up.

Will you have access to everyone that you consider appropriate?

Your Expectations

It would be best if you made your expectations clear to avoid misunderstandings. These are mine and are placed in a written contract for services that includes the scope of work:

1. I must have complete access to every person I believe necessary.
2. They will supply a private meeting space for interviews. All interviews are explicitly confidential unless permission is granted to break confidentiality. Exceptions include threats to harm persons or property and previously unreported vulnerable person abuse. I will not advocate for or against the positions or proposals of any party, but I will challenge the thinking behind a proposal if I consider it necessary (a technique known as reality testing).[1]
3. I advocate for godly peace, forgiveness, and reconciliation through the Holy Spirit. I will not make personnel recommendations, with one exception: If, by my training and experience, I believe that one of the major figures is mentally ill in ways that may be intractable and which directly lie at the cause of conflict and its continuation, I will make that conclusion known to the governing board so it can follow up as it believes proper.
4. The governing board, clergy, appropriate staff, and others I identify through the interview process must commit to one full day of intensive intervention work as a group.
5. My confidential written report will be distributed to the governing board and clergy. The report will include recommendations for procedural and substantive changes and will propose a date for any necessary follow-up work.
6. They agree to pay my fees and expenses upon submission.

1. Reality testing is a technique for testing positions and ideas for soundness.

If possible, all contact with the people involved should be made face to face. I generally plan for at least five days in the affected church, not including travel time.

It's been said that the janitor will know everything you need to know. It's not true, but my practice is to personally interview every church staff member and employee, from janitors to pastors, governing board members, and those identified as conflict leaders. I want to see them in person to catch clues that I might otherwise miss, such as subtle eye and facial changes, tensing at specific questions, and to gauge credibility. I try not to interview children as this is neither their fight nor is their testimony reliable unless the questioner has specialized training in conducting child interviews and follows those protocols. I was blessed to be trained in child interview techniques, but it was a long time ago, and I am not confident that what I remember is accurate.

I try to interview two or three people per hour, meaning I can interview up to twenty congregants in one day—but that day may run from 7:00 AM to 10:00 PM, depending on their availability. By the end of the second day, I will have a reasonably clear picture of what is going on. I will know who the antagonists are, the factions' positions, how the conflict unfolded, and how far apart they are emotionally and positionally. I will have also identified many underlying needs that have given the conflict energy and gained insight into how they might be resolved.

I interview the pastor(s) last, as they usually have the most to gain or lose. They often have valuable insights into relevant personalities and backgrounds. A warning: I learned early on that, in too many cases, the lead pastor or an associate pastor were the instigators, quietly manipulating everything from concealment. It happened again just two weeks ago. While this is unusual, it happens often enough that we must be aware and look for signs of it. Don't take anything you are told at face value. Verify everything if you can. Sometimes, the pastor is attacked for legitimate reasons, but there is a large enough percentage of pastors with mental disorders that you need to be very careful. For more information on this phenomenon, see my 2020 book, *Let Us Prey*.[2]

2. Puls, *Let Us Prey*.

Communication Skills

We must have the communication skills necessary to assist the group. Teaching or public speaking experience can be beneficial in this area.

We must be able to:

Reflect: Listen profoundly and paraphrase what we have heard, asking for clarification or if we have understood correctly. The purpose of reflection is to ensure that we understand what is being said and to let the participants know they are being heard. Example: "I heard you say you are considering leaving if this is unresolved. Is that correct?"

Clarify: Ask open-ended questions that seek more information that cannot generally be answered with a simple yes or no. The purpose is to gain a greater understanding of what is being said and to reinforce to the participants that we care and are fully engaged in hearing them. Example: "You suggested that the membership of the elder board should be updated. Can you tell me what you mean by that? What would that look like?"

Reframe: This may be the most difficult skill, as it takes what is said and retains the original meaning but places the statement in a different light. The purpose is to demonstrate to the participants that we truly understand what is being said and the impact of the problem. Reframing can also help them see their statement from a different viewpoint. Reframing is used throughout the process. Remember that parties often express what they want by saying what they don't like.

- Reframing can take the sting out of a comment or concern and make it easier for another party to hear and consider.
- Reframing can help clarify the issue or problem at hand.
- Reframing can help the parties focus on the future rather than the past.
- Reframing can shift the focus onto the issue rather than the person.
- Reframing can help identify a party's genuine interest.

Reframing Examples:

"No one treats me like I belong in this group. You must serve a full three-year term before they accept you."

Possible reframe: "You feel like you're being shut out because you haven't been here long enough."

> "He is such a dictator! No one is allowed to have any ideas or thoughts of their own unless they agree with him. It's not worth it anymore. Maybe I should resign."
>
> Possible reframe: "You feel that he does not listen to or consider ideas from others, and you have almost given up on working well with him."
>
> "We keep going around and around in circles. I don't see how we are going to resolve this."
>
> Possible reframe: "You're very frustrated and feel like nothing is happening. It's important to you that this be resolved."

Practice reframing statements made to you by others. Remember, reframing restates what was said but looks at it from a different viewpoint, e.g., a negative is turned into a positive.

DANCING IN THE MINEFIELD OF CHURCH CULTURE

Every organization develops an overarching culture that is visible and another, perhaps several others, invisible but continually operating in the background. Within this duality are micro-cultures consisting of groups of people with certain interests. The strongest of these micro-cultures are informal power centers that influence other cultures. Their power is not necessarily dependent on their positions within the organization but is drawn from invisible communication lines inside and outside organizational boundaries.[3]

The investigation process will usually reveal these invisible forces. One of the best sources of the "projected culture" is the church website. This is where they tell what they want the world to know about them, particularly the image they want the world to see. In that sense, the website projects the desired church culture to every web visitor. They want you to believe this, but in many cases, it is little more than wishful thinking. I began digging for their belief statements and other posts that would give me a flavor of the place and people. Just remember, what is on their website reflects how they wish to be seen by outsiders and may not reflect reality.

Congregational cultures reflect the surrounding culture, but only to a limited degree. One of the reasons people join these faith communities

3. See Cameron and Quinn, *Diagnosing and Changing.*

is their uniqueness. Even congregations within the most inflexible belief systems will differ and often advertise their distinctives. Four congregations on four adjoining street corners will be distinctly different from one another, even if their underlying belief systems are almost identical. Our task is to work separately from the culture but in such a way that we do not offend cultural norms.

Internal peacemakers have an advantage over outsiders. They know the people and the culture, which allows them to work from within. They can intervene in valuable ways, starting when they learn about the conflict. Their disadvantage is that they are already known, which lowers their credibility to a limited degree.

The damage is generally real and deep when outside peacemakers are called in. The congregation and its leaders are wounded, emotionally bleeding, and wary. Trust had been broken in perhaps the last place the congregants believed it could happen. The senses of betrayal and confusion are strong and profoundly influential. They are in emotional and spiritual pain, and they are grieving what has been lost: friendships, peace, trust . . .

They don't know or trust the outsider. Even if they know you, they may not trust you. Trust must be earned.[4]

Therefore, we must live and breathe gentle hope and encouragement. We must be committed to bringing about lasting peace. Like frightened creatures trapped in a corner, they look to us to see if we will bring more pain or help them heal. In the meantime, they stay as far away from us as possible, growling softly in the background, ready to bare their teeth if necessary.

No one said this was easy!

The interventionist/peacemaker needs as much information as possible from the outset. In gathering the data, the interventionist must be aware that probably all of it is skewed by the emotional experiences of the people providing it. Conflict skews the senses more than standard situations, morphing what we observe into biased memories. We find the facts in the patterns of information and common threads woven through it.

Building trust may be the greatest challenge. This takes patience and complete transparency.

4. Some peacemakers/interventionists believe that trust should be automatic because they are professionals on the scene to help. This is a fallacy. Conflicted groups are usually at a point where trust has been so shattered that they trust no one. Trust can only be won by consistent, trustworthy behaviors over time.

7

Afflicted: When the Pastor Is the Problem

I know that after I leave, savage wolves
will come among you and not spare the flock.

~Paul of Tarsis, Acts 20:29

Books about church conflict rarely address one of the most soul-searing issues I and others have faced, usually discovered by accident: the pastor is the problem. Raising this problem is generally avoided as long as possible, but it is real and must be confronted when uncovered. The issues are sometimes what we expect, such as when the pastor may have a different vision for the future in a faith community that sees no need to change. It may be that their teaching and preaching style grates on the nerves, is too flashy, or congregants risk going into a coma when listening. It could be disagreements about pay and benefits, lifestyle, or theology, such as having a puritanical pastor in a liberal church (it happens!). It could be almost anything.

None of the religious conflict management books I have read even mention mental health issues affecting the minister beyond brief mentions of depression, burnout, or compassion fatigue. While each problem is serious, they also overlap in cause and effect and may be symptoms of something much more serious. None mentioned serious mental illnesses such as personality disorders.[1]

1. See Adams et al., *Clergy Burnout* and Puls, "Narcissist Pastors."

The following information is not intended to help anyone make a diagnosis. It is intended to acquaint the reader with some of the symptoms of several mental disorders so that informed recommendations can be made for professional help when the symptoms are recognized.

BURNOUT

"Burnout" is the most common mental health complaint among pastors. According to *Psychology Today*, burnout is not a simple result of long hours; it is the result of being unable to control your job because you constantly work to meet other people's expectations. You are forced to work toward goals that don't resonate with you or you disagree with and respond to a lack of social support for your actions. It could even be that the work wears you down and you have lost your passion for it. (This happened to me after working for the same large corporation for twenty-six years.) Many people experiencing burnout try to compensate by working harder and longer hours, but the opposite is needed: rest and time away.[2]

A few years ago, I was at a church outside of Dallas, Texas. As is my practice, I interviewed elders, deacons, congregants, and the associate pastor. I always save the senior pastor interview for last; by then, I usually have a clear picture of the conflict. I went to present it to the senior pastor and cooperatively map a pathway out of the mire. In this case, the deacons and elders had several misunderstandings that escalated into open conflict. A few procedural violations had worsened things, but I was impressed by how much the church had grown in recent years. The people I interviewed indicated that the senior pastor, Rob, did not know how to handle their conflict and told them to work it out themselves. My alarm bells started softly chiming.[3]

After interviewing the elders, deacons, staff, and several members, I finally sat with Pastor Rob. The opinion that he did not know how to intervene was correct, but what else I learned was much more troubling. He was uninterested in dealing with the matter, even with my help in the background. He had only angry energy, stayed in his office as much as he could, and had no interest in going out and meeting with his church members. In addition, he was sleeping poorly, had stopped working out,

2. Barna Research, "Pastors Share Top Reasons."

3. Young, "Burnout."

and was overeating. He was angry at the board members and had difficulty putting together his Sunday sermons.

I asked him when he had last taken his four full weeks of vacation. He did not know. Was it eight years ago or ten? He had taken ten nonconsecutive *days* in the last year but said his workload did not allow him to take more. I suggested this might be part of his problem, but he quickly insisted this was not the case. He was frustrated with the situation but seemed to fear what might happen if he was gone too much (this is a common, self-inflicted injury). He looked at me with horror when I suggested he was long overdue for a sabbatical. He agreed he was experiencing "some burnout" but insisted he could handle it. In his words, "I just need to tough it out." Welcome to Texas!

When I finally put everything together, he seemed to be a victim of success. The church had doubled over the last few years, and families were streaming in as new subdivisions popped up. But the entire church had grown beyond his ability to pastor it. Despite this, he was determined not to hire an executive pastor who could take over the day-to-day functions, allowing him to spend much more time in the areas he valued.

I explained what I thought we should do, and on Saturday evening, we moved forward with a reconciliation process.

The Saturday evening reconciliation process was long and intense but paid dividends. As we neared the end, several deacons and elders embraced each other while seeking forgiveness and reconciliation. That is until Pastor Rob stormed out while muttering, "This is all bullshit." With that, we identified the primary cause of their problems.

The respected Barna research organization offers some startling findings: As of March 2022, the percentage of pastors considering quitting full-time ministry within the past year was 42 percent. This is consistent with data from fall 2021 when Barna first reported on a sharp increase in pastoral burnout, and it confirms the growing number of pastors who are considering resignation—a rise of 13 percent to 42 percent in January 2021. Over half of pastors considering quitting full-time ministry (56 percent) say "the immense stress of the job" has factored into their thoughts on leaving. Beyond these general stressors, two in five pastors (43 percent) said, "I feel lonely and isolated," while 38 percent named "current political divisions" as reasons they have considered walking away.[4]

4. Barna Research, "Pastors Share."

What are the differences between simple stress and burnout? Dr. Sherrie Bourg Carter writes in *Psychology Today*, "[T]he difference between stress and burnout is a matter of degree, which means that the earlier you recognize the signs, the better able you will be to avoid burnout."[5]

Signs of physical and emotional exhaustion (adapted from Carter):

- Chronic fatigue. Increasingly tired most days, eventually leading to feeling completely drained and overwhelmed.
- Insomnia: Difficulty falling or staying asleep even though exhausted.
- Forgetfulness and Poor Concentration: Difficulty remembering tasks and focusing.
- Physical Symptoms: chest pain, heart palpitations, shortness of breath, headaches.
- Increased Illness: The immune system weakens with exhaustion, increasing illness.
- Loss of Appetite: This is especially significant if you love food.
- Anxiety: Mild worry intensifying to interfere with daily life.
- Depression: Increasing feelings of sadness, hopelessness; can develop into severe depression; suicidal thoughts.
- Anger: irritability can become serious outbursts and conflicts at home and work.

Signs of Cynicism and Detachment

- Loss of enjoyment. You no longer enjoy things and turn down invitations. Eventually, loss of enjoyment can affect all areas of life.
- Pessimism. At first, this may present as negative self-talk and/or moving from a glass-half-full to a glass-half-empty attitude. You begin to see life and relationships as trials to be endured. At its worst, this may move beyond how you feel about yourself and extend to trust issues with coworkers and family members and a feeling that you can't count on anyone.

5. Carter, "Tell-Tale Signs of Burnout."

- Isolation. Increasing disinterest in socializing with friends or colleagues.
- Detachment. Detachment is a general sense of feeling disconnected from others or your environment. It can take the form of the isolative behaviors described above and result in removing yourself emotionally and physically from your job and other responsibilities.

Signs of Ineffectiveness and Lack of Accomplishment

- *Negative feelings:* Feelings of apathy and hopelessness. It presents a general sense that nothing is going right or matters. Life comes to a point where we may ask, "What's the point?"
- *Increased irritability*. Getting angry at little things that do not matter.
- *Lack of productivity and poor performance*. No matter what you do, you can't climb out of the hole.[6]

Burnout is generally identified as having four personality dimensions: the desire to please others, guilt or shame proneness, lack of self-compassion, and lack of differentiation of self from the role (this is particularly true for men, who tend to see themselves as inseparable from what they do).

On the desire to please others: "Clergy with a high desire to please others neglect their hobbies, families, and spirituality, fear letting down congregants, and have difficulty saying no to requests. Clergy low in the desire to please reserve time for their personal lives without feeling selfish or anxious about disappointing others."[7]

Guilt and shame are distinct emotions. "Researchers have described *shame* as a feeling that is deeply associated with a person's sense of self apart from any interactions with others; guilt, on the other hand, emerges as a result of something I have done that negatively affects someone else; *guilt* is something I feel because I have *done* something bad. *Shame* is something I feel because I *am* bad."[8] Psychiatrist Willem Martens says, "Shame is felt as an inner torment, as a sickness of the soul. It is the most poignant experience of the self by the self, a wound felt from the inside,

6. Carter, "Tell-Tale Signs."
7. Barna Research, "Pastors Share."
8. Thompson, *Soul of Shame*, 62.

dividing individuals from themselves and each other."[9] Guilt is separate from us and what we did—it does not make me worthless and can be repaired. Shame, on the other hand, is all about who I am—broken, useless, and beyond restoration.

Self-compassion entails being kind and forgiving to oneself during times of failure and disappointment. We learn from our mistakes and move on. People low in self-compassion tend to berate themselves for extended periods for even minor shortcomings. They are more prone to depression, self-criticism, thought suppression, and anxiety, while high self-compassion reverses these.

Men are particularly bad at differentiating themselves from what they do. We tend to see what we do as being who we are, and failure at what we do means we are failures as a state of being. By separating from the role, failure becomes a temporary setback. Clergy who can distinguish their personal identity and values from their role and effectiveness as clergy members often experience lower levels of burnout.[10]

As you can see, burnout is a spectrum disorder that may include depression, anxiety, and compassion fatigue.

Diagnosable depression is further along the spectrum than simple burnout.

A depressive disorder is an illness that involves the body, mood, and thoughts. It interferes with daily life and normal functioning and causes pain for the person with the disorder and those who care about them.[11]

A depressive disorder is different from a passing blue mood. It is not a sign of personal weakness or a condition that can be willed or wished away. People with depressive illness cannot merely "pull themselves together" and get better. Without treatment, symptoms can last for weeks, months, or years. Depression is a common but serious illness, and most people who experience it need treatment to improve. Appropriate treatment, including medication, can help most who suffer from depression.

Major depression is manifested by a combination of symptoms that interfere with the ability to work, study, sleep, eat, and enjoy once-pleasurable activities. Such a disabling episode of depression may occur only once but more commonly occurs several times in a lifetime.

9. Martens, "Shame and Narcissism," 11.

10. Wasberg, "Differentiation of Self."

11. Barnard and Curry, "Relationship of Clergy Burnout."

Dysthymic disorder, also called dysthymia, involves long-term (two years or longer) less severe symptoms that do not disable but keep one from functioning normally or from feeling good. Many people with dysthymia also experience major depressive episodes at some time in their lives.[12]

Symptoms vary and may include:

- Persistent sad, anxious, or empty mood.
- Feelings of hopelessness or pessimism.
- Feelings of guilt, worthlessness, or helplessness.
- Loss of interest or pleasure in hobbies and activities that were once enjoyed, including sex.
- Decreased energy, fatigue, being "slowed down."
- Difficulty concentrating, remembering, or making decisions.
- Insomnia, early morning awakening, or oversleeping.
- Appetite and/or weight loss or overeating and weight gain.
- Thoughts of death or suicide, suicide attempts.
- Restlessness, irritability.
- Persistent physical symptoms that do not respond to treatment, such as headaches, digestive disorders, and chronic pain.[13]

Anxiety

According to the American Psychiatric Association, anxiety is a normal stress reaction and can be beneficial in some situations. It can alert us to dangers and help us prepare and pay attention. Anxiety disorders differ from normal feelings of nervousness or anxiousness and involve excessive fear or anxiety. Anxiety disorders are the most common mental disorders and affect nearly 30 percent of adults at some point in their lives. However, anxiety disorders are treatable, and several effective treatments are available. Treatment helps most people lead normal, productive lives.[14]

12. Sawchuk, "What Is Depression?"
13. Mayo Clinic, "Depression."
14. American Psychological Association, "Anxiety."

How Common Are Anxiety Disorders?

In any given year, the estimated percentage of US adults with various anxiety disorders is:

- 7 percent to 9 percent: specific phobia
- 7 percent: social anxiety disorder
- 2 percent to 3 percent: panic disorder
- 2 percent: agoraphobia (extreme or irrational fear of entering open or crowded places, of leaving one's own home, or of being in places from which escape is difficult).
- 2 percent: generalized anxiety disorder
- 1 percent to 2 percent: separation anxiety disorder

Women are more likely than men to experience anxiety disorders.

Anxiety refers to the anticipation of a future concern and is more associated with muscle tension and avoidance behavior.[15]

Fear is an emotional response to an immediate threat and is more associated with a fight-or-flight reaction—either staying to fight or leaving to escape danger. Fear-based anxiety disorders can cause people to try to avoid situations that trigger or worsen their symptoms. Job performance, schoolwork, and personal relationships can be affected.[16]

In general, for a person to be diagnosed with an anxiety disorder, the fear or anxiety must:

- Be out of proportion to the situation or age-inappropriate.
- Hinder the ability to function normally.

The demands placed on the clergy, by themselves and others, put pastors at greater risk for depression than individuals with other occupations. The depression rate among clergy was 11.1 percent—double the then-national rate of 5.5 percent. It has since doubled again. "Twenty-six percent of U.S. Protestant pastors say they have personally struggled with some type of mental illness, including 17% who say it was diagnosed and 9% who say they experienced it but were never diagnosed."[17]

15. Duckett, "Clergy More Likely to Suffer."
16. Lifeway Research, "Pastors Have Congregational."
17. Postell, "Stress Tops Mental Challenges."

The anxiety rate among the clergy was 13.5 percent. More than 7 percent of clergy simultaneously experienced depression and anxiety.[18]

Job stress was identified as the predominant cause. The minister's role encompasses several stressful activities, including grief counseling (for which a majority feel they are not adequately trained), balancing the competing demands of congregants, and the weekly sermon. On top of this is the "business end" of the church: finances, budgets, board meetings, committee meetings, staff meetings, personnel issues, and so on, for which most pastors have little to no training. "The strain of these roles is further amplified by having to switch rapidly between them, which other studies have shown to exacerbate stressful experiences."[19]

A minister's job demands can be overwhelming, particularly if the minister is not adept at time or boundary management. "The top predictor of depression is the minister's guilt about not doing enough at work, followed by a lack of social support from the congregation. The top predictor of anxiety was doubting their call to ministry."[20]

COMPASSION FATIGUE

Compassion fatigue is one of the recent diagnoses contributing to burnout and depression among the clergy. It results from pouring compassion into others while receiving little to none in return over an extended period.[21] Compassion fatigue can be defined as the emotional price one pays for caring for others without sufficient returned caring. It is also known as vicarious or secondary trauma, referencing the way that other people's trauma can become one's own. "The symptoms of compassion fatigue make it more difficult to provide patient care and to perform other duties."[22] Compassion fatigue is often combined with or diagnosed as post traumatic stress via vicarious trauma, which is trauma experienced through the stories of others. Compassion fatigue and vicarious trauma appear as problems for professional providers such as nurses, physicians, counselors—and ministers.[23] It has also been noted in emer-

18. Lifeway Research, "Pastors Have Congregational."
19. Postell, "Stress Tops Mental Challenges."
20. Adams et al., "Clergy Burnout."
21. Canadian Medical Association, "What Is Compassion Fatigue?"
22. Tunajek, "Compassion Fatigue."
23. Slocum-Gori et al., "Understanding Compassion Satisfaction."

gency first responders such as paramedics and police officers, resulting in severe changes in clinicians over time as a result of working with trauma victims.[24] Anyone from any profession can experience secondary stress and PTSD symptoms. As a former police officer, I can attest to this reality as several scenes have stayed with me in vivid color, sound, and smell since the mid-1980s, though I no longer dream about them.

Note that compassion fatigue (CF) is defined as the emotional "cost of caring" for others and is a stress response that appears suddenly and without warning and includes a sense of helplessness, isolation, and confusion. CF is unique to the "caring professions," where the caregiver is constantly in compassion mode, with little compassion being returned. Their "compassion tank" eventually runs dry like a reservoir with a slow leak and no incoming water. If not attended to, CF may lead to depression and stress-related illnesses.[25]

Pastors are often called upon to work with traumatized people and find themselves sharing the emotional burden of their parishioners to ease the healing process. Compassion is more than empathy or sympathy—compassion demands actions to alleviate suffering, and pastors often find themselves immersed in the grief and pain of those who call upon them. The cumulative effects can be crippling. Friends of mine, both therapists, worked with traumatized victims of the 9/11 terrorist attacks in New York City. In so doing, they witnessed the reality of those terrible and traumatic events. They found it impossible to keep clear barriers between themselves and their clients and eventually found themselves suffering from vicarious trauma. Vicarious trauma is now viewed as an occupational hazard of clinical work that addresses psychological trauma.

If this can happen to trained and experienced therapists, how much more vulnerable are pastors, who have little to no training in countering compassion fatigue but are on call day and night to respond to the suffering of others?

PERSONALITY DISORDERS

The public has little understanding of leader mental illness and tends to be naïve about how it works and how it affects people such as ministers.

24. Flanelly et al., "Correlates of Compassion Fatigue."
25. Flanelly et al., "Correlates of Compassion Fatigue."

We tend to attribute mental illness to people within the lower echelons but not at the top. Instead, we attribute top leaders' unusual behaviors to eccentricities connected to leadership qualities. I wish it were so! According to the Mayo Clinic,

> A personality disorder is a type of mental disorder in which you have a rigid and unhealthy pattern of thinking, functioning, and behaving. A person with a personality disorder has trouble perceiving and relating to situations and people. This causes significant problems and limitations in relationships, social activities, work, and school. In many cases, the person may not realize that they have a personality disorder because their way of thinking and behaving seems natural to them. And they may blame others for the challenges they face. [26]

I was forcefully made aware of one of the most dangerous and destructive mental illnesses in pastors about twenty years ago when I worked for an aging senior pastor who was trying to hang on to his shrinking congregation. At first, I wrote off his behaviors as eccentricities or responses to stress, but faint alarm bells gradually became louder until I could not ignore them any longer. The clincher for me was when he verbally attacked me more viciously than anyone had ever done before, which is not easy. It was only later, when I was researching his condition with the help of some mental health professional friends, that I realized how seriously ill he was. I had no idea how many ministers might have the same or similar conditions, and neither did anyone else. There was—and is—almost no research on it.

In this case, I am writing about narcissistic personality disorder (NPD), a mental disease that is almost untreatable but more destructive to organizations and the people in them than almost anything else. NPD is associated with "Cluster B" in the *DSM5*.[27] "Cluster B personality disorders are characterized by dramatic, overly emotional, or unpredictable thinking or behavior. They include antisocial personality disorder, borderline personality disorder, histrionic personality disorder and narcissistic personality disorder."[28] What makes this confusing and difficult to accept is that most of these people appear normal, if somewhat eccentric,

26. Mayo Clinic, "Personality Disorders: Symptoms."
27. Zimmerman, "Overview of Personality Disorders."
28. "Personality Disorders," 645.

at first contact. They are neither normal nor eccentric—they are actors, and many are dangerous predators.

Unfortunately, we have found that ministry is highly attractive to those with personality disorders, particularly NPD. But think a little deeper. What other profession places people in power positions, makes them privy to deeply held secrets, and invites them as honored guests into the happiest, saddest, and most poignant moments of our lives? It is common for someone with one of these disorders also to have symptoms from at least one other disorder, and perhaps more.

In its usual understated way, the Mayo Clinic lists the symptoms of NPD below (my expanding remarks are in italics):

- Belief that you're special and more important than others. *Wants to associate only with people judged to be at his (between 50 percent and 75 percent are men) high level or above; expects his orders to be followed without question; brags about his intelligence and achievements; takes credit for the work of other people; never takes responsibility for mistakes or failure and always has a scapegoat to blame.*
- Fantasies about unlimited power, success, and attractiveness. *In the most severe cases, he or she will believe whatever their fantasies tell them, and act accordingly. Sees himself as so attractive that he will ignore normal social boundaries; believes the rules do not apply to him. Must always be in control; "gaslights" those close to him to confuse, diminish, and control them.*
- Failure to recognize others' needs and feelings. *Does not experience empathy, compassion, or guilt; sees others as three-dimensional cartoons to be exploited and thrown away; knows that he hurts others constantly but does not care; terrible parents and relational partners.*
- Exaggeration of achievements or talents. *Exaggerates is a weak term—he lies constantly about anything and everything to get what he wants, then denies it when caught in blatant lies; achievements and talents are wildly exaggerated; claims friendships with powerful and wealthy people; claims degrees and awards never earned.*
- Expectation of constant praise and admiration. *Must always be the center of attention; gets rid of or emotionally destroys anyone too close who he perceives as a threat; takes credit for the work of others but never the blame for failures; constantly denigrates the work and achievements of underlings and rivals; actually does very little work*

and the product is mediocre; lazy, mediocre student. Constantly feels underappreciated.

- Arrogance. *Wants everyone to know how superior he is; will not tolerate any form of criticism or challenge; never forgives, always seeks revenge; his ideas are always the best; will not hesitate to tell you how inferior you are; everyone is expected to bask in his presence and kowtow to his every whim.*
- Unreasonable expectations of favors and advantages, often taking advantage of others. *Emotionally seduces people who have something he wants, then casually throws them away when he has it; everything he has is "the best"; will not hesitate to cut in line; his time is more important than yours; expects you to work unreasonable hours while he will not; believes that his sexual prowess is unmatched.*
- Envy of others or belief that others envy him. *Envies others of higher social status or greater wealth and power; is absolutely certain that others envy him, but also sees this as a threat because what he envies, he tries to take, and he assumes the same of others; tends to be paranoid and convinced that there are conspiracies against him; explodes in narcissistic rage when he feels threatened, which he frequently does.*[29]

Yes, I am writing about pastors. I have met them, worked with and for them, and counseled some out of the ministry.

Narcissists can be incredibly charming, but it is the seductive charm of a cobra rising to strike. They are full of grandiose ideas. Problems and failures are never their fault. And they will do whatever they can to seduce you to drop all defenses if they see you as useful—or destroy you if they see you as a threat. One of the more fascinating things about them is that no matter how they see you, you are useful only so long as you give them what they need: praise, a sense of superiority, and unquestioning loyalty. They see me and those like me as a threat. Their favorite tactic with me when I am called into their church is to shower me with praise to disarm me.

"I am so amazed that God has sent us such a godly and gifted man such as yourself. I've looked you up and your reputation makes me humble just to be here with you. By the way, I'm feeling a bit burned out—I never get any appreciation here—so would you please be my counselor?"

29. Mayo Clinic, "Personality Disorders: Symptoms."

Those are the actual words of a narcissistic pastor to me when his church called me in. I was a threat, and he was trying to protect himself through manipulation. He was trying to manipulate and control me to neutralize the threat that I presented.

Unfortunately, those with NPD almost never enter counseling voluntarily because it threatens to unmask them. Their egos are so brittle that they can shatter by experiencing what others have called their "true self." This leaves that faith community with three choices: fire him, force him into retirement, or learn to live with increasing destruction.

When I presented these options to two church boards, their response was the same: They knew that this was what they were dealing with and needed to act to save the church but needed an outsider to tell them.

If you suspect a pastor has a personality disorder, consult an experienced mental health professional before making recommendations. It's their diagnosis, not yours.

A NARCISSIST AS LEAD PASTOR

Lead pastors tend to be extroverted, but distinguishing between narcissistic and self-confident leaders can be very difficult.

The extroverted narcissist is full of self-promotion, can be exceedingly charming, and is full of grand ideas. He or she is also vindictive, greedy, dishonest, manipulative, and insecure enough to take pre-emptive actions to protect himself. They are always scanning the environment to detect potential threats and will not hesitate to act against anyone they believe is hostile.

The percentage of pastors suffering from NPD is unknown, but it is clearly higher than in the general population. "One challenge for researchers is that narcissists, although not in fact humble, are sometimes adept at feigning humility."[30] In this, they are consummate actors—the last thing they want anyone to see is them as they truly are, so they become experts at creating façades of confidence and success to distract others.

The narcissist demands absolute loyalty from everyone. Orders are to be followed immediately and without question. Anyone who questions him is at once under suspicion and becomes increasingly likely to

30. Huprich and Nelson, "Malignant Self-Regard."

be forced out. One interesting quirk is that they often delegate the dirty work of firing someone to others so that they can say it was a personnel decision, and they had nothing to do with it.

One might conclude that a narcissist CEO would improve the company's bottom line, but that is not the case, nor is it the case for narcissist pastors. Narcissists "are associated with significantly lower stock-price performance in absolute terms and relative to the S&P 500. The median annualized stock-price performance for CEOs in our sample with higher narcissism is four percent compared with the median annualized stock-price performance of 27% for CEOs with lower narcissism."[31] They tell a big story but do not deliver.

Narcissistic pastors set out to control the board of elders soon after ascending to their position. They use charm to learn about each board member, focusing on how they might be useful by learning about their strengths and weaknesses. They then set out to exploit them by using this knowledge to flatter, gratify, and even threaten them into following their lead. If that does not work . . . One new elder asked to see the budget. The next day, he received a call informing him that he was no longer an elder.

CONCLUSION

About fifteen years ago, I was contacted by elders from a local church. People were leaving, the new associate pastor was thinking of moving back to California, and female staff members were "creeped out" by the senior pastor. They refused to work late because "the Ghost" was always moving silently about somewhere in the building, and they sensed he was watching them. In the morning, they would find items on their desks moved about. He would either criticize their work or take personal credit for it.

The associate pastor was fully ordained and recruited from a southern California church. He told me that the senior pastor wanted to control everything down to the smallest detail and strongly criticized him for showing any initiative. After less than a year at the church, he was discouraged and ready to return to California with his wife and two young sons.

The senior pastor, the object of this investigation, told me that his staff was disloyal and the new associate pastor was incompetent. He

31. Larcher et al., "Are Narcissistic CEO's All That Bad?"

never got the credit he so richly deserved because he had to watch over everything and everyone so closely that he was at the church at all hours, not getting enough sleep and feeling burned out. Then, he asked me to be his counselor, which I declined.

He was determined not to leave, even though he could activate his retirement, because the associate was incompetent and never should have been called. So, in his words: "Jesus was only crucified once, but this is my third crucifixion." That statement shocked me. It seemed he was saying Jesus had it easy . . .

I consulted with a Christian psychiatrist, who concluded that the senior pastor was a "covert narcissist" who would stay until he was fired, forced into retirement, or died.

I took these findings to the board of elders and explained the consequences of each course of action. The response was, "We knew. We just needed an outsider to tell us." They gave the senior pastor two options: retire and have a huge retirement party or face charges before the congregation. He retired but refused to attend his retirement party because "They are such ingrates!"

A few weeks later, I successfully led the elders through the forgiveness and reconciliation process.

As I stated, a church with a narcissistic pastor has few options.[32] A sabbatical is often suggested but usually rejected outright. Therapy is generally a waste of time and money as the narcissist believes he is well and all others are sick, leaving no need for therapy. As time goes on, he becomes less and less able to control his predatory impulses, and people begin to leave. The options are to fire him/her, force him/her into resigning or retiring, or let it continue and suffer the damage.

For a deeper understanding of predatory pastors, please see my 2020 book *Let Us Prey: The Plague of Narcissist Pastors and What We Can Do About It.*

32. Puls, "Narcissistic Pastors and the Making of Narcissistic Churches."

8

What Do You Do with a Moral Failure?

Things that grow in a secret garden always grow mutant.

~Unknown

We come to our churches and faith communities with certain expectations, including a tendency to look up to the pastors as being on a higher plane than the rest of us. Whatever the "domini" said was straight from God during my childhood. We expect our priests and pastors to be humble, honest, caring, compassionate, morally strong, and without the temptations we face. I have heard it suggested that we create idyllic mental images of our pastors as having the qualities we wish we had but whose absence we are too embarrassed to acknowledge. We wish we were not so easily tempted to be unfaithful to our husbands and wives; we wish we were not so quickly drawn to lies to cover our weaknesses and infidelities; we wish we were stronger in the face of temptation to cheat on our income taxes and to pad our time sheets at work. Somehow, many of us seem to have concluded that our pastors have moved beyond all this and are now immune to the wiles and ways of temptation. Even though we intuitively know this is wishful thinking, we need to believe that our ordained clergy have risen above it all and stand as powerful examples of grace. Otherwise, why would we listen to them week after week?

Our pastors may have a higher calling but come from the same tide pool as the rest of us. And, like the rest of us, they have secrets. According to one source, 81 percent of pastors have been tempted to engage in inappropriate sexual behavior with someone in the church but have resisted.

However, 31.75 percent of the clergy surveyed admitted to having sexual intercourse with a church member who was not their spouse.[1]

We know this, and it is the difference between reality and wishful thinking. In some ways, we *need* pastors to be morally better than us; otherwise, why should we listen to them? Their words must be hollow if they crave as we crave. If this is true, what they offer has little value. But we deny this for a simple yet powerful reason: many look to them as anchors in a world increasingly adrift. If that anchor loses its grip, we begin an inevitable drift onto the jagged rocks that will eternally sink our souls. The cognitive dissonance between how we need our pastors to be, and the reality of their humanity, is too much.

A particular outrage is when they preach against moral failures and are caught in the throes of the sins they condemned. We are enraged at the revelation, for it undercuts everything we believed and wanted to believe until it seems everything we have been taught and have believed is now collapsing. Our only choice is short and brutal: Get rid of them! It makes no difference that Galatians 6:1–2 says that we are to "gently restore" those caught in sin. It's easier to crucify than restore.

We tie our spirituality to theirs, and it shatters when they shatter. In short, we *need* our pastors to be humbly holy instead of arrogantly foolish. It is a matter of spiritual survival.

The consequences of pastoral moral failures are higher than most realize.

The Evangelical Council for Financial Accountability (ECFA) has named pastoral/church leader moral failure one of the "greatest financial risks to churches."[2]

These incidents leave the church and the board of elders collectively and sometimes individually liable for civil and punitive damages.

I became aware of the undercurrents of church intrigue as a young boy. My father was chairman of the board of elders at our small church in Grand Rapids, Michigan. It was typical for church members and even groups of members to stop by to meet privately with my dad. I knew they were usually there to complain about something the pastor had done, but I never knew the details of their complaints or what they wanted done about them. The one thing I understood was the tension their visits brought into our small home.

1. Krejcir, "Statistics in the Ministry 2025."
2. Martin, "Reinforcing the Foundation of Trust."

Sometimes, there would be a series of meetings between elders and congregation members in our basement. When they left, Dad's face was often a mixture of sadness, disgust, anger, and confusion. As the board chair, he was responsible for finding the truth and reporting those findings to the entire elder board. If action against the pastor was necessary, he and two or three other elders (including his friend Howard, who eventually became my father-in-law) would confront the pastor. More than once, after such a meeting, the pastor abruptly resigned and left town with his family. I do not recall the congregation ever being told the reasons (this was before specific privacy laws were in place).

I must set something straight before we go further: In my experience, most clergy are caring people profoundly sensitive to their congregations' needs. They work long hours, and their families are often neglected. I am not writing about them.

I suspect we have all read or heard about high-profile pastors and their moral failures. Here are a few that were highly publicized from 2024.

Gateway Church founder and senior pastor Robert Morris resigned following a report he repeatedly sexually molested a twelve-year-old in the 1980s.[3]

In September 2024, Gateway asked another one of its executive pastors, Kemtal Glasgow, to resign after an undisclosed "moral failing" that the church said was not related to Morris's alleged abuse, but it may be that two predatory pastors were selecting their victims from the same church.

According to a September 2024 article in *Christianity Today*, "Stonebriar Community Church, founded by Chuck Swindoll, fired one of its longtime associate pastors in July after an undisclosed moral failure. Three other pastors of large churches were arrested. The senior pastor of North Dallas Community Bible Fellowship, Terren Dames, was arrested in May for soliciting a prostitute, and the church fired him. The founding pastor of Koinonia Christian Church, Ronnie Goines, was arrested for sexual assault in late July. Lakeside Baptist Church's youth pastor, Luke Cunningham, was arrested and charged with sexually assaulting a child after church leaders learned he had been accused of abuse at a previous church and reported him to police."[4]

3. NBC News, "Pastor Robert Morris Resigns."
4. Belz, "Deep in the Heart."

In late July, Josiah Anthony, lead pastor of the Cross Timbers megachurch in Denton, Texas, resigned for actions that were "inappropriate and hurtful" to church staff, elders of the megachurch said in a statement. They later added that they learned he had a pattern of inappropriate communication—sometimes sexual—with women in the church and on staff.[5]

Tony Cammarota "confessed to church leadership of a moral failure." Cammarota, pastor at a Frisco, Texas megachurch for more than seventeen years, was removed from his job.[6]

In September 2024, Pastor Steve Lawson was quickly and quietly removed from his church in Dallas, Texas, after it was discovered that he had an "inappropriate relationship" with a woman.[7]

According to a November 2020 statement from Hillsong Church Global, staffer Carl Lentz, best known as Justin Bieber's former spiritual mentor, was fired from his church for "moral failures" and "breaches of trust."[8]

In 2019, James MacDonald, the founding pastor of a Chicago area megachurch, was forced out as senior pastor for what church elders called "highly inappropriate comments" and other misconduct. MacDonald was pastor of Harvest Bible Chapel, a church he founded in Rolling Meadows some thirty years before. He grew the church from eighteen members to more than 13,000 across nine campuses in the Chicago area. MacDonald had been on an "indefinite sabbatical" amid allegations of financial mismanagement when, in a letter to the congregation, church elders said the decision to fire MacDonald was accelerated by "highly inappropriate recorded comments" he had made.[9]

In 2018, Bill Hybels, superstar founder and pastor of the Willow Creek megachurch in Chicago, resigned after sexual misconduct allegations were made against him. "Hybels's resignation is particularly significant because Willow Creek is a paradigm for evangelical megachurches across the United States." Hybels's entire board of elders resigned *en masse* for their failure to properly supervise Hybels and hold him accountable.

5. Blair, "Founding Pastors Resign."
6. Hastings, "Texas Megachurch Pastor Tony Cammarota Fired."
7. Eturralde, "Steven Lawson Removed."
8. CP Staff, "Dallas Pastor Steve Lawson Removed."
9. Staff, "Founder of Harvest Bible Chapel Fired."

Willow Creek reported an average of 18,000 attendees on weekends in 2018, but that dropped to 7,740 in 2023.[10]

Then there is Mark Driscoll, founder of Mars Hill Church in Seattle, Washington. Driscoll resigned in 2014 after it came to light that he had paid a marketing company $200,000 in church funds to fraudulently boost sales of a book he had co-authored with his wife and had plagiarized up to ten pages from other writers. An investigation concluded that he was quick-tempered, arrogant, and domineering. He resigned.[11]

But Driscoll was not finished, nor had he changed his ways. In 2016, Driscoll founded The Trinity Church in Scottsdale, Arizona, two years after the scandal at Mars Hill. It was only a short time before complaints of the same types of behavior surfaced. The church board wrote, "We are troubled that he continues to be unrepentant despite the fact that these sins have been previously investigated, verified, and brought to his attention by his fellow Elders, prior to his abrupt resignation . . . Accordingly, we believe that Mark is presently unfit for serving the church in the office of pastor."[12] Those are strong words rarely offered in these situations. Instead, churches tend to soften the message by wrapping it in forgiveness, woundedness, and the hope of reconciliation.

Finally, there was the pastor of a Spanish-speaking strip-mall church who, according to the Commodity Futures Trading Commission, convinced 1,515 mostly Latino church members and others to invest at least $5,900,000 in Bitcoin by promising huge returns every month—and kept the money for himself. As this is written he has been charged in US District Court for Eastern Washington for "engaging in a fraudulent digital assets multilevel marketing scheme worth at least $5.9 million."[13]

> In its continuing litigation, the [Commodity Futures Trading Commission—CFTC] seeks restitution to defrauded customers, disgorgement of ill-gotten gains, civil monetary penalties, trading bans, and a permanent injunction against further violations of the Commodity Exchange Act and CFTC Regulations.
>
> As alleged in the complaint, Pinillo, individually and doing business as the Solanofi entities, mainly targeted Spanish-speaking customers who had little to no experience or understanding

10. Burton, "Megachurch Pastor Resigns."
11. Shellnut, "Former Mars Hill Elders."
12. Shellnut, "Former Mars Hill Elders."
13. Department of Justice, "Former Tri-Cities Pastor Indicted."

> in digital asset transactions or commodity interest trading. He abused his position of trust as the church pastor to attract customers and claimed to be the CEO of the Solanofi entities that had an automated computer trading system which he called Solanofi. Pinillo claimed to operate a leveraged staking trading platform which rewarded users through an interest pool based on high performance trading of cryptographic assets. He further claimed it was risk free and guaranteed profits of up to 34.9% compounded monthly.
>
> Pinillo provided customers with access to an online dashboard with account statements showing their purported account balances and profits. He encouraged customers to involve friends and family in his fraudulent scheme by offering to pay a 15% referral fee to them for referring additional customers. These representations and account statements were false. During the relevant period, there was no trading platform, no trading took place, no profits were generated, and Pinillo misappropriated all assets that customers transferred to him.[14]

We could go on for a hundred more pages, but the point is made: While the people I have listed were all pastors, the problem of abusive authority exists at every level of Christianity. The megachurch scandals just get the headlines.

Why Do Pastors Succumb to Moral Failure?

It is easy to wander off into the weeds while looking for plausible reasons why so many high-profile pastors succumb to moral temptations, but the weeds are the wrong place to look, for our pastors are just like us. They may be more "religious" than we are in terms of visible trappings, but they come from the same societal and cultural backgrounds as you and me, and visible religious trappings are often a defensive veneer covering inner weaknesses.

How much physical, emotional, and spiritual pressure can you withstand, and how far can you bend under it before you break?

According to one study, "The demands placed on clergy are becoming increasingly distressing to religious organizations . . . They are often required to be available both day and night. They may be called upon to function as pastor, marriage counselor, individual psychotherapist, 'CEO'

14. Commodity Futures, "CFTC Charges Washington State Pastor."

of a complex church organization, dispute mediator between divisive groups in the congregation, accountant, friend, and surrogate parent."[15] Eventually, they may feel a loss of passion and purpose. With that loss comes a deadening emptiness they may try to fill with alcohol, drugs, or illicit sex. I believe this is one of the defining issues overshadowing pastoral misconduct, and little has been done to alleviate the problem. Further, it can be argued that we do not *want* to know and actively avoid any source that might force the knowledge upon us. "Thus, confusion reigns amidst ambiguity, and people may either step away to avoid any responsibility of discernment or choose sides based upon personal relationships over truth."[16] A large part of this discomfort stems from the fact that few models exist on how to handle the moral failure of a pastor or church staff person. Compounding the issue is ambiguity on how to treat the guilty one.

There can be multiple reasons why a pastor might succumb to moral failures: human imperfection, high expectations, pressure, lack of accountability, isolation, burnout, struggles with personal demons, and sometimes a sense of entitlement due to their position within the church; essentially, they are human beings with vulnerabilities just like everyone else, but often face unique challenges that can lead to moral missteps if not properly addressed.

How do congregations react? Exactly as we might expect when morally insulted: denial or affirmation—"I can't believe it," or "I kind of thought that/suspected . . ."; Anger—"How could he be so selfish?" or "I can't believe they won't let him stay . . ."; Justifying—"If only he or we or they would have . . ."; Depression—"I'm so hurt, sad" or "I just want to give up," as well as "I miss him, them, the way it was . . ."

In terms of personal impact, the experience can be compared to the unexpected death of a close family member.[17] When someone close to you dies, your world changes. You are in mourning—feeling grief and sorrow at the loss. You may feel numb, shocked, and fearful. You may feel guilty for being the one who is still alive. You may even feel angry at your loved one for leaving you. These are all normal feelings. There are no rules about how you should feel. There is no right or wrong way to mourn.

15. Crisp-Han et al., "Professional Boundary Violations."
16. Rhodes, "Why Preachers Fail Morally."
17. National Institute on Aging, "Coping."

When grieving, we can feel both physical and emotional pain. Grieving people often cry easily and can have trouble sleeping, lose interest in food, experience problems with concentration, have a hard time making decisions, ride an emotional roller coaster, and so on.

But this is bigger than an individual loss. This is grief on an institutional scale. The entire congregation experiences the shock of betrayal by perhaps the one person they may have trusted the most. Yes, the pain lessens over time but is often replaced by cynicism and suspicion, which carry over into the pastoral call process, so the next pastor may find herself trying to live up to impossible standards that assure failure.

Complicated Grief

We mourn what we have lost, but we each mourn differently and need different amounts of time to pass through our grief into the sunlight again. Perhaps the most poignant and painful relational ruptures are birthed by moral betrayal from someone once greatly admired. Unfortunately, some people become stuck in the deep emotions of grief. They have lost something so precious and essential to them that they cannot find their way home again. This prolonged and intense reaction to loss is known as complicated grief. People with this condition experience intense sorrow and emotional pain, may be unable to understand or accept the loss, and have trouble resuming their own lives and planning for the future.

Many people find the corporate grieving process so uncomfortable and even threatening that they try to hasten the end point of their roller coaster of emotions by pushing forward at the highest possible speed.

There is very little an outsider can do under these circumstances, beyond assuring them that their reactions are all normal and suggesting a grief support professional to help them re-engage.

Warning: Reefs Ahead

It has been said that the best defense is a good offense. In this case, let me recast it this way: Prevention is a better strategy than mass grief therapy.

Phil Cooke is a church consultant who has helped multiple churches through the maze of questions, accusations, anger, and bewilderment brought on by pastoral moral failures. He identifies six habits to watch for that may indicate a pastor is headed for trouble in a 2022 article on Ministry Watch.

1. Abusing alcohol and/or sleeping pills
2. Crude or sexualized joking with staff members
3. Spending too much time away from a spouse
4. A fascination with pornography
5. Really stupid decisions
6. No one can question the boss's decisions[18]

Interventions are better than infections. Galatians 6:1 lays it out: "Brothers and sisters, if someone is caught in a sin, you who live by the Spirit should restore that person gently. But watch yourselves, or you also may be tempted" (NIV).

18. Cooke, "Top Six Risky Habits."

9

The Hidden Challenges of Leader Transitions

I have never yet known the Spirit of God to work
where the Lord's people were divided.

~D. L. Moody

A transition is the time and process of changing leaders, in this case, ministers, from the announcement of the coming vacancy through the first several months or even years after the new minister is on the scene. Transitions are a time of unease for congregations, and sudden transitions from the forced exit of the leader are chaotic. Transitions introduce change into what may have been a stable system and open the door to strong resistance. The conflict-generating power of transitions is much stronger than most people suspect.

Many believe the transition process is simple: advertise the opening, winnow the candidates to four or five, conduct interviews, perhaps have the candidates preach, and then decide. That understanding is common but dangerous. Further, the pastor who has announced the leaving date is the wrong person to lead the transition as he or she has a vested interest in preserving their legacy. We will return to this.

OVERVIEW

Every church wants a great "transformational" leader to grow the church and expand its ministry. "Transformational leadership is a leadership style that can inspire positive changes in those who follow. Transformational leaders are generally energetic, enthusiastic, and passionate. Not only are these leaders concerned and involved in the process, but they are also focused on helping every member of the group succeed."[1] Marisela Jiménez writes, "Organizational change requires managers' cognitive and affective abilities to understand stakeholders' reactions."[2]

Unfortunately, truly transformational leaders are not common. In my experience, very few pastors are transformational. Sometimes a transformational leader is the problem

Humans generally do not like change, and congregations do not like the transition period. It is uncomfortable and often perceived as unstable. A common error is a push to "lean forward into the future" and rush the replacement process. Moving too fast leaves much of the congregation confused and sad. They are grieving their losses but are rarely given an avenue to share their grief or even have it acknowledged.

EMOTIONS OF THE TRANSITIONAL PROCESS

The transition process for staff and congregants includes grief, denial, anger, bargaining, and so on. The longer the minister has been in place and the better he or she is liked, the higher the levels of grief and resistance to change, and the more intense and challenging the transitional process is likely to be. The people and their remaining leaders rarely understand the corporate grieving process, let alone employ it during the transition. They find it uncomfortable and may try to hurry through it quickly. Grieving is then truncated, and the emotional needs of the people are still unattended.

In my estimation, the usual, uncomplicated transition period is about one to two years, although it can be much longer. One particularly challenging transition I was part of lasted for six years. Without thorough planning and careful execution, transitions easily become a time of organizational drifting with the currents, resulting in a loss of purpose and direction.

Understanding and intervening in transitional issues call for an integrated approach that covers the entire system from bottom to top. Fortunately, a few pioneers have blazed a trail. Organizational development

1. Cherry, "What Is Transformational Leadership?"
2. Jiménez, "Leadership Style."

pioneer William Bridges created a vocabulary for understanding and discussing organizational change. He helped us understand how people experience change and what they need to get through it, whether the change is personal or organizational. Bridges was among the first to show that while change is situational, transition is psychological[3] and needs to be better understood and attended to, especially in American churches where change is both endemic and rapid. (The average minister stays in one place for slightly more than three years before moving on.) Bridges described the process by which organizations and the individuals within them experience transitional change and further segmented it into three major stages: first as an ending, second as an indeterminate period of confusion and distress that he termed the neutral zone, and third, completing the cycle with a new beginning.[4]

Each stage has multiple tasks to complete before moving to the next, with each task accompanied by simple rituals marking endings and beginnings. Rituals promise continuity, order, and predictability, and they are essential in times of change and transition.[5] Bridges noted that Western culture offers few rituals to mark safe passage through these stages, leaving people drifting with unfinished business on an unfamiliar sea where the shortest course to the desired landfall may crash them onto the reefs of confusion and decline. Transitions are inherently uncomfortable, and there is a strong tendency to hurry through the neutral zone without understanding that its insecurities are a normal and necessary part of the transitional process and that it offers a time for losses to be mourned and opportunities to be found. Bridges asked individuals and organizations to intentionally spend time in the neutral zone, sorting through the remains of the old to psychologically accommodate the space between old and new and successfully mourn their losses. This is best accomplished face-to-face but often in guided silence. "Therapeutic silence in traumatic grief and loss thus takes the theological task of wholeness very seriously. Yet this wholeness is often affected by empathic speech, instead emerges from the intentional acceptance of the difference presented by the loss."[6] To emphasize, the process must not be rushed. It is helping them give birth to something new, and, as someone once said, it takes nine months to make a baby no matter how many people you put on the job.

3. Bridges, *Managing Transitions*, 3.
4. Bridges, *Managing Transitions*, 4–6.
5. Black, "Ancient and Modern Ritual."
6. Capretto, "Empathy and Silence in Pastoral Care."

Bridges's work was expanded by C. Otto Scharmer, who charted the flow of dialogue and the tasks of the transitional process into three major components: The Flow of Dialogue During Transitions, The Transition Process, and The Tasks of the Transition Process.[7] As one can see, these correspond to Bridges's three levels of transition. All three processes are active at the same time. The challenge is normalizing the processes to those going through them and gaining enough time and commitment to complete the various tasks.

Task One: Letting Go of the Past (Grieving)

Grieving is how humans recover from loss. The most important task at the beginning stage is to properly identify and respectfully unload or let go of the past; that is, to identify, acknowledge, mourn, and release what is being lost. There will be mourning of losses even when the community is overjoyed to see their leader leave. Unfortunately, it seems that very few faith communities mourn these losses intentionally; instead, they tend to "move forward" by whitewashing the blemishes of the past in hopes the overall communal narrative will survive intact. In leaving the past behind without meaningful recognition of it, the wounds experienced may scab over, but they do not fully heal.

There are effective ways to do grief communally. One is to hold a "goodbye celebration" for the outgoing pastor. In this, people are asked to share what makes them happy and sad. It is important to name what is being lost communally. Perhaps foremost is the loss of relationships. Some stalwart members will quickly pull up stakes and leave, while others will leave during the first few months with the new leader. People who have been together for years and have formed strong bonds fear the loss of these important relationships. If the exiting leader has been there for any length, he or she will have formed relationships within the congregation that will now be severed. Despite promises to "keep in touch," they know that this does not happen often and that the last time they experience what may have been a fulfilling relationship will be the last day the person is there. This is true even in those cases where the leader is forced out. No matter how many negatives a person may have, there are also positives that people have grounded their relationships upon. For some, the leaving will be particularly traumatic, as the leader was their genuine

7. Scharmer, *Theory U.*

confidant with whom they entrusted their deepest secrets and received support and understanding. If they have been in conflict, multiple relationships have already been damaged, and a significant portion of the congregation has likely left.

Talking about what the transition means to them individually rather than collectively produces more personal and honest answers. What is ending, and who is losing what? These simple questions and conversations may dispel a generalized sense of loss and foreboding. Ask, "What is over for everyone?" This will give a greater understanding of corporate loss and create a tighter focus on what is not changing.[8]

Who should lead this process? Perhaps a noted therapist in the congregation or a highly regarded associate pastor can do the job. Or an outside facilitator may be needed.

Intentionally employing deepening dialogues seems to be the most effective and efficient means of satisfying the grieving process. Social scientist Bill Isaacs defines dialogue as the art of thinking together, a challenging but attainable goal.[9] During the early stages of change, the dialogic flow consists of polite and nonreflective shared monologues, with blame placed on the past and now-distant people to justify a proposed different future. However, several proposed futures are usually present, and they tend to clash. Whether the transition is planned or unplanned, the primary features of this first stage are uncertainty, grieving, and fluid background conversations.

There will be quiet resistance fueled by unspoken questions such as, "Where do I fit in? Will there be room for me? Will I still have a role? What will change? What if we don't get along?" These anxieties will persist until satisfactorily answered. Resistance tends to lessen as leaders keep them informed along the way. One of the main resistance points is easy to name: the present is known and, to some extent, comfortable because it is known, while the coming change introduces uncertainty, which is inherently uncomfortable. Change resistance is based on negative past experiences and is therefore rooted in the past.[10]

As stated earlier, several approaches can be combined to ease grief, calm the background noise, and start new conversations:

8. Dudley and Ammerman, *Congregations in Transition.*

9. Isaacs, *Dialogue.*

10. Salmond, "Managing the Human Side of Change," 42.

1. name their fears and discomfort,
2. accept that time-honored rituals will change,
3. acknowledge losses,
4. expect and accept grieving,
5. mark the endings,
6. expect overreaction, and
7. ensure the important things will continue.[11]

Churches and secular organizations rarely acknowledge what is being lost during leader transitions and tend to fixate on the pivot toward something new. The past must be honored, accepted, and allowed to leave. In a real sense, this is a time of mourning, and someone familiar and trusted is most helpful in guiding church members through the grieving process. Part of this process is marking the endings, which allows new beginnings to not compete for space with the old.

Acknowledge the losses. Never denigrate the past, even if it is described as hellish. All losses are subjective, so accept the reality and importance of subjective losses. Don't argue with what people tell you; it will stop the conversation, and you need more conversation, not less. Some see the world in stark black and white with nothing in between. They also tend to believe that their "objectivity" is truly objective and not influenced by their internal biases. They are wrong. Bridges writes that loss and grief are subjective experiences and that their "objective views" are just subjective views hiding behind a thin curtain of objectivity—which makes the "objective view" an irrelevant opinion.[12]

Most transitional faith communities try to project a positive sense of welcoming something new without honestly acknowledging what they are losing. This failure ignores a crucial part of the human psyche: we must say goodbye to the past before embracing the future. We must mark the ending through contemplation, discussion, prayer, and ritual. We must normalize this unrecognized grieving process for what it is: a reality that needs a ritual to release us from its grip. Then, we can let the past rest in peace while opening ourselves up to a new future.

Naming their fears and discomfort in a protected setting normalizes those fears and reduces their power. By openly expressing their uncertainties, people find that these fears are shared, which tends to bring

11. Bridges, *Managing Transitions*, 22–26.
12. Bridges, *Managing Transitions*, 24–32.

people together in a common area where uncertainty is allowed to become accepted and normal.

If we are grieving, it is because we have lost something important. One of the easiest ways to identify the focus of grief is to have them name what they see as losses. It does not matter if others perceive the losses as real; they are real to the person expressing loss, and naming the losses brings them into the open for all to examine. In most cases, there will be nods of agreement upon hearing what it is named. Once it is named, it is no longer without shape, form, or substance; naming it makes it real. Once we have named it, we have also claimed it as our own, while bringing it into the group also brings it into a circle of corporate grief.

Faith communities have rituals that connect the past with the present and the present with the future, with the goal of connecting with each other and with God. Rituals give comfort and continuity, and major changes done too swiftly are resisted.[13] Understanding that some rituals are likely to change simply because of a new minister's personality and practices allows them to institute incremental change with minimal resistance. "If the transition management strategy used symbolic rituals such as testimonials or funerals, the ending of these events can be used as the launching point from the past to the future."[14]

Overreaction is normal during the transitional process. Some will struggle with the changes and push back against them. Those who cannot accept the changes tend to leave.

The neutral zone is the unmarked crossing point between two clear borders, where false security is found in routine. In a very real sense, the neutral zone is like the Sinai wilderness through which Moses led his people. The purpose was not so much to get the people out of Egypt as to get Egypt out of the people. It took forty years.

Routine matters take on greater importance than their apparent worth as they provide continuity, a connection with the old and the not-yet, and routine soothes and assists in coping with the neutral zone. There is a certain dull safety in routines that require little of us but the motions. It is neither life nor death but a gray place with little variation or energy. Congregations in transition will often find themselves in this undefined place, feeling alone and separated, unable to cross over the chasm to the new land. Ambiguity increases, and so does the longing for answers.[15]

13. Gino and Norton, "Why Rituals Work."

14. Salmond, "Managing the Human Side of Change," 42.

15. Buchanan, *Your God is Too Safe.*

However, if they have been prepared for it and know that the community's essential functions are continuing, their borderland experience can be accepted as a normal, though challenging, part of transitioning.

The tension of politeness that marked the beginning of conversations is here replaced by more straightforward, even confronting, conversations. This is where facilitation skills become instrumental in keeping the flow going in the right direction and creating a safe space that allows people to express themselves honestly. Normalizing their uncertainty and the resulting tension is one way to make it acceptable.

Unresolvable opposing points of view are called polarities, and seeming polarities will arise.[16] Polarities demand responses of yes or no, but this is deceptive. These tensions can be normalized as a natural phenomenon where the answer is neither yes nor no, but yes/and. This calls for new ways of thinking and sparks creativity in many.

The uncertainty principle says that even the most secure people in the old organizational structure become increasingly insecure when a major transition is announced. Deeply personal questions must be asked and answered, such as: Where will I fit in? Will there be room for me? Will I still have a role? What am I losing? Will my friends still be here? What will it be like working for the new pastor? What if we don't get along? These anxieties inevitably cause resistance and even active push-back until answered adequately.

Their best opportunity to redefine themselves as a church will come after the new pastor has been there for a few months. As such, it should be led by the new pastor if possible, or the pastor with the help of others experienced in group work. This is a process of taking stock, identifying, and sensing their new calling and is highly creative. With their new calling comes the opportunity to identify new core values and rejuvenate their identity. This opens a new course and trajectory into the future. This may seem a daunting task in a large church, but one church I worked with had more than 100 members come together over three consecutive Saturdays to define the new core values and succeeded.

Becoming

The most challenging task confronts them: becoming, which is the process of change and reunification. The focal point of becoming is to wrestle

16. Johnson, *Polarity Management.*

with such fundamental questions as: Who are we being called to become? What are we to do? Where do we belong in God's unfolding story? The process involves ever-deepening dialogue to share fears, hopes, aspirations, and dreams of what can be.[17] It requires that the people be fully present as it is largely a time of silence, dialogue, meditation, and prayer as they seek the heart of God rather than definitive answers. Becoming goes further as it seeks answers to an existential question: What questions lie at the heart of whom we are called to be? This existential examination has no clear and concise answers. As the question states, it seeks deeper questions of who they are as a community.[18]

The New Journey

Journeys into the unknown can be unsettling or exciting; the difference between them is in planning and attitude. A facilitated Future Search can bring out new ideas and dreams that can be solidified into new goals.[19] The conversation gains passion and shifts from asking questions to a generative dialogue that creates as it goes and where all are welcome.

The most interesting marvels I have seen when a faith community has reached this point are high levels of courage and energy in generating and adapting new models of ministry in place of old models that no longer worked. They keep what is good and jettison the rest with proper ceremony and respect. There is a new sense of freedom propelled by much higher energy levels throughout the organization. They embody the voice of freedom to be what God created them—and their community—to be. It is one of the very few places where the concept of "synergy"[20] can function.

Yes, there will still be problems, but the goal is a better set of problems!

17. Scharmer, *Theory U.*

18. Scharmer, *Theory U.*

19. Weisbord and Janoff, *Future Search.*

20. "Synergy: the interaction or cooperation of two or more organizations, substances, or other agents to produce a combined effect greater than the sum of their separate effects" (Synergy Services, "What Does Synergy Mean to You?").

10

Easing Transitions: Succession Planning

In preparing for battle, I have always found that plans are useless, but preparation is indispensable.

~ Gen. Dwight D. Eisenhower

Reality: Your pastor will leave. The only variables are when and how. It's like marriage: 48 percent of marriages end in divorce. The other 52 percent end in death. Either way, they end.

You want a smooth transition from your pastor to the successor. Otherwise, it can be drawn out, uncomfortable, and a source of serious conflict.[1]

Pastoral transitions do not have to be traumatic or overly disruptive. The primary reason they tend towards both is the lack of a realistic succession plan created well before it is needed and the failure to prepare the congregation for what is to come. A well-designed and executed succession plan supplies a specific framework for replacing pastors. In its simplest form, a succession plan is an action plan to follow when senior leaders plan to leave. A more comprehensive succession plan would center around an internal and methodical process of naming and developing potential leadership successors through systematic appraisal and training.

According to one study, 60 to 75 percent of nonprofit executives plan to leave their organization in the next five years (churches are nonprofits).

1. Puls, "Leadership Transitions."

Usually, such turnover occurs without succession planning or knowledge transfer for the new pastor. Within faith-based nonprofit organizations, the baby boomer generation is facing a crisis where its founding leaders are now retiring and having difficulties transitioning responsibilities to the next generation. On top of that, 77 percent of faith-based nonprofits operate without a succession plan.[2]

The lack of a workable succession plan is particularly damaging when the pastor suddenly dies or resigns. This leaves the remaining leaders scrambling to decide what needs to be done and who will do it. They must quickly decide on the minimum candidate qualifications for the position, how the recruiting process will be done, the timelines for the process, the makeup of the hiring team, interview questions, whether to hire a consultant, a budget for the team, and so on. Under these conditions, people tend to hurry and, in a rush, make mistakes. Knowledge transfer may be almost nonexistent under these circumstances, leaving the new pastor significantly disadvantaged from day one.

A realistic succession plan will eliminate much of the uncertainty of an unplanned exit.[3] My church went through it as I was writing this book. Our pastor was in his early sixties and much loved in the church and respected in the community. The church had grown exponentially under his leadership and is now one of the largest in the area, though size was not his goal—introducing people to Jesus and discipling them was the goal.

About a year ago, we received an email from the executive pastor of our church informing us that Pastor "Bob" was on a six-month sabbatical for health reasons. The succession plan had been activated, and the various pastors shifted roles and responsibilities to keep the church functioning at a high level while Pastor "Bob" was off. While there were questions, there was no confusion or "Oh my gosh! What do we do now?" That is the advantage of succession planning. Note: We all prayed that Pastor "Bob" would return to the pulpit, but that was not to be.

The traditional church approach centers on replacement, not succession; knowledge transfer is often only minimally considered.

- Focus is limited to executive-level positions, mostly external.
- Focus is on identifying immediate and short-term replacements.

2. Cited in Puls, "Leadership Transitions."
3. Shadow, "Exploration of Knowledge Transfer."

- Plans are limited to naming one or two potential successors for senior positions through an elimination process.
- Plans are linked to individual job requirements and job descriptions.
- The job is advertised with a glowing description of the church to attract as many applicants as possible.
- Potential candidates are found based solely on the application, recommendations, and work history.
- The candidate field consists of applicants who are seeking new employment.
- Interview questions tend to be based on job descriptions and standardized questions anyone can find online, usually with the "best" answers attached.

For example, about twenty years ago, I was on a search team seeking a new senior pastor. We advertised the position and received hundreds of applications. While this may be the easiest way of finding candidates, it does not answer an unasked question: Why are we looking for a person who is looking for a job? More importantly, why are they in the active job market? We eventually recruited a successful pastor who was happy in his current position but ready for a greater challenge.

Preparing the successor is more than naming them—they must learn the actual expectations and intricacies of what they must do, a process known as knowledge transfer.[4] No matter whether the candidate has held similar positions, every position is different and imposes a steep learning curve. Even though they may have held the same position elsewhere, the people, cultures, and expectations differ. How will the new person gain the knowledge necessary to lead effectively within this new context?

I recently went through the succession process with knowledge transfer. I was the dean of academic affairs at Pacific Northwest Christian College. PNWCC is a very young college; I was the first academic dean in its history. Over time, I developed the position's roles and responsibilities and the policies governing academics while spearheading our successful multi-year drive for accreditation. My plan had always been to retire when accreditation was awarded.

I was the only person who knew what the position entailed, how policies and procedures were applied, and myriad other details of operating

4. Daley Jr., "Succession Planning."

a small college. We developed a plan and timeline for knowledge transfer. The new dean would be an internal promotion, and I had approximately eight months to prepare her to take over from me.

I made lists of everything I did and everything I was responsible for. I was surprised at the length of the lists and the complexity of some roles. We met every week to explore what she needed to know and answer her questions. I compiled and supplied comprehensive notebooks for her reference. She was a quick learner and asked many excellent questions as we clarified roles, responsibilities, policies, and procedures. Of course, I could not transfer my years of experience to her, but I would still be available to her as I stayed on the faculty with an office on campus.

While knowledge transfer is imperfect, it gives the successor a running start and a greater chance of success in the new position. Yes, it usually means having both pastors on the payroll for a time, but it is an investment in the future, and the payoff is greater than the cost. The college, students, and new dean benefited from our process, and I remain available for consulting, policy development, and special projects.

The succession plan must be realistic. It should name the person who will be the interim leader, name a search committee, develop minimum qualifications for the position that include education, experience, and certifications, and a general timeline for completion. One megachurch simply named a respected leader who would be in charge while they sought a new pastor. That is not a succession plan.

Comprehensive succession planning includes five steps or stages. As summarized by the Treasury Board of Canada Secretariat, it looks like this:[5]

STEP 1. Identify Key Areas and Positions

- Key areas and positions are those that are critical to the organization's operational activities and strategic objectives.
- Identify which positions, if left vacant, would make it very difficult to achieve current and future goals.
- Identify which positions, if left vacant, would be detrimental to the constituents' health, safety, or security.

5. Vasudev, "Beyond Shareholder Value."

STEP 2. Identify Capabilities for Key Areas and Positions

- To establish selection criteria, focus employee development efforts, and set performance expectations, you need to determine the capabilities required for the key areas and positions identified in Step 1.
- Identify the relevant knowledge, skills (including language), abilities, and competencies needed to achieve organizational goals.
- Use the Key Leadership Competencies profile (see Appendix 1).
- Inform employees about key areas and positions and required capabilities.

STEP 3. Identify Interested Employees and Assess Them Against Capabilities

- Determine who is interested in and has the potential to fill key areas and positions.
- Discuss career plans and interests with employees.
- Identify the vulnerable areas and positions and the candidates who are ready to advance or whose skills and competencies could be developed within the required time frame.

STEP 4. Develop and Implement Succession and Knowledge Transfer Plans

- Incorporate strategies for learning, training, development, and the transfer of corporate knowledge into your succession planning and management.
- Define the learning, training, and development experiences that your church requires for leadership positions and other key areas and positions.
- Link employees' learning plans to the knowledge, skills (including language), and abilities required for current and future roles.
- Discuss with employees how they can pass on their corporate knowledge.

STEP 5. Evaluate Effectiveness

- Evaluate and monitor your succession planning and management efforts to ensure the following;
- Succession plans for all key areas and positions are developed;
- Key positions are filled quickly; and
- New employees in key positions perform effectively.

Boards traditionally defer to the lead pastor, but that is changing as they begin to better understand their legal responsibilities as fiduciaries and the knowledge that they might be held individually and personally liable for damages under certain circumstances.

This raises an important question: Should the current pastor be involved in choosing his/her successor? If yes, how much involvement and influence on the outcome should they have?[6] A case can be made for either choice. Also, denominational protocols must be considered. Some denominations regularly move their pastors and assign a new pastor with little or no input from the receiving congregation or leaders. Some denominations and independent churches allow the local pastor to select the successor and then mentor them. In contrast, still others create selection teams to winnow through the applications and select a group of finalists for interviews with the current pastor not being involved.

While the outgoing pastor will have some influence, the pertinent question is, how much influence? A spectrum of pastoral influence in the succession process must be considered.

Some boards still defer to the recommendation of the outgoing pastor. In the business world, this is often determined by their success and length of tenure, with successful CEOs receiving greater deference from the board to participate in or make the decision. Current governance standards have moved away from this practice. Today, the board is expected to be heavily involved in succession planning for top executives. This includes ensuring that the company has a sound process for evaluating their progress and consulting with third-party advisors.

Candidates may be recruited from outside, there could be an internal promotion, or both paths can be travelled simultaneously. However, a current executive or associate pastor may not have the knowledge, skills, or disposition for the senior position. They may be very good in their

6. Treasury Board, "Succession Planning."

current position but fail when promoted because they lack the leadership or managerial qualities necessary to succeed at the very top.

Long-term pastors are also concerned with their personal legacies and may want nothing to change after they are gone. One who was approaching retirement said he would rather see the church turned into a grain elevator than have it change from the direction he had implemented, even though the church was losing members and needed change. His natural inclination was to find someone who would be his "mini me." Or, and I hesitate to raise this, the outgoing pastor might want their successor to fail—or perform worse than they did—to validate their legacy and importance to the church. I have seen it. I recently consulted with members of two churches where the senior pastor actively sabotaged his chosen successor and forced him out.

Newly "planted" churches are growing while most established churches are losing members, especially in the "mainline" denominations (Presbyterian, United Methodist, etc.). The founding pastor in a church plant may become so accustomed to having his way that he sees the church as something he owns. The result is often "founder's syndrome" where the founding leader believes he has every right to control the outcome of a successor search. Founding pastors may believe it is their right to control the process and handpick their successor, and they may be more likely to choose someone like themselves to carry on their legacy.

This process is challenging, as previous success does not guarantee future success. More rigorous research is needed to establish success and failure rates for CEO-selected successor clergy. Chino Walters argues that the current evidence regarding CEO-selected successor clergy is not promising.[7] He notes that Black churches do not generally have retirement plans or 401k access and concludes, "To have an effective succession, there must be a retirement plan in place . . . We cannot wait until the predecessor decides to retire."[8]

The absence of succession strategies highlighted some significant indications: pastoral succession was not taught, and pastoral retirement was unacceptable within the Black Pentecostal church culture. Also, the participants who were products of a pastoral succession revealed that not only was there no utilization of structured succession strategies to

7. Larcher et al., "Outgoing CEOs."

8. Walters, "Exploring the Absence."

facilitate the process, but there was also no documented succession plan established at all.[9]

This leaves most of the planning and preparation for succession up to the local church. Unless your denomination appoints the minister, the local church must determine the minimum qualifications for the eventual successor, decide on the process, authorize the financial package, agree on who will be part of the process, define the scope and role of the current pastor's participation, and operate the process when the time comes.

Preparing the Congregation for Change.

Significant changes require significant leadership. Lifeway Research's 2021 "Greatest Needs of Pastors" study found that 47 percent of US Protestant pastors say leadership is a skill they need to invest in developing. Another 46 percent of pastors say dealing with resistance to change in the church is one of the most challenging people dynamics they face in ministry. Two major issues are guaranteed to arise during the actual succession process: any changes that must be made, and how to deal with upset people.[10]

1. Be certain the change you're considering is what needs to be done.
2. Gain preemptive support from leaders.
3. Remember Egypt: Consider when Moses led Israel out of bondage. At one point, all of Israel agreed that leaving Egypt was the right plan. But before long, they were all grumbling because they were uncomfortable. If you don't remind your people what Egypt was like, you'll have a lot of grumblers on your hands.
4. Transparency. Communicate clear expectations for completion.
5. Overcommunicate. It's easy to give too little information but very difficult to give too much.[11]

9. Walters, "Exploring the Absence."
10. Lifeway Research, "Greatest Needs."
11. Boyles, "5 Steps for Leading."

ONBOARDING THE NEW PASTOR

Internal Promotion

Do not skip onboarding if an internal candidate is appointed to the senior pastor position. While skipping it seems to make sense, going deeper reveals significant flaws. A December 16, 2016, article in the *Harvard Business Review* argues, "An internal candidate has already navigated a career with the company, so onboarding may seem superfluous."[12] However, few inside people have ever been in a CEO position before "and must learn to handle a level of responsibility for which they have had little preparation. Furthermore, they will inherit a team made up of former peers, some of whom may have been rivals for the top job and will benefit from assistance in dealing with that dynamic."[13] Likewise, in a church their relationship with the board of elders will change dramatically "because reporting to and managing a board is vastly different from making periodic presentations to it."[14]

The article offers a startling statistic and the reasons behind it:

> According to some estimates, one-third to one-half of new chief executives fail within their first 18 months. Some of these flameouts can be attributed to poor strategic choices by the new leader, and some result when the board makes an imperfect choice—overestimating a candidate's abilities and potential or hiring a leader whose skill set doesn't fit the context. Sometimes the new leader is obviously responsible for a handoff gone wrong, and other times the board is rightly blamed. But a close look shows that it's rarely that simple. When a succession fails, the responsibility is almost always shared.
>
> Why do they fail? They may be experts in finance or marketing, but their style does not fit the culture well. While this may seem unimportant to some, it means that the new person will destabilize the culture, and the culture will always fight back. Helping new leaders understand the culture and improve their "soft skills" to successfully navigate it may be the best way to increase their chances of success.[15]

12. Ciampa, "After the Handshake."
13. Ciampa, "After the Handshake."
14. Ciampa, "After the Handshake."
15. Krell, "Weighing Internal vs. External Hires."

External

The external candidate holds an advantage, but it is not exhaustive or deep. The congregants do not know them; therefore, there is no internal reputation to live up to or drag them down. They have not made friends in the congregation or earned enemies. They can start with a slate relatively clean from grudges held against them. They will have an easier time making changes (although there will still be resistance). Their "honeymoon" with the church will likely be longer than an internal candidate's, allowing them to gain confidence and build an inner circle of wise advisors. However, being expected to lead through an unfamiliar culture can be a minefield of unexpressed expectations. "Cultural fit is the most important factor when you are considering hiring somebody externally. When you promote people internally, one of the biggest advantages is that they already know how to work in the environment."[16]

In other words, you may not want your new pastor dancing in a minefield of unexpressed expectations.

KNOWLEDGE TRANSFER: THE FINAL PIECE OF THE TRANSITION PUZZLE

This final section focuses on the issue of knowledge transfer. How much do you expect the new leader to know about the church and how it functions? How do they know if they are hired from outside?

Key Mistake: Not instituting a comprehensive knowledge transfer process.

New pastors do not know what they need to know on arrival. They may be familiar with established goals and objectives and know how to pursue them—but they will not know the silent expectations that form yet another minefield. They do not know the quirks and variations that make your church function. They may have a track record of success, but they are strangers to your people and processes, which places them at an immediate disadvantage.

The missing piece is "knowledge transfer."

Knowledge transfer takes time and costs money, but its dividends far surpass the initial costs.

16. Krell, "Weighing Internal vs. External Hires."

Knowledge transfer occurs when the departing leader spends enough face time with the new leader to share the knowledge necessary for success. It can involve various methods, such as mentoring, training, coaching, and sharing information and insights one-on-one.

Knowledge transfer ensures that critical knowledge is passed on and retained within the organization. By sharing knowledge and experience, individuals can build upon their successes and avoid the mistakes of others, leading to better decision-making and improved performance.[17] This extended "who does what and how things work" approach accelerates relational cohesiveness and efficiency.

Companies prioritizing knowledge transfer are 4.5 times more likely to have highly engaged employees. Knowledge transfer can also lead to a 25 percent increase in productivity and a 35 percent decrease in employee turnover.[18]

Example: As noted earlier, I had been dean of academic affairs at a small, private college for seven years and was preparing to retire. I was the college's first academic dean, had written most of the college policies and procedures, and had coordinated our successful quest for accreditation. These had been my goals from the outset. Having completed them, I gave eight months' notice of my retirement and submitted a succession and knowledge transfer process.

To organize the process, I gathered important documents into three-ring binders and recorded the unwritten protocols, problems, and observations I had developed. I was surprised at how many there were.

We decided that the college registrar was the best person for the job. She accepted our proposal, and the knowledge transfer process was activated.

We met weekly for an hour or so for the next seven months to discuss everything she needed to know. In between our meetings, we communicated by phone and email.

The knowledge transfer process was invaluable. She confidently stepped into the position in June 2022 and is doing well. We still meet occasionally for technical issues.

17. Gallemard, "Basics of Knowledge Transfer."

18. Gallemard, "Basics of Knowledge Transfer."

11

Distinctive Characteristics of Faith Community Disputes

Family quarrels are bitter things. They don't go according to any rules. They're not like aches or wounds; they're more like splits in the skin that won't heal because there's not enough material.

~ F. Scott Fitzgerald

CHURCH CULTURE

Organizations are hybrids of the surrounding cultures. Every organization has its own internal culture, of course. While many characteristics are common across organizations, certain distinctives in faith communities tend to set them apart from secular organizations.

The apostle Paul coined the term "body of Christ" as an illustration of unity where each limb, organ, and cell is interdependent with other limbs, organs, and cells. Nothing functions alone, nor can it. Cells rely on oxygen delivered by blood that obtains and delivers oxygen from the lungs, and the lungs require the heart to keep blood flowing. We will die if any of these stops working.

A different but also accurate analogy for the church is that of family. In this case, it is a collection of individuals who create tight bonds with others based on a shared belief system. As a family, it accepts those with a "blood connection." In the church, the blood connection is through Christ. Within this family are mothers, fathers, grandparents, aunts, uncles, brothers, sisters, cousins, and so on. Each has a role to play, and, as in any family, that role changes depending on the connection/role of the person they are interacting with.

Family arguments and disputes are part of everyday living. I suspect we are all familiar with the term *family feud*. A family feud is a long-standing argument or conflict between two or more family members or between two families. Feuds can cause a lot of anger and sometimes violence. Few disputes are as bitter as family feuds. Why? Proximity. We live together, we eat together, and we *know* each other on a deeper level than non-family. We *depend* on each other. Society tells us to trust our families through such phrases as, "Blood is thicker than water," meaning our allegiances should be to family over everyone else.

Few fights are as discouraging as family feuds. They take away what might be our last vestiges of emotional safety, replacing them with a cup of bitterness. They destroy relational security and close the door to emotional safety.

Unfortunately, too many churches are like dysfunctional, feuding families.

Why? Read on:

Ongoing Relationships and History. Congregational disputes contain highly charged interpersonal issues and relational history that can promote or hinder potential resolution. While in most secular groups, the primary focus is on getting the work done, in churches, the emphasis is on emotional and spiritual experience. The emotionality of common experience allows deeper relationships to develop among people who might otherwise have little to no contact. A typical dispute may be experienced less as an opportunity to resolve specific issues and more as an unpleasant strain on an ongoing relationship—or as an opportunity to settle a long-standing grudge.

Family systems theories are helpful in locating power centers within the congregation. People solicit each other's attention, approval, and support and react to each other's needs, expectations, and upsets. This connectedness and reactivity make the functioning of family members interdependent. Reciprocal changes predictably follow a change in one person's functioning in the functioning of others. Families differ somewhat in their degree of interdependence, but it is always present to some degree. As in blood-related families, in a church there may be identifiable matriarchs and patriarchs, mother and father figures whom people look to for wisdom and authority. They are revered, and their advice is taken seriously. There will be siblings and sibling rivalries. As in many families, the sibling there the longest is given the most responsibility, the middle is often the "black sheep" or provocateur who refuses to conform and who causes endless heartaches for the parent figures, and the last, or "lost," child, to whom the rules mean little, is the "be-perfect" nonconformist. Add on aunts, uncles (including the "funny" uncle no one invites home for dinner), and cousins, and you will get the complexity of family systems theories in conflict analysis. Families feud and hold grudges, and so do faith community members.[1]

Church Culture. The internal culture of a church has profound effects on relationships and is often much more important than the cultures of the organizations where the members work at their jobs. People want to feel respected and accepted in the congregation, and a culture that promotes respect and supplies ongoing recognition is likely to have a high cohesiveness. The effect is reasonably unified if congregants can articulate the other person's value and how they benefit from the relationship. Conversely, the absence of respect and recognition makes it more difficult for conflicting value systems to coexist. Members may view disputes in competitive, "zero-sum" terms where one person or group can win something only by causing another person or group to lose.

Reluctance to Participate. It has been said that truth is the first casualty of war. It isn't. Trust is the first casualty, leading to deception as a defense against perceived but hidden threats.[2] Members may be reluctant to take part in collaborative problem-solving processes. They may feel coerced into participation, fear retaliation, or be concerned about confidentiality. These are real concerns and cannot be ignored with impunity.

Distrust. I treat you differently if I do not trust you compared to how I treat those I trust. And I sense it when you do not trust me and act accordingly. Trust violations and the suspicion of trust violations are the primary triggers of faith community conflicts. The lack of trust naturally generates tensions that grow stronger if not confronted and broken.[3]

1. Bowen Center, "Introduction to the Eight Concepts."
2. Isaacs, *Dialogue*, 66.
3. Bansal and Zahedi, "Trust Violation."

COMMON SOURCES OF FAITH COMMUNITY CONFLICTS:

1. Founder's Syndrome. The people who created the congregation or who form a bloc of long-time members want to keep control and resist efforts to expand or bring in new ideas or processes. This can become strong when new families arrive and have ideas for change. The founder's syndrome solution is for the new arrivals to conform or leave.[4]
2. "Different" people arriving. An influx of Gen Xers into an elderly congregation, different racial groups coming into a single-race congregation, new members who differ widely in age and ethnicity, or the arrival of a bloc of highly educated people into a working-class church will create tension and conflict.
3. The minister.
4. Power struggles between the elders and deacons.
5. Change in mission.
6. Change in structure.
7. Lack of a realistic mission or vision. "Where there is no vision, the people perish" (Prov 29:18).
8. Lack of clarity in mission or vision.
9. Change in music styles.
10. What worked in the past no longer works.
11. Financial decisions/financial stress/building projects.
12. An aging congregation.
13. Changes in leadership, power shifts, and ministerial transitions. As I wrote earlier, few people understand that transitioning from one minister to another is a complex task that can take years to complete. They want to declare the transition finished when the new minister is on the job, but that often is only the beginning of the process. Not understanding the transition process and the time it takes is a common source of conflict.
14. Communication style. How people communicate is often more important than what they say.[5]

4. Yankelovich, *Magic of Dialogue*, 134.
5. Yankelovich, *Magic of Dialogue*, 134.

Boundary Management: One of the more effective means of forcing an agenda onto another is to invade their boundaries in terms of space, time, and personality. Effective work groups manage their relationships with respectful boundary management, encompassing work and personal space. Personal boundaries are often different and tend to be highly cultural in origin. For example, an American used to an arms-length distance of personal space will be decidedly uncomfortable in a Japanese subway, where people are commonly packed together like sardines in a can. Likewise, other cultures may see the arms-length standard as unfriendly and stand-offish. Unknowingly violating personal space requirements causes significant but usually silent discomfort. Knowingly doing so is rightly understood as aggression.[6]

Data Filtering and Biases

Disputes arise and escalate because of mental leaps toward untested assumptions about other people and their intentions. Since our brains work by synthesizing and categorizing input from our surroundings and then generalizing from this knowledge, the opportunities for drawing untested conclusions are endless. Consider the following logical sequence:

- The truth is obvious.
- Our beliefs are the truth.
- Our beliefs are based on real data.
- The data we select are real data.
- Our logic in data selection and interpretation is correct.

Unfortunately, this seemingly logical sequence is deeply flawed. We come to each of these levels with layers of presuppositions and biases running silently in the background, like the operating system on a computer. We do not notice or think about it until it malfunctions, and then we may be bewildered and not know how to proceed.

Dozens of biases constantly work in the background of our thought processes. We often do not even notice them, even though they significantly affect our decisions and interactions with others. We are likely to make serious errors if we do not confront them.

6. Filippova and Pivnenko, "Psychological Boundaries."

1. Confirmation bias. Our first challenge is called confirmation bias. We come to every problem with pre-existing beliefs based on our experiences, observations, intellect, and what we have been told. While we may believe that we are examining data dispassionately, the opposite is true—our subconscious preexisting beliefs are pushing us to conclude favorably or unfavorably, reinterpreting what the data may say to fit what we already believe. Confirmation biases tend to confirm that what we already believe is fact and disregard, diminish, or even discard contrary data. We do not naturally seek out knowledge that contradicts our beliefs; we tend to reject it when we find it.

2. Belief perseverance. Belief perseverance occurs when we hang on to what we believe despite strong contradictory evidence. We experience an emotional reaction against contrary data, not so much for what it says as for what it is: a contradiction of foundational beliefs that have emotional power against change. This is showcased in the debates between those who believe in a young Earth, seven literal twenty-four-hour days of creation, and those who believe the Earth is billions of years old, and "days" as used here are not literal twenty-four-hour cycles. Of course, opposing "facts" cannot be factual, leaving each group to disregard the others based on their presuppositions about what is a fact—or they can invent their "facts," known as "alternative facts." This technique is common but unsupportable.

3. Belief bias. The third challenge is belief bias. Reading something that supports our beliefs makes sense, and we do not see internal weaknesses. When we read something we disagree with, it is easy to see the flaws and reject its validity while ignoring or minimizing its strengths.

4. Attribution distortion. If someone we like and admire says something controversial, it is far more likely to be viewed positively, or at least the wrongfulness of it is minimized or disregarded. If someone we despise or fear does the same thing, it is viewed with suspicion, if not outright rejection. Attribution distortion has more to do with trust than it does with facts.

5. Self-serving bias. All of these come together in self-serving bias, a bias towards evidence that confirms what we already believe and disregards whatever is in opposition.[7]

7. University of Reading, "Values, Beliefs and Attitudes."

The problem is that the data we discard also have validity, leaving our viewpoint skewed. This is why people with identical data can reach wildly different conclusions. Each conclusion is the "truth," *as they understand it.*[8]

INTERESTS: THE HEART OF THE MATTER

Every conflict has three levels running simultaneously: positions, issues, and interests.

Positions are a specific point of view, stance, or argument adopted by a person as "the answer" or "solution" to an issue or problem. Positions are concrete and clear proposals of what is wanted or needed to resolve a specific issue but are also flexible and fluid. A good example is negotiating to buy a used car. You can be sure that the seller will set the opening price higher than what he expects to get. Knowing this, you counter with an offer lower than what you are willing to pay. An agreed-upon price is reached through offers and counteroffers, and the car is yours.

In conflict, positional attempts to solve the identified problem often obscure what is essential and may have nothing to do with what is truly desired. People usually don't know how to quantify what they genuinely need when it is intangible, such as respect, and so find themselves making demands that others can relate to, such as money, which has nothing to do with the underlying need.

Issues are the identified problems behind the proposals. They tend to be less concrete than positions but often give clues to the identity of the underlying need. For example, the position might be for a 10-percent raise, and the issue is stated that the raise is deserved based on performance. Attention to the stated need can open an otherwise buried pathway to the heart of the matter: interests.

Interests are deeply held values or needs. They are intangible and difficult to measure; interests defy objective criteria. They include innate needs for survival, safety, recognition, respect, and acceptance. Interests cannot be negotiated away but can be substituted with other interests. Interests are identified by the emotions attached to them and come out through careful questioning:[9]

8. Program on Negotiations Staff, "Four Conflict Negotiation Strategies."
9. Program on Negotiations Staff, "Four Conflict Negotiation Strategies."

> Peacemaker: "Sharon, I can see that you are struggling with this proposed change in liturgy. Can you tell me what you are feeling and why?"
> Sharon: "I'm afraid that we are going to dump all of our traditions, and they mean so much to me."

In the above example, careful questioning revealed a much deeper need and the hopes and fears that drove it. For many people, traditional liturgies provide a sense of security and stability in an insecure and unstable world. They can count on them, and they offer comfort. These are emotional responses to actual changes and must not be discounted. Instead, reassurance and compassion can often alleviate the underlying fear.

The tenor of the conversation changes when the underlying interests are named and spoken. In this instance, the question is formed into a statement: "What I hear you saying is that the liturgy we have used has deep meaning to you, and you are afraid of losing that meaning. Am I correct?" You have just opened the way for them to expand on their underlying tensions while legitimizing their emotions, both inviting deeper disclosure. You have respectfully spoken into her fear and made it permissible and even welcome in the conversation. In that case, her answer will almost always be a higher frequency "Yes! I just feel that we are losing too much!"

While not everyone can relate to positions, interests are universal and foundational to every human being. Bringing interests into the conversation greatly increases the chances that they will move away from their opposing positions to find and agree cooperatively on a workable solution.

Interests are the key to understanding what is really behind the fight and why so much emotion has been poured into it. Interests give conflict its emotional impact and fulfilling them is foundational. A person whose interests are not met or are threatened is in a constant state of fight or flight, which is psychologically, spiritually, and physically damaging.

How the question is asked makes a significant difference. *Do not* just ask, "What do you want?" It is much more important to ask, "Why is this important to you?" or, "What does this mean to you?" These deeper, probing questions seek out underlying interests, which are non-negotiable and highly emotional.[10] The answers to this type of question often lead to creative solutions where everyone's needs are met without giving up what is most important to them.

10. Program on Negotiations Staff, "Four Conflict Negotiation Strategies."

The key to breaking the conflict cycle is to focus as much as possible on the interests, for they are the driving forces behind the emotions of conflict. Focusing on positions will rarely get to a deep solution that brings about lasting cohesion, for positions are only one way in a cornucopia of possible solutions that rarely reach the deeper levels of resolution, let alone the deepest level of reconciliation.

Asking these questions and others like them will uncover whether the group you are working with has the authority to decide. In most cases, they will, but often within defined parameters. These questions will also uncover weak points in the strategy for carrying out decisions. Each of these issues must be tackled before an informed decision is reached.

The second issue is how to decide.

Someone will inevitably answer "majority vote." I highly recommend that a majority vote *not* be used in making important decisions, as it leaves too much room for dissent and sabotage. It further entrenches the "tyranny of the majority" that cuts off discussion before consensus can be reached. Moreover, some hierarchical organizations will allow decision-making authority only in the hands of those who must implement the decisions.

Helping Them Reconnect

Unless they have already negotiated an agreement that spells out how they will deal with the present issues and future problems, you will need to guide them through this process. Aside from matters of church dogma (which can be difficult to define even within a small group), there are three basic rules for negotiations:

1. Everything is negotiable.
2. Everything is renegotiable.
3. You cannot lose what you do not have!

During the negotiation phase, the peacemaker helps the parties brainstorm possible solutions and solve problems. The peacemaker should encourage the parties to direct their comments toward each other and work together to resolve each issue and named interest. Here is where the parties should work harder than the peacemaker—this is their conflict, process, and resolution. Try to encourage the parties to use Fischer and Ury's "win-win" approach towards meeting each other's needs rather than dickering.[11] The peacemaker can keep the momentum for resolution moving forward by identifying mutual, shared interests that create common ground, emphasizing the parties' interdependence, identifying factors motivating the parties to reach a resolution, and asking what will happen if the situation is unresolved.

Behaviors That Inhibit Reconnection

- Blaming the other person: "It's all her fault." *Response:* "Fault is no longer the issue. What can you or both of you do to improve the situation?"
- Clinging to past hurts: "He was so cruel to me!" *Response:* "We can see that you are deeply hurt over what happened in the past. You are in charge of the present and the future. What can we do now to make things better for the future?"
- Denying the dispute: "I don't see what the problem is." *Response:* "What information do you need to understand their viewpoint?"
- Clinging to distrust: "She has made those promises before and never kept them. Why should I believe her now?" *Response:* "What would it take for you to trust her? What needs to happen? What can she do that will create trust?"
- Denying feelings: "I am not angry—I just want what's fair!" *Response:* "You seem angry, so we know this is important to you. What would a fair resolution look like?"
- Threatening revenge: "I'll make him pay for this!" *Response:* "It's obvious that you feel very strongly about this. Will you please help us understand what you are feeling right now?"
- Setting unrealistic goals: "We need to be finished by noon today." *Response:* "Is that possible or reasonable? What is the next best thing?"

NOTE: There is no such thing as "constructive criticism." It is self-canceling by nature.

11. Fisher and Ury, *Getting to Yes.*

Guidelines for Giving Feedback

Readiness of the Receiver—Give feedback only when there are clear indications that the receiver is ready to be aware of it. If the receiver is not ready, she or he will be apt not to hear it, will misinterpret it, or become defensive.

Descriptive, Not Interpretive—Giving feedback should be like acting as a camera plays back the scene. Give a clear report of the facts, rather than your ideas about why things happened or what was meant. It is up to the receiver to ponder the why's or the meanings or to invite you to ponder this with him/her.

Recent Happenings—The closer feedback is given to the event's occurrence, the more accurate and useful it will be. When feedback is given immediately, the receiver is most apt to be clear on what is meant and understand the emotions associated with the event. Delayed feedback is not received well.

Appropriate Times—Feedback needs to be given when there is a good chance it will be helpful. Feedback will not be viewed as helpful when other work or events demand the receiver's current attention or when critical feedback is given in front of others.

Things That Can Be Changed—Feedback can only lead to improvement when given about things that can be changed. Feedback is of little use if nothing can be changed.

Demanding a Change—Feedback should not be confused with requesting a person to change. The decision to change is up to the receiver. You may include your reaction to the receiver's words or behavior, but to say, "I've told you what you need to do to change, now do it!" is not likely to help. Instead, reaffirm group norms, particularly about making decisions.

Avoid Overload—We tend to overdo it when we first learn to give feedback. The receiver likely cannot handle a laundry list. Give feedback in small bites and make them pleasant to the emotional palate.

Give Feedback to Be Helpful—Consider your motivations for giving the feedback. Are you really trying to be helpful? Are you just getting rid of your own frustrations or feelings? Are you trying to persuade someone to do something that you want them to do? Are you trying to make yourself look better by comparison? Remember, this is not about you!

Resistance

Resistance is a natural, emotional reaction against having to leave one's comfort zone and face difficult issues. Resistance is a necessary part of the learning process. Feelings of resistance need to be expressed before a party or group is ready to accept and genuinely use what someone else has to offer.

Some will offer open resistance. The ones you really need to be aware of are the saboteurs. Their body language can usually pinpoint them, but not always. They tend to hang back, sit towards the back of the room or close to exits, may offer some criticism, or may even offer praise to throw you off their scent. Reaching sufficient consensus is useful to limit the ability of saboteurs to operate as it places their commitment before the entire body, which then acts as an accountability check.

There are a variety of constructive ways to confront resistance or opposition:[12]

- Be able to identify when resistance is taking place. Name it and confront it immediately, e.g., "You seem to be upset with the direction we are going. What is bothering you?"
- View resistance as a natural event and a sign that you are dealing with sensitive and often volatile emotions.
- Support the group in expressing resistance directly.
- Do not take expressions of resistance as a personal attack or a challenge to your competence as a peacemaker, even though they may be framed that way.
- Identify what form the resistance is taking (pick up cues).
- Name the resistance to the group.
- Be quiet after you name the resistance. Let the group respond to you.

Faces of Resistance:

- Constantly demanding more details.
- Flooding you with details.

12. Harvard University, "What Is Integrative Negotiations?"

- Inauthentic time constraints.
- Impracticality.
- Attack.
- Opens with, "I'm not surprised by this . . ."
- Confusion.
- Silence.
- Intellectualizing.
- Moralizing.
- Wooden compliance.
- Questioning methodology.
- Flight into health issues.

Concerns Underlying Resistance:

- Control or lack of control.
- Vulnerability.
- Being dependent.
- Need for confirmation, not change.
- Fear of the unknown.

The goal of this chapter has been to provide the reader/interventionist with a basic understanding of the various dynamic possibilities underlying church conflicts. Multiple factors interact to produce complexities that may not exist in secular organizational fights. For example, secular corporations rarely concern themselves with spiritual warfare. Likewise, it is much more common to have a mass exodus of members from a faltering church than to have half the workforce of a corporation suddenly quit due to internal conflict.

We also challenge the concept of "truth." If my "truth" and your "truth" clash, at least one is partially or completely false. Even facts are subject to challenge. Much of what I was taught as fact in high school chemistry and physics has been greatly modified or even disproven. What we believe as fact must be viewed in light of the caveat, "based on what we know at the moment." The effect tends to soften the positions we take and open us to new information.

Not everything listed here will be at play in each conflict, nor should the reader be expected to remember everything here. The goal is to create awareness.

12

The Big Tent

Adversity is the refiner's fire that bends iron but tempers steel.
~ James E. Faust

It takes courage to venture into the next level of group conflict resolution, which is to bring everyone who chooses to take part into the same room. Your goal is to ease into a conversation designed to lead them to an ever-deepening dialogue, bringing mutual understanding of how they have emotionally injured each other—and opening the "hope gates."

The most critical factors for success are the humility and compassion of the facilitator/peacemaker.

THE CULTURE OF POLITENESS

One of the larger blockers in group contexts, particularly congregations, is the problem of "politeness"; that is, discussions always occur within the permitted polite culture of that congregation, even if that politeness is "weaponized."[1] In my experience, we dance around the core of the conversation without addressing it until someone gets angry enough to blurt it out. In this sense, we deal with only the sides of the conversation. In critical times, a culture of politeness "may impede honest, meaningful feedback and may impact feedback seeking, receptivity, and bidirectional feedback exchanges. It is essential to understand the institutional

1. Shonk, "3 Types of Conflict."

feedback culture before it can be successfully changed."[2] What might happen if we abandoned the sides of the conversation and explored only the center? Might we not get to a deeper and more honest dialogue without the layers politeness imposes? We seek dialogue where we genuinely hear each other and the emotions underneath the words but without judging them. Dialogue is somewhat of a "foreign language" that must be led with simple, agreed-upon rules.

When we are actively aware of our biases and perspectives, we are better able to consider and understand different viewpoints simultaneously, without necessarily agreeing with them, which allows for a more open-minded and inclusive approach to various situations. Awareness of our personal biases will enable us to entertain and understand opposing viewpoints and see what possibilities lie within them without compromising our own beliefs. However, it does tend to "loosen our grip" on the idea that we are "right" and they are "wrong," which then encourages empathy and a more remarkable ability to see from the other person's perspective.

We must not ignore the politeness culture as it works in the group. Early on, the Litany of Misery (Chapter 15) largely bypasses the politeness problem by making things universally real. It is the primary tool for breaking through the bone of politeness to the marrow of what is happening.

Communications expert Daniel Yankelovich finds four blockers to deeper dialogue that often accompany the potholes of politeness.

1. Holding back. When Yankelovich asked people why they were not more forthcoming, particularly at the beginning, they often said something like, "You have to be comfortable enough to speak." The role of the facilitator/peacemaker is to create a safe space where people feel free to express their thoughts without being judged.
2. Being locked into a box. We tend to look for answers in the places we already know. Thinking "outside the box" is a common phrase but an uncommon ability. Yankelovich suggests also looking to the broader community for possible solutions that may not fit our current thinking.
3. Prematurely moving to action. Some people want to move to action steps very quickly. Too quickly. The group must explore the

2. Ramani et al., "About Politeness."

intended outcomes of any proposed solution and the potential unintended consequences. "A focus on swift action short-circuits the process of probing the depths of the participants' thoughts, perceptions, feelings, and assumptions that can provide a foundation for informed decision-making."

4. Listening without hearing. "One of the most common potholes is an unwillingness to make an extra effort to understand others when they are not wholly articulate . . . Empathic listening requires patience and an ability to tune in to other people's feelings."[3]

BEGINNINGS

Every process has a beginning, and how this is begun sets the tone for everything that follows.

Once the participants are in the circle, their religious leaders enter and open in prayer, asking for divine guidance, aid, comfort, and courage. They then introduce the peacemaker and sit with the others. This effectively transfers the mantle of authority to the peacemaker.

Acknowledge everyone and tell them what you have done so far. Much of their hope is gone, and many are here out of curiosity rather than believing that a resolution is possible. You must live and breathe quiet hope!

Explain the process for the day. Your role is to ease, encourage, and advocate for their ability to resolve their differences. The only cases where resolution failed were when the participants were there only out of curiosity, as they had already decided that they were done trying and no longer had any interest in seeking authentic peace. (Stating this reality challenges those in this camp to engage.)

Ground Rules

Though tempting, you do not need to supply ground rules; rather, ask them how they wish to be treated and write their answers on large Post-it notes that will be hung on the walls. Every religion seems to have some version of the Golden Rule: Treat others as you wish to be treated. Have

3. Yankelovich, *Magic of Dialogue*, 130–36.

them define what that means to them, and you will have a list looking much like this:

- Treat me with respect.
- Listen to what I have to say—don't cut me off.
- Speak only from your own experience.
- Do not assume that you know what I mean—ask!
- If it's important to me, it's important.
- No interruptions.
- We can disagree without being disagreeable.
- Please be curious about what I say.

Each of these is a sign of how they feel they have been treated.

Opening Lines—The Litany of Misery

Once they have agreed upon their ground rules, it's time for what I term the Litany of Misery, which goes something like this:

> I have been among you for several days. I have listened deeply to what you said, and in those conversations, I also heard your pain and confusion, your fear and frustration, your desire to return to peace, and your belief that things can never again be the same. Some of you have lost all hope while others cling tenaciously to what can still be your future, a future together and not splintered and split.
>
> There is hope! This can be resolved in ways that heal, but it is not easy. It is a path of deep but gentle honesty, self-reflection, repentance, and confession, of meeting your enemy head-on, for your enemy is you. You have done this to each other and yourselves, and the damage is breathtaking, but healing is possible, forgiveness is real, and while it is true that life can never be the same as it was, I hold out this promise to you: It can be better than it was!
>
> In each interview, I asked you to share with me the physical, emotional, and spiritual discomforts you have felt and which you feel now. I also asked what you would each do if this matter was not resolved.

> I will read exactly what you told me without embellishment.
> This is your reality, for this is what you said.
> (Read out loud everything in the Litany.)

NOTE: As you read through the list, many will begin to nod their heads, if only slightly, when they recognize their answers. The circle allows them to see each other, and cognitive dissonance occurs when they see their "enemies" have also been experiencing the same lament. They have dehumanized their "enemies," and this realization of shared misery begins to return their humanity. By the end, they will have started seeing each other in a different, more humane light. What they thought was their private misery is universally shared. You have brought them back together to a place they can now use as an anchor point.

> No one has been having fun. Not one person told me what a wonderful, exhilarating experience this fight has been. Everyone has been miserable, top to bottom and back through the middle. Everyone wants it to stop.

> You have the keys to unlock your future together. You intuitively know what must happen. My job is to help you move away from hardened positions and hurt feelings toward creative solutions and reconciled relationships. Together, we can find our way home.

THE PROBLEM-SOLVING PROCESS

A problem is simply a gap between what is desired and what currently exists. Problem-solving can be done through a systematic approach. To have an effective process, all members of the group must focus on the same issue at the same time even if there are related collateral issues.

Please do not then tell them what they should do. Instead, inquire, "How do you want life to be? What does that look like?" They will tell you because it is different from the way their lives have been. In doing so, they keep control of their lives and environment at a time when many or most will believe they have lost all control. They will also create a vision of how life can be. That is where we are going.

Have them list the problems at the center of the conflict but in non-confrontive terms. Write each on a separate piece of giant Post-it and hang it on a wall.

- Name what the problem is, not *who* the problem is!
- Attempt to define why it is a problem.
- Brainstorm possible solutions.
- Work to uncover the underlying interests that have been violated—this will produce lasting solutions.
- Examine the unanticipated consequences as well as possible benefits.
- Evaluate effectiveness later.

Do this for each identified problem. This may not take as long as you think!

A significant chasm opens before you when the stakeholders ask for your recommendations. That is not your role! If you make recommendations, you had best be as wise as Solomon, for they will start through the gate you have opened. You will also diminish their ownership and accountability. E.g., "This is what the peacemaker told us to do. I told you it wouldn't work, and it's all her fault."

They may ask, "How should we work together in the future?" Our response is simple and empowering: ask them how they would like to work together. Keep asking them questions like these:

- What would you like to do?
- How would you like to work together?
- What would that look like?
- What will it take to get there?
- What are you willing to do to get there?
- What are the potential consequences of success? Of failure?
- How will you make decisions?
- What decisions will you make?
- What are your expectations of each other?
- Are there individual and group accountability issues we need to deal with?
- What does it look like to be accountable?

. . . and so on.

The key is not to answer their questions but to ask the right questions and allow them to find their own answers. This creates ownership, resilience, and long-term commitment.

You have described life as it is.

We will shift the focus from the present to the future when you ask them how they would like life to be.

13

Facilitating Change

You don't have to take giant leaps to make the quickest progress. You have to take baby steps and keep on taking them. Great and lasting success is achieved through small, consistent steps.

~ Marci Shimoff

To see how change plays out, we will briefly examine what has come to be called the Beatitudes (Matt 5:3–12). "Blessed are the poor in spirit," they begin. Each statement opens with "blessed," which means happy or satisfied. It seems something weird is happening here, though, as we don't believe the poor or those in mourning are happy or satisfied, do we? Each statement is in the form of a couplet, meaning two lines. I suggest you open your Bible and read each couplet—but stop for several seconds between each and let it resonate within you.

The couplets form a progression from what we would term negative to positive. Augustine of Hippo lived in fifth-century North Africa and is described as a brilliant theologian and philosopher. His writings shaped much of Christianity as we know it today. However, his teachings on the Beatitudes have been largely lost. Where we tend to see them as separate, even stand-alone, statements, Augustine saw them as a progression of belief and holiness, a set of stairs leading toward heaven. Or a set of small baby steps, moving from infancy to adulthood.[1]

1. Brent, "Augustine of Hippo."

Augustine's stairway concept perfectly illustrates facilitating groups from where they are to where they wish to be via small steps.

Facilitating groups as they work toward a better future is easier than most people believe. It primarily consists of asking questions and offering observations as a process guide. It requires excellent listening skills but rarely requires deep subject matter expertise. If you choose to move into the facilitator role for something like a future search, remember that this is not about you.

The peacemaker eases change. Here are some ways.

Observe

- Watch for non-verbal clues to what is happening, particularly discomfort, frustration, and anger. Confront: Jim, you appear frustrated. What's going on?
- Model good listening.
- Watch for resistance and defensiveness; be ready to clarify perceptions and assumptions.
- Listen for "gifts" from one side to another (e.g., a willingness to make concessions or agree to the other).
- Ask open questions, paraphrase, and summarize to build understanding and generate discussion.
- Help the parties see the issues in a neutral and consensual way—separate the people from the problem.
- Use hypotheticals to get them to look at other perspectives.
- Always be attuned to the parties' need to save face.

Support

- Build rapport and use *appropriate* humor.
- Encourage the parties by focusing on the future.
- Discourage "bottom lining" and ultimatums.
- Acknowledge and affirm their interests.

- Use reframing to refocus the parties from negative to positive, position to interest, past to future.
- Help the parties save face by recognizing their emotional and psychological interests as authentic.
- Neutrally describe disruptive behavior and specify what would help.
- Be flexible in your process management.
- Focus the parties on areas of mutual gain.
- Help the parties develop multiple options.
- Encourage maximum specificity in agreements.
- Help the group name a process for future dispute resolution.

Suggestions for Questions

We manage the past by moving toward the future. It is too easy to get stuck in the muck and mire of a group's discord. If they had found their way out, they would not need you, but here you are!

We know what happened, who did what, and the damage and loss they have experienced.

Everything now turns towards the future! There are two main questions (with variations) that will get them there:

1. What do you want the future to look like?
2. What needs to happen for that future to become real? (NOTE: Some will want to talk about what they do not want; turn them toward what they want. This change from negative to positive produces creative thinking.)

Having them describe their collective dream of the future gives it a sense of "We can do this!" An excellent question to get them started is, "What does that look like? Let's describe what you are seeing."

Questions help move the process forward during the problem-solving phase. Questions, rather than statements, help them own the problem and its solutions. Emphasize their responsibility to resolve their dispute. Acknowledge each agreement and each progressive step, no matter how small.

Examples of useful questions:

- What is the best possible future?
- What are its parts?
- What are your major concerns?
- I'm not clear on . . . Could you explain further?
- What do you need for this to work?
- What does ___________ look like to you?
- What must happen for you to feel satisfied with the outcome?
- Is this taking you where you want to go?
- What do you see that she or he needs from you?
- What would help both of you meet your needs?
- Help me understand . . .

Address each of the major identified issues in this way. However, rather than homing in on solutions, go for the underlying interests, e.g., Why is this important to you? What does this mean to you?

Listen carefully for the emotional response—the emotion you must satisfy. Just be prepared for surprising twists when they finally do reach solutions!

Guidelines for the Peacemaker

1. Maintain a nonjudgmental mindset throughout the process.
2. Be optimistic about the chances for a resolution.
3. Help the parties reach an agreement that satisfies them, not you.
4. Fractionalize the issues and take one piece at a time.
5. Normalize their feelings.
6. Use role reversal—imagine life as the "other" throughout the conflict.
7. Use hypotheticals and visualization when helpful.
8. Use metaphors, e.g., tell a brief story to illustrate a point.
9. Be incredibly careful with humor!

10. Expand the pie—"In the best possible world, what would that look like?"
11. Seek common ground. Remind parties of their similarities or shared values and goals.
12. Reduce confusion. Summarize the discussion and any resolution(s) reached.
13. Empower the parties to resolve problems—on their own.
14. Help the parties develop trust, e.g., What does trust look like? Are you willing to do that? Are you willing to be held accountable?

VALUE DISPUTES

Solving problems is one thing. Resolving values disputes is an entirely different animal! Some of the most demanding situations are those that surround conflicting values.

But are they conflicting *values*?

Our values define who and what we conceive ourselves to be. We often reach for the most potent arguments and authorities in defending our values. Scripture and dogma are usually shaped and put forward in faith communities as proof statements in the prophetic tradition: "Thus saith the LORD!"

Every congregational conflict I have experienced was a value dispute rather than a matter of fundamental religious belief or practice. Yes, they argued over issues and positions, but the fundamental disagreements were found in their foundational values. Values are the most basic operating system, the DOS 1.0 of congregational conflicts, the background operating system that silently keeps everything working. Values are conclusions taken as facts about the way things "should be."

A value is a belief, a principle, or a pattern of behavior that a person has come to hold as extremely important and worthwhile. Examples of values are honesty, fidelity, sincerity, religion, etc. Values often involve moral, cultural, or ethical beliefs. Many values are so deeply held that there is little chance of compromise. Fortunately, most values are shared at their deepest levels. Unfortunately, values are usually not clearly stated or, if they are clearly stated, are not defined—in this case, the devil is in the definition.

Value disputes can arise over religion, gender, political beliefs, teaching content, philosophy, personal ethics, parenting style, cultural beliefs, lifestyle, morals, etc. "Disputes involving values tend to heighten defensiveness, distrust, and alienation. Parties can feel so strongly about standing by their values that they reject trades that would satisfy other interests they might have."[2]

Value statements identify value disputes, e.g., "That's not fair." Fair play is a value, but precisely what constitutes fair play has differing definitions. Likewise, statements with "should" are usually value-laden, e.g., "You should have known."

Value differences often arise because they are assumed to be universal when they are not. Value issues are deep-seated and are frequently not examined by the person holding them. They are often based on assumptions about how people "should" feel, think, and behave. "People's values, beliefs, and attitudes are formed and bonded over time through the influences of family, friends, society, and life experiences. So, by the time you're an adult, you can hold very definite views on just about everything with a sense of 'no one is going to change my mind.'"[3]

We feel justified in defending our positions with great vigor when the conflict concerns values, as we tend to reduce complex issues to right-or-wrong, black-and-white statements and positions. Value disputes result in unyielding positions defended with great energy. If someone refuses to be bound by our values, the conflict intensifies. This is particularly true when one of the disputants sees the problem as preferences rather than values, and the other sees it as values rather than preferences. An example is the debate as to whether homosexuality is a preference or genetic in origin. If preference, it is characterized by many as wrong or sinful. Pushing these beliefs forward into unyielding positions creates a win/lose scenario that often appears unresolvable as one party uses values to try to trump the beliefs and behaviors of another.

Values vs. Preferences.

There is a difference between preferences and values. Preferences are easily changed, while values at their core act as anchors and are tied closely to morality and personal ethics. Values are closely related to interests and

2. Shonk, "3 Types of Conflict."
3. Babu, "Beliefs, Values, Attitudes."

can be identified by emotional markers, but tend to come from deeply held beliefs, e.g., all life is holy; honesty is essential; image is everything. Values tend to be marked by "is" and "should" statements.

Values appeal to the sense of higher authority, though their authority often stays unexamined. Religious disputes are challenging because Scripture, at least on the surface, sets out the fundamental values. Religious values usually add layers to the underlying values about how the world works and how things should be. People will often hide behind Scripture and use it as a weapon to escape the underlying value conflict—it can quickly degenerate into who is "right," frequently using the same text as the authority.

Conflicts in value-based organizations such as churches can quickly divide them into competing groups. If one of those groups must lose, it is likely to leave *en masse* and either begin a rival church or join another existing church.

The good news about these conflicts is that focusing on the underlying interpersonal values will often bring resolution, as the superordinate (superior) values are used to justify the positions taken. The superior values recede once the underlying conflicts are resolved, as shields are no longer needed.

The bad news is that many people who need to be right and control the behavior of others will not even consider opposing positions. This is usually more about keeping power than reaching an understanding. These religious power struggles ignited wars throughout recorded history during the Protestant Reformation, the Crusades, and "holy" wars. They often escalate steadily to organizational destruction. I have seen it happen. Do you remember Maryann and the shrub? They were so far down the path of destruction when I was asked to help that no one could have saved it.

So sometimes you will find hardened positions that are not reconcilable. In churches, these problems usually stem from doctrines and the interpretation of scriptural texts. These intense disagreements escalate quickly, often ending in bitter resentment between former friends. Each group is convinced they are right, and the spiritual stakes are so high that the spark of conflict can instantly ignite an all-consuming conflagration. In these situations, the peacemaker can only slightly affect the outcome. However, on a more positive note, the focus of blame may become the peacemaker, making him or her the "scapegoat," which leaves them a face-saving escape route.

Options for Values Disputes

Consider interests and values separately: Separate the person from the problem and engage issues individually. Determine what value your counterparts attach to their positions and respond accordingly.

Engage in relationship-building dialogue: Build relationships by establishing rapport or a common cause, bringing your counterpart to your side while helping yourself understand her interests and values.

Appeal to overarching values: Appealing to common or shared values can help bridge the gap by bringing you and your counterpart closer together in terms of bargaining interests. By establishing a common negotiating ground, you can create value (and claim more value) than may have been apparent previously.

People often are unclear about their values—even to themselves—as they have not been in a position where they previously had to examine and enunciate these foundational beliefs. Lack of clarity produces the appearance of inconsistency between words and actions, thus creating more significant confusion and the potential for deeper conflict. Values can often be ferreted by questions such as, "What is the most important part of this to you, and why is it so important?"

It is easy to argue over positions and proposals, but values tend to be universalized and unarguable. Values are the most basic of needs, but we often have difficulty focusing them into concrete proposals because they do not lend themselves to solidity. Values such as the need for respect are universal, but how we apprehend what respect looks like must be said before we can understand how the person requesting it will know they are respected. It is assumed that we all know what "treat others as you want to be treated" looks like, but we do not. Respect is often an individual understanding, but it comes with family and cultural roots that shape it. The same is true of integrity. In the West, integrity means carrying through on promises, being honest, and not taking what is not yours. In some Middle Eastern honor and shame cultures where authority is essential, taking something that does not belong to you is not connected to integrity. We assume that our definitions of values are universal, but how they are defined must be explored to work effectively with value disputes.

Values are tightly connected to strong emotions, so value conflicts can quickly escalate into hardened and supposedly nonnegotiable positions.

The job of the peacemaker is to bring the underlying values to the surface and describe them. Understanding eventually begins to supplant anger as the parties find their values are shared at the deepest levels. These values are often in the realm of the importance of family, respect for individuals, emotional and financial security, and so on. These deep discussions and the more profound listening that goes with them lead to deeper dialogue about the meaning of each one's life and place in the world and, by extension, within the group.

Once value barriers are breached, people become aware that the other side wants the same things. A new energy can become a profound force in the room as they find commonalities.

In this sense, it is very similar to those moments where proper understanding breaches the barriers of fear and deeply touches the soul. The peacemaker must be very gentle at this decisive moment yet must help the group find a new focus. It is not unusual for the group members to cross their battle lines at this point and offer comfort and acceptance to each other.

You have reached a healing breakthrough when this happens. It is unforgettable.

Covenants

Settlement agreements for faith community disputes are little different from those in interpersonal or organizational mediations—they spell out who will do what to whom and with what in the future. Each section must be in their words, not yours, though you can suggest phrasing and diction.

I prefer the term "covenant" for obvious reasons. It has a touch of the sacred, requires higher agreement and commitment, fits better into a religious environment, and seems to allow for more significant spiritual discourse during negotiations.

Each agreement should be written down as it is reached, using the most precise language to get the essence. The group, or a subgroup, will work with you on the final language. What gives the covenant power is having every person sign it.

Commitment: Even though only the congregation governing board may have the legal authority to sign binding agreements, a covenant is an agreement of a different sort. It is a holy pledge between the people of

God to *teshuva* (Hebrew: return to the path of the LORD). Under these circumstances, every participating person should sign it in a formal ceremony. The peacemaker signs only as a witness.

Signing their names to the document vastly increases the likelihood of following it and produces a mechanism for enforcement.

Are we there yet? Not quite, but we are closer than we were. Forgiveness and reconciliation must be attended to—if they are ready.

Accountability, simply put, is the sum of their expectations of each other in carrying out decisions and how they will be enforced. Too often, these expectations are not stated, and they frequently lead to further problems. We will address accountability in the forgiveness and reconciliation process.

Each group member must discuss and agree on how they will hold each other accountable and support each other. Unexpressed expectations often create problems in the first place, so the expectations must be brought into the open. This discussion will reveal differences in conflict styles, allowing the peacemaker to devise acceptable confrontation strategies.

THE MINEFIELD

Pastors come and go. Sometimes, we are sad to see them go, while at other times, we will gladly help them pack their bags and escort them to the freeway on-ramp.

There are two types of leadership exits: forced and voluntary. Both trigger fundamental changes throughout the church.

The interim between the announced leaving and when the organization is comfortable with the new leader is called "transition." The standard, uncomplicated transition period is about one to two years, although it can be longer. Without thorough planning and preparation followed by careful execution, transitions can quickly become a time of organizational drift, resulting in a loss of purpose and people.

Organizational development pioneer William Bridges concluded that while change is situational, *transition is psychological* and creates needs that must be attended to. As we have seen, Bridges described three significant stages: the ending (the leader leaves), the neutral zone (an indeterminate period of confusion and distress), and a new beginning. The neutral zone is the most emotionally intense and least understood.[4]

Voluntary endings cause minimal disruption but forced endings are abrupt and are marked by significant chaos, confusion, anxiety, sadness, and distrust, even among those who welcome the change.

Most churches view transitions as simple and sequential: advertise the opening, see who applies, sift the candidates down to four or five, conduct interviews, and then the hire/call. This approach is quick and efficient but often ignores the emotional dynamics set loose in the congregation.

The neutral zone can be compared to an emotional minefield because the danger is unrecognized until the first mine is stepped on—and explodes.

Leadership changes often lead to instability and vulnerability, with emotions like discomfort and frustration intensifying each other. When staff and volunteers perceive instability, they begin asking anxiety-driven questions such as, "How will this affect me?" or "Should I leave now?" This uncertainty can result in fear, panic, decreased commitment (and finances), and increased job searching. Forced departures provoke the strongest reactions, and as tensions escalate, there is significant pressure to shortcut the process.

Mistake #1: Not asking or answering why we are looking for someone who already needs a job. There are reasons why they are out of work or want a new situation, and you need to find the reasons behind it. Candidates will couch it in the most favorable terms and gloss over any negative factors. References are only the first level—ask each for the names and contact information of others to interview, digging down to the third or fourth level. Pursuing this could quickly shorten the candidate list.

Mistake #2: Not taking active measures to reassure and keep employees and stakeholders informed, which results in anxiety, increased staff and volunteer turnover, increased costs, and more confusion.[5]

The more respected and long-tenured the departing leader, the greater the grief and resistance, prolonging and complicating the transition. Neglecting emotional needs can result in depression, absenteeism, reduced productivity, high turnover, organizational instability, and

4. William Bridges Associates, "Bridges Transition Model."

5. Walk and Handy, "Job Crafting."

increased costs—replacing employees can cost from 50 percent to 200 percent of their annual salary.[6]

There Be Dragons Here: Navigating the Neutral Zone Minefield

The neutral zone is the unmarked crossing point through the wilderness between the "ending" (the leader leaving) and the "new beginning" (the new leader settled in). In a sense, the neutral zone serves as a buffer, like the Sinai desert through which Moses led his people out of Egyptian slavery. As I've said previously, the purpose was not so much to get the people out of Egypt but to get Egyptian culture out of the people. It took forty years.

Whether the transition is planned or forced, the primary features of the neutral zone are uncertainty, anxiety, and grieving.

Mistake #3: Not acknowledging, understanding, or guiding the corporate grief process.

Grieving is the natural way to process loss, even when a community is happy to see a leader go. The key is to let go of the past thoughtfully and respectfully—by recognizing, acknowledging, mourning, and intentionally releasing what is being lost. Grief follows no fixed timeline and cannot be hurried. It creates an open, uncertain space for something new to emerge, much like how it takes nine months to bring a baby into the world, no matter how many people are involved; people in transitioning organizations often feel isolated and lost in uncertainty, with rising insecurity and a desire for clarity and closure.[7] This neutral zone is like Sheol, a gray, lifeless place where the souls of the dead await a better future.[8] Addressing two key concerns can reassure: 1) Will essential functions continue? 2) Who will handle them? If the remaining leaders are well-prepared and assure continuity, the challenges become a manageable part of the transition.

Mistake #4: Not making it safe to have opposing conversations.

Early transitional conversations tend towards tense politeness but, over time, become more straightforward, energetic, and even

6. UC Berkeley ExecEd, "Impacts of Poor Mental Health in Business."

7. Gino and Norton, "Why Rituals Work."

8. Sheol in the Hebrew Bible is the underworld place of stillness and darkness where the souls of both the righteous and the unrighteous dead go, regardless of their moral choices in life. As a rabbi explained it to me, Sheol is a place of shadows, a place of "asking," with little life force.

confrontational. Allowing the people to express their hopes and fears safely enables the flow of dialogue to expand and move through a four-stage progression:

1. Talking Nice. Group harmony is maintained at the expense of diving into the real issues.
2. Talking Tough: Group harmony gives way to debate, which fails to work through the issues because each side tries to prove itself right and the others wrong.
3. Reflective Dialogue: Listening takes over, and individuals can start conveying their perspectives without trying to convince others or feeling judged.
4. Generative Dialogue: The dialogue moves beyond personal conversations, allowing a truly collective experience of meaning-making, discovery, and transformation.[9]

Mistake #5: Interpreting rigid but opposing standpoints as unchangeable yes-or-no polarities rather than opportunities for creative change while envisioning the future.[10] Interjecting the concept of yes/and can ease these tensions.[11]

Mistake #6: Not acknowledging the legitimacy of anxious or contrarian questions. The remaining leaders fear they may no longer be needed. Anxious questions may not have answers: Will there be room for me? Will I still have a role? Where will I fit in? What do I stand to lose? Will my friends still be here? What will it be like working for the new boss? What if we don't get along? Acknowledging these as legitimate eases anxiety and resistance.

Mistake #7: Whitewashing grief.

A common misconception is that faith communities mourn their losses more effectively than secular organizations. In a forced exit, they often whitewash their public image to cover up any negative aspects but rarely have guided opportunities to express their grief communally.

When the pastor leaves a church, congregation membership can often decline. Some members may choose to leave the church with them, seek out another church with a similar style of ministry, or simply become

9. Jaworski and Scharmer, "Leadership in the New Economy."

10. Johnson, *Polarity*.

11. Block, *Answer to How Is Yes*.

less active due to the emotional impact of the departure. All of these are products of grief.

Every church has rituals that should be continued through the neutral zone. Rituals anchor stability in change and transition. "Because rituals promise continuity, order, and predictability, they are important in times of change and transition."[12] Openly name the losses, acknowledge their value, and declare them concluded through a ritual.

Simple questions can bring private fears into the open to discover that they are shared.[13] Once shared, the sense of isolation is transformed into one of community. Some examples:

- How is all of this affecting you?
- What is over, and what are you losing?
- What is your greatest concern in all this?
- How can we support each other through this?
- What is vital that we continue?

Talking about what the transition means to them individually or in a group produces more personal and honest answers. Losses and concerns take on shape, form, and substance when they are named; naming makes them real and legitimate. Naming also claims them as our own, creating a circle of shared ownership. It then becomes easier to name and focus on what is continuing—and what is coming.[14]

Mistake #8: Publicly criticizing the past, even if described as hellish.

Bridges writes, "Loss is a subjective experience, and your 'objective view' (which is really just another subjective view) is irrelevant."[15] All losses are subjective, so their reality and importance, even if outlandish, must be respected.

Mistake #9: Not building in or allowing silence.

The leader of this process must be an empathetic listener and comfortable with silence. Peter Caprello from Vanderbilt University suggests that intentional silence, combined with grief, fosters healing—not through words, but by accepting the changes and losses that come with

12. Briller and Sankar, "Changing Roles."

13. Puls, "Leadership Transitions and Faith Community Conflicts."

14. Dudley and Ammerman, *Congregations in Transition.*

15. William Bridges Associates, "Transition Model."

it.[16] Profound silence is part of the Jewish tradition of "sitting shiva" with the friends and relatives of someone who has died. The ritual has its roots in the ancient book of Job. Job had lost his vast fortune, his children, and his farms. His friends came and sat with him, sharing his grief in comforting silence for *seven* days.[17]

C. Otto Scharmer expanded Bridges's work by charting the flow of dialogue and the tasks of the transitional process, illustrating it in the shape of the letter "U" (see Appendix). Scharmer also named three central components of transitional processes that correspond with Bridges's three levels of transition: 1) The Flow of Dialogue During Transitions, 2) The Transition Process, and 3) The Tasks of the Transition Process.[18] All three processes are simultaneously active, but the emphasis shifts. The challenge is normalizing the processes for those going through them and gaining enough time and commitment to complete the various tasks.

In sum, several approaches can be combined to ease grief, calm the background noise, and start new conversations:

1. name their fears and discomfort,
2. accept that time-honored traditions will change,
3. acknowledge their losses,
4. expect and accept grieving,
5. mark the endings,
6. expect overreaction,
7. ensure the important things will continue, and
8. look to the future.

Rituals recognizing, honoring, and releasing the past help the grieving process while opening portals to a new future.[19]

16. Capretto, "Empathy and Silence."

17. Job 2:12–13. "Sitting *shiva*" is a Jewish mourning ritual involving a week-long gathering to grieve, reflect, and heal. The term comes from the Hebrew word *shiva*, which means "seven" and symbolizes the seven days of mourning. During *shiva*, mourners typically gather in the deceased's home and sit on low benches or stools as a sign of humility and grief. They also refrain from their everyday activities, such as work, using cosmetics, and going out. Shiva is a time to create space for grief, talk about the loss, and receive comfort from others.

18. Scharmer, *Theory U.*

19. Lang, "Helping Churches Respond."

Acknowledging fears and discomfort in a safe environment helps normalize them and lessen their impact. When people openly share their uncertainties, they realize others share similar concerns, fostering a sense of connection and making uncertainty feel more manageable.

Becoming

"Becoming" follows the neutral zone. This highly creative task involves Scharmer's four-stage progression of ever-deepening dialogue to share fears, hopes, aspirations, and dreams of what can be.[20] Becoming asks a challenging question: What questions lie at the heart of who we are called to be? This existential assessment has no clear and concise answers. Instead, it seeks deeper questions about who they are as a community with a new calling.[21] This becomes an opportunity to identify new core values, rejuvenate their identity, and chart a new course for the future.

THE NEW JOURNEY

Journeys into the unknown are often unsettling or exciting. The difference results from preparation and attitude. The conversation shifts from asking questions to Scharmer's generative dialogue that creates as it goes. It is common for people to become passionate here. A facilitated "future search" can bring out new ideas and dreams that can be given solid form in new goals.[22]

Keep what is good and jettison the rest with proper ceremony and respect. Higher energy levels propel a new sense of purpose. They embody the voice of freedom to be what they—and their community—can be. There will still be problems, but the expectation is for a better set of problems![23]

20. Block, *Answer to How Is Yes*.
21. McNeal, *Present Future*.
22. Weisbord and Janoff, *Future Search*.
23. McNeal, *Present Future*.

14

Forgiveness and Reconciliation

True reconciliation is never cheap, for it is based on costly forgiveness. Forgiveness depends on repentance, which has to be based on acknowledging what was done wrong, and therefore on disclosure of the truth. You cannot forgive what you do not know.

~Desmond Tutu

THE POWER OF FORGIVING

Forgiveness is part of every religion. It is the center of Christianity. Interestingly, secular philosopher Joanna North has written, "It seems that Jesus of Nazareth discovered the power of forgiveness 2000 years ago." Convinced that Jesus was right, she goes on to say,

> Forgiving a person for a wrong he has done has often been valued as morally good and indicative of a benevolent and merciful character. However, while forgiveness has been recognized as valuable, its nature as a moral response has largely been ignored by modern moral philosophers who work outside the confines of a religious context. Where it has been discussed, forgiveness has been thought particularly difficult to define, and some have thought the forgiving response paradoxical or even impossible . . . [T]he value of forgiveness lies in the fact that it essentially requires recognizing the wrongdoer's responsibility for his action. Secondly, that forgiveness typically involves an effort on

> the part of the one wronged: a conscious attempt to improve oneself about the wrongdoer.[1]

Only recently has clinical science put together the pieces of what Jesus taught and placed them into a coherent whole that describes what it means to forgive, the benefits to the forgiver, how it works, what blocks it, and how to overcome those barriers.

Regardless of how you view Jesus of Nazareth, he described the forgiveness process accurately. I wish that we Christians would practice it more.

That said, we will focus on the clinical studies related to biblical principles. I have every reason to believe they will fit nicely into your beliefs.

Judaism: Psalm 86:4–5. "Gladden the soul of your servant, for to you, O Lord, do I lift up my soul. For you, O Lord, are good and forgiving, abounding in steadfast love to all who call upon you."

Christianity: Matthew 18:21–22. "Then Peter came and said to Him, "Lord, how often shall my brother sin against me and I forgive him? Up to seven times?" Jesus told him, "I do not say to you, up to seven times, but up to seventy times seven."

Islam: Quran. "Those of you possessing affluence and ample wealth should not make oaths that they will not give to their relatives and the very poor and those who have made hijra in the way of Allah. They should rather pardon and overlook. Would you not love Allah to forgive you? Allah is Ever-Forgiving, Most Merciful."[2]

Hinduism: Vidura said: "There is only one defect in forgiving persons, and not another; that defect is that people take a forgiving person to be weak. However, that defect should not be considered, for forgiveness is a great power. Forgiveness is a virtue for the weak and an ornament of the strong. Forgiveness subdues (all) in this world; what can forgiveness not achieve?"[3]

Buddhism: "Think of your nearest and dearest people. Forgive them for anything you think they have done or are doing wrong. Fill them with your forgiveness. Let them feel that you accept them. Let that forgiveness fill them. Realizing that this is your expression of love." [4]

1. North, "Wrongdoing and Forgiveness."
2. Quran, Surat An-Nur 22.
3. Mahabharata Udyoga, Parva, Section XXXIII.
4. Still Water Sangha.

Did you notice that the same healing chord runs through all of these?

Defining Forgiveness

How we conceive forgiveness makes it easier or more challenging to accomplish. It helps if we do not connect it with reconciliation. For our purposes, and from the literature, they are separate and distinct. Understanding this distinction can bring clarity and guide our journey toward forgiveness and reconciliation.

What do we mean when we use the word *forgive*? It seems there are as many definitions as people trying to answer the question. We have failed to understand forgiveness, what it is, how it works, and why it benefits us. This sows confusion, and we draw back from it because we sense we will lose something in forgiving another person, but we don't know what it is. This phenomenon has built a mythology that offers apparently reasonable explanations for why we should not forgive. They seem logical until they are examined closely, and then they disintegrate.

Forgiving is often confused with condoning, excusing, forgetting, or justifying the offense. Forgiveness does none of these but requires that each is attended to in specific and deliberate ways.[5]

Forgiving requires confronting the act and the damage it caused without denial or defense. The power of forgiving lies in its ability to overcome these barriers.

Objection: If I forgive, he gets away with it.

Response: What is he not getting away with now? How does hanging on to all your pain and misery affect him? Hanging on to your misery does not affect him. It is more choice than result.

Objection: We must forgive and forget, and I can't forget. Therefore, I cannot forgive.

Response: God did not give us the ability to forget, nor does Scripture require it. Instead, we must remember what was done to us. Otherwise, there is nothing to forgive. Therefore, remembering is the gateway.

Objection: I will forgive him when he is sorry and asks for forgiveness.

5. Russell, *Real Forgiveness.*

Response: What if he never comes to you? What if he is never sorry? Do you believe God intended you to carry all this pain with no way to heal it unless someone else does something you cannot control?

Objection: Justice first, then forgiveness.

Response: What if justice does not meet your needs? What if there is no justice? Are you to live in an emotional prison because no one lets you out? The key to your cell door is in your pocket.

Objection: Forgiveness requires reconciliation, and I want nothing to do with her.

Response: Forgiveness is a solo gift you give to yourself. Reconciliation requires full commitment of both/all. You can forgive and sever the relationship, but you cannot reconcile completely without mutual forgiveness and full commitment.

Objection: I can't forgive myself for what I did.

Response: You don't have to. Even though the person you harmed may not forgive you, God forgives you. All you need to do is seek it, accept it, learn from the past, change, and move forward in freedom.

Why Forgive? The Surprising Answers!

Many do not see a connection between their unforgiveness and their emotional, physical, relational, and spiritual health problems. Research shows that informing them of the benefits of forgiving makes it easier to forgive. It's called "enlightened self-interest." Here are results from some of the studies:

- Conditional forgiveness (I will forgive if/when) is associated with higher mortality rates—you die sooner![6]
- Those whose religious practice includes forgiving discipline have reduced internal hostility, which is directly related to better health.[7]
- Religiosity is related to greater forgiveness, greater forgiveness is linked to reduced hostility, and reduced hostility is tied to better subjective health.[8]
- Emotional forgiveness replaces negative, unforgiving emotions with positive, other-oriented emotions. Emotional forgiveness involves

6. Toussaint et al.,"Forgive to Live."
7. Koenig, "Religion, Spirituality, and Health.
8. Wohl et al., "Looking Within."

psycho-physiological changes, and it has direct health and well-being consequences.[9]

- Learning to forgive relieves stress.[10]
- Learning to forgive has been shown in clinical studies to relieve guilt and emotional distress.[11]
- Forgiving helps the victims of sexual violence resume everyday, productive lives.[12]
- Forgiveness therapy is a highly effective antidote for chronic disease and mental health in that disease symptoms are decreased, and positive mental health is increased.[13]
- Forgiveness is an effective way of moving from anger over a transgression and shame for being on the receiving end to self-love and acceptance.[14]
- Anger is associated with more toxic stress conditions that produce adverse changes in cardiac and vascular regulation, while forgiveness is associated with a healthier heart. These findings suggest that interventions aimed at decreasing anger while increasing forgiveness may be clinically beneficial to heart health. [15]
- Forgiveness is associated with lower blood pressure levels, heart rate, and rate pressure product. Increased blood pressure recovery after stress is also linked to forgiveness. Forgiveness may produce beneficial effects directly by reducing the cumulative burden of chronic stress and life events associated with betrayal and conflict indirectly through reduced perceived stress.[16]
- Women who received an apology showed faster recovery from the offense than those who did not. In contrast, men who received an apology showed delayed recovery from the transgression compared to men who did not receive an apology. These results show

9. Worthington Jr. et al., "Forgiveness, Health, and Well-Being."
10. Lawler et al., "Unique Effects."
11. Johns Hopkins Medicine, "Forgiveness."
12. Davidson et al., "Associations."
13. Elliott, "Forgiveness Therapy."
14. Burrow and Hill, "Flying the Unfriendly Skies?"
15. May et al., "Effect of Anger."
16. Hannon et al., "Soothing Effects of Forgiveness."

potentially healthful benefits to forgiveness and apology, but the relationship is influenced by the situation and by gender.[17]

- Empathy is associated with forgiving. Women were more empathic than men, but no gender difference in forgiveness was apparent.[18]
- Learning to forgive substantially increases the ability of addicted teens to break further addiction.[19]
- Forgiving breaks the descent into bitterness and revenge-seeking while increasing the ability to trust again.[20]
- PTSD sufferers who forgive have their symptoms reduced to such an extent that they are often able to return to everyday lives.[21]
- Learning to forgive reduces death anxiety in the elderly.[22]
- Forgiveness is an effective treatment for depression.[23]
- Learning to forgive strengthens the immune system.[24]

And these are just a sample! To sum it all up, forgiving is good for you! But what is it? It's time to define forgiveness.

Individual forgiveness is a conscious decision to release anger, resentment, fear, pain, and the desire for revenge against another. What they did was real; it caused pain, was unjustified, and was wrong. Nevertheless, we choose to release all these toxic emotions we are holding against those who hurt us. In doing so, we break the emotional chains binding us together.[25]

Notice that this is entirely one-sided and does not involve the offender!

Congregational forgiveness: Forgiveness is an act that joins moral truth, forbearance, compassion, and commitment to repair torn human relationships. It requires a truthful examination and turning from the past that neither ignores past wrongs nor excuses them, neither overlooks

17. Whited et al. "Influence of Forgiveness."
18. Toussaint et al.," Forgive to Live."
19. Lin et al., "Effects of Forgiveness Therapy."
20. Enright, *Forgiveness Is a Choice.*
21. Witvliet et al., "Posttraumatic Mental and Physical Health."
22. Krause and Ellison, "Forgiveness by God."
23. López et al. "Forgiveness Interventions."
24. Turner, "Health Benefits of Forgiveness."
25. Puls, *Road Home.*

justice nor reduces justice to revenge, that insists on opponents' humanity even in their commission of dehumanizing deeds, and that values justice that restores above justice that destroys.[26]

South African Nobel Peace Prize winner Nelson Mandela said, "Forgiveness liberates the soul. It removes fear. That is why it is such a powerful weapon."[27]

Here is the secret: the healing power of forgiving is directed primarily at the forgiver rather than the one forgiven. Forgiving is in your own best self-interest. It is good for you, your family, your church, and your community. Archbishop Desmond Tutu succinctly states, "Thus to forgive is indeed the best form of self-interest since anger, resentment, and revenge are corrosive of that *summum bonum*, that greatest good, communal harmony that enhances the humanity and personhood of all in the community."[28]

26. Puls, *Road Home*.

27. Henley, "Invictus."

28. Tutu, No Future Without Forgiveness.

15

Forgiveness Examined: Turning

Nothing erases the past. There is repentance, there is atonement, and there is forgiveness. That is all, but that is enough.

~Ted Chiang

WHAT IS TRUTH?

The healing process is well underway. The Litany of Misery brought home the damage inflicted and received. Explaining the benefits of forgiving has brought each person's self-interest into the center of awareness.

Now, we move forward with the more intense, formal forgiveness and reconciliation process, which I call TRUTH. The word is an acronym for the five main stages of the process: Turning, Remembering, Understanding, Transforming, and Healing.

Turning has been underway for some time, but now it takes an unexpected change in direction. They know the pain they have received; now, it is time to accept the pain they have given.

One of the central realities of congregational conflict is that no one is entirely innocent. They have all contributed to the problem by what they did, what they did not do—and what they thought, for their thoughts shaped their attitudes, and their attitudes shaped their behaviors.

The forgiveness process tends to follow a bell curve. A few will forgive without help because that is their nature, or they recognize what unforgiveness is doing to them. Some forgive in the beginning stages of the process, more in the second stage, most in the third stage, fewer in the fourth, and fewer in the fifth. In a mirror image of the beginning, a few will never forgive.

Putting Miles Behind You

We will start with the gateway to forgiving: finding and expressing empathy for the offender.

Empathy is not one key among many—it is the most potent key![1] If we see what rage, hate, and vengeful thinking do to our relationships, we find ourselves isolated in self-created prisons, gasping for sunlight and fresh air. We crave life and freedom, which forgiveness promises to us. An apartheid torture victim in Soweto, South Africa once told me she forgave to get her life back. Forgiving is as much a practical matter as it is a spiritual one.

An old saying warns us not to judge people until we have walked a mile in their moccasins. It suggests trying to understand the lives of offenders and what it must be like to be in their shoes. The issue is not guilt or innocence but identifying why they did it.

Jesus told his followers, "But I tell you, love your enemies and pray for those who persecute you, that you may be children of your Father in heaven" (Matt 5:44). Praying for those who have hurt us starts this process. It is challenging to pray for someone's welfare and healing without seeing them on a more human plane than where we want them to be. In praying for them, we find a different, less violent way of viewing offenders, leaving us more open to forgiving.

The key, then, lies within our hearts.[2] In other words, the challenge for anyone who would help people overcome their self-imposed barriers to forgiveness, be they individuals, groups, congregations, or nations, is to trigger empathy across conflict boundaries. Gaining empathy for an opponent requires imagining life and the incident from the other person's perspective and seeing them as a distinct individual with human needs and weaknesses. It's not as difficult as one might think.

Empathy helps us see others in much the same way as we see ourselves, lessening the tendency to exaggerate what they have done into who they are. Without empathy, we see perpetrators as an "it," something not worthy of love or respect. We begin to see them as things that are

1. Every, "Growing Scar Tissue."
2. Rohr, *Quest for the Grail*, 20.

not fully human. Empathizing changes our perspective from "I-It" to the more intimate and equal "I-Thou" described by Jewish mystic Martin Buber.[3] With empathy, we wonder why they needed to steal instead of labeling them thieves. By inquiring about why they stole, we can see the human needs that drove them.

As we consider what happened from different perspectives, we begin to see that mitigating factors may have escaped us. This does not make what happened right, but it can radically alter our understanding of the act and the actor.

What must it be like to be the other person? Why did they do it? Answering these questions is not for the faint of heart—it can be a shocking revelation to conclude that we might have acted the same way under similar circumstances.

Empathy then allows us to reframe what they did and the damage it caused into something more easily understood and, therefore, more easily forgiven, helping both.[4]

The Light of God Within

Foundational to a Christian worldview is the view that every individual, regardless of what they may have done, must be viewed as a human being who is a child of the living God. Somewhere within, perhaps hidden by filth and sin, lies a holy spark. Focusing on the divine spark within the offender rather than what they did grants them the opportunity to change. Suppose we see what they did as who they are. In that case, we deny them both the opportunity and incentive to change, becoming oppressors ourselves by locking them into the prison of perpetual "offenderhood." It changes the exclusive isolationism of "me" and "you" to the inclusive "we."

The Barrier of Self

Empathizing with others isn't easy when we are absorbed in ourselves and our issues. We become selfish when we feel wounded and wronged, focusing on our needs and excluding others. In truth, it can be nearly impossible on our own to focus on the humanity of the offender while

3. Buber, *I and Thou*.
4. Stone et al., *Difficult Conversation*.

we are screaming in physical or emotional pain. Our motivation to focus on the offender often is to inflict as much pain back to them as possible!

Creating a sacred space where it is safe to tell—and understand—their stories diminishes emotional pain and the pressure to "get even." We can prime a healing wellspring by asking such questions as, "Has there been a time when forgiveness was granted to you when you did not deserve it?" If we are honest with ourselves, we must answer "yes." This answer can open an unexpected bridge to common ground.

Once they see themselves as guilty of something, somewhere, "somewhen," and even if they see their offenses on a lower plane than the offenses of others, empathy becomes more decisive in moving them towards each other and forgiving.

From Shame to Guilt

As we saw earlier, reframing turns the picture from a negative to a positive. For instance, a victim might say, "You stole the meat and bread. You're a thief." The offender responds, "You didn't need it all." Hearing the underlying need, the peacemaker reframes, "You took it because you were hungry." The offender responds, "Yeah! I hadn't eaten in three days! I'm sorry, but it hurt so bad!" The matter has suddenly shifted from theft to desperate hunger, something much more straightforward to forgive, as almost everyone knows some manner of hunger. Effective reframing changes the focal point from "I am the offense" to "I did the offense," separating the person from what she has done, allowing healthy guilt instead of shame.

Shame strikes most profoundly into the heart. Wounds inflicted from the outside hurt the ego, but shame is a gaping wound inflicted from the inside that injures the soul. Shame leaves us standing naked and defenseless in the court of human judgment. It is humiliation on a grand scale.[5] Shame says we did something because we are defective and beyond help.

Guilt says that what you may have done is not who you are. You have value, and you can change.

Shame offers no such possibility, as it is about whom you are at the core. Shame has been connected to direct physical, verbal, and symbolic aggression; indirect aggression through harming something meaningful

5. Choi, "Feeling One Thing and Doing Another."

to the person; malicious rumoring, displacing aggression to another person; ruminative anger; and self-aggression.[6]

The interventionist's job is to help them move from "I am . . ." to "I did . . ." If successful, this allows them the freedom to change and increases the victim's ability to empathize and forgive.

Mutuality

All nonviolent conflicts have at least two sides, each seeing the other as the aggressor. Discussions of "offenders" and "victims" are usually misleading. The roles of offender and victim usually become inseparable, meaning everyone is responsible for the problem *and the solution.* The intellectual and emotional dawning that we are both victims and oppressors in the same persons cultivates more empathy from all sides, greatly easing the resistance to forgiving.

Compassion is empathy in action. Empathy without action passively understands what another feels, like listening to music, while compassion hands us an instrument and places us in the middle of the orchestra. Empathy costs little and requires nothing, while compassion pulls us from the safety of the spectator seats onto the dirt and sweat of the playing field. Compassion has a price tag!

Compassion requires action.

Some may argue, "Leave it to God," but that mistakes passive peacefulness for peacemaking. We can and must do more than that; otherwise, we risk remaining where we are.

Turning Towards Home

Each layer of the process requires a new and higher level of repentance.

Have you ever been driving somewhere and found yourself becoming less and less sure of your direction? You were initially certain, but now the landmarks you remember are not there, and the landscape looks increasingly unfamiliar. You slowly realize that you are going the wrong way and turn around. Likewise, repentance is a change of mind followed by a change in direction.

The first level of turning involves engaging all the parties at once. It turns them inward and away from the conflict, helping them find their

6. Hendricks, "Shame and Aggression."

guilt before turning outward again. It spurs empathy, which spurs healthy guilt and helps them repent.

We have helped them acknowledge their collective misery by guiding them inward to their shared suffering, which they fear doing. Since this first level is passive and shared, resistance was minimal.

The peacemaker helped them reach this first turning point by repeating back what they had described to him or her: their woundedness in all of its rawness, fully explaining the physical, spiritual, and emotional damage wrought by the conflict. It is jarring as participants begin to see heads nodding in acknowledgment, especially those they thought were unaffected by it all—where they thought they were alone, they find a shared crucible of suffering.

The narrative ends their isolation and begins bringing them back together.

Curiosity is engaged, and they begin to see each other as frail and human, traits they had long before stripped from their opponents and hoarded to themselves. This first level of turning is the change of mind from denial to acceptance that one has participated in the conflict and that their participation was hurtful at some level.

Turning to Action

The second level of turning completes the turn and spurs action.

Ask them to silently pray or meditate for three to four minutes for the well-being and healing of those who hurt them. Warning: three to four minutes seems a very long time!

Once they are done praying/meditating, ask them to consider who prayed for them. This is a jarring change in perspective, but the fact is that they have been someone's enemy, and those people are now praying for them. It shifts their view from innocent victimhood to a more encompassing view of mutual pain and wrongdoing, which moves them closer to forgiving.

As compassion grows out of empathy, repentance reflecting the love of God comes closer.

The focus of turning is very tight. It is primarily a peacemaker-led journey into the self to confront the pain one has endured, to begin owning their hurtful behaviors, and to recognize that their pain is universal.

Turning is the beginning of beginnings. Without it, nothing else can occur; forgiveness will be forfeited, and true reconciliation will become a fleeting illusion.

Turning and Hope

It is vital that the peacemaker radiates hope. You can see it when the participants enter. They are war-weary. They are refugees, boat people rafting away from their own suddenly unfamiliar and threatening country. They want their discomfort to stop, the conflict to go away, and everything to return to how things were. They are lost in a dark sea and can't find the harbor entrance. They may have a chart to show them the way, but they need a light to see it. Hope is their lighthouse.

As congregants become more aware of their mutual woundedness, love and compassion become easier. As compassion grows, hope also grows and compassion grows again—they feed off each other while producing more than they consume.

Each level of the crucible requires turning inward and then outward. As each level progresses, they become more and more open, vulnerable, transparent, and thus more forgivable and forgiving, while increasing empathy in that part of each that is a victim, turning them away from anger towards compassion, increasing the ability and willingness to forgive. Thus begins the increasingly intimate dance of forgiveness.

The Turning Narrative

Don't let the length of the turning narrative intimidate you—it is the most extended narrative within the process. Everything builds on the turning narrative.

The peacemaker begins by describing faith as appropriate for the group. For Christians I use Hebrews 11:1: "Faith is the substance of things hoped for, the evidence of things not seen." Though faith has been diminished, it is still alive and well. God can heal. The peacemaker prays for the well-being of each participant as they begin the journey to healing.

The turning narrative must include the following:

- the results of the conflict without ascribing blame;
- behaviors that hurt people without identifying details;

- the complete list of physical and emotional manifestations of the conflict felt by the congregants, e.g., headaches, nausea, sleeplessness, anxiety, fear, digestive problems, hurt, and grief.
- the woundedness of relationships and the confusion and fear that occurred when friends turned on each other;
- the economic impact on the church from the conflict and the general estrangement that has enveloped the congregation; and,
- the likely outcome for the congregation and the church if the conflict is not healed.

The Turning Narrative (Example)

Good morning and thank you for being here. Many of you have spoken with me or members of my team about what you have experienced here. We listened very deeply to every one of you, and to those who we did not speak to, I think you will find your experience reflected here.

We took everything you told us and compiled it into this report. There are things you will hear that will be difficult to accept, but it is the truth of your experience as a congregation. We spoke with eighty-five adults through telephone and personal interviews. No one's position was so high as to dominate our report, nor so low as to be left out. We placed all the comments together, and patterns appeared that showed us some very good news: you are normal people trying to deal with a difficult situation. Unfortunately, the ways in which we deal with conflict are not always constructive. Hurtful statements have been made by and about many people. If that was all we looked at, it would be very discouraging, but we looked beyond to where you want to be and know that we can help you get there.

I am simply going to describe back to you what you described to us. There are some things you will not like to hear, and there are others that offer hope. All we ask is that you listen carefully. We report nothing that did not come from you. This is your truth. What you find may surprise you.

The conflict was difficult for everyone. No one enjoyed it. Not one person told us that this was a good thing and that they were having a good time. Despite how some people may have appeared to react on the surface, we saw nothing but confusion, pain, and misery underneath. You have much in common that you may not have realized.

You share the symptoms of stress overload. You told us of not being able to sleep at night because your minds could not shut out the images and words you experienced. The result for some was terrible fatigue and an inability to concentrate. It affected your ability to do your jobs. For others, simply getting out of bed became a huge effort, as all you wanted to do was sleep. You reported the same inability to concentrate, and some of you experienced minor accidents that could have been major. You feel so tired that you want to crawl into a hole and pull the top in over you and disappear. You share a terrible sense of sadness and loss.

Almost all of you have physical symptoms that have been anything but pleasant. Many have digestive problems such as nausea, acid stomach, diarrhea, and vomiting. Some are on the verge of ulcers and colitis. Others have fierce migraines that drop them to their knees in pain, causing them to withdraw from friends and family to be alone in a darkened room. Some of you have lost all appetite—what once was delicious now holds no attraction, and you have lost enough weight that losing any more could present a health risk. Others have tried to compensate by eating, and eating, and eating, but you can never get full because what you seek is not food, but comfort. You are ashamed of yourselves for your weakness.

Many of you are mourning the loss of friendships, and it is very difficult because so few of your friendships outside this congregation really mean that much to you. Here you have friendships with substance more than style, but many of those friendships seem gone, destroyed in the heat and anger of conflict. And so, you mourn the loss of friends that you valued deeply, even loved.

Many of you find your entire view of the church shaken, and some are fast losing their faith. Unity now seems like a dream dissipating on awakening to a cold and cruel reality. You crave unity, but everyone in the conflict has made it a place of discord. I do not mean to offend those of you who just heard what I said and reacted by thinking that it was others more than you who brought discord into the house of God, but what I said is true. The sad news is that everyone in this room has had a part in the conflict. No? Then answer these questions honestly and you will have your truth. Did you ever, even once, react in anger? Did you ever, even once, pass on a rumor or gossip? Did you ever, even once, react to something by telling someone else rather than going to the person who offended you? Did you ever, even once, categorize someone as a jerk, an idiot, a schemer, as dishonest, or some other negative? If so, then you are part of the conflict.

Here is the one thing that is perhaps most difficult to accept: did you just stand by to see what happened, and believe that you are therefore not part of the conflict? If so, then you deceived yourself, for in doing little or nothing, you allowed the conflict to consume your friends and destroy relationships. You did not stand in the gap as a peacemaker, and you are part of the conflict.

Finally, did you just give up on someone as being beyond hope? Did you write them off? If so, you are part of the conflict.

All of you in this room share a commonality of pain and suffering. Though many want to point their fingers in blame, there has already been enough blame. Part of the problem is that your blame is usually pointed outward. Blaming each other is useless, because all are to blame, which is why Jesus commanded us to examine ourselves for sin before we ever think of looking at our neighbors. My job is to name it: it is sin. There was a target, and you missed it.

Though some of the rhetoric of this conflict has been dressed in rich spiritual clothing, it is the thin veneer of hypocrisy. Jesus described this as being like a painted grave vault—beautiful, clean, and noble on the surface, but rotting inside. Scripture has been twisted and used as a weapon, when the purpose of Scripture is salvation and holy living.

Some of you have hurt others intentionally. You did it when you were angry. You did it when you felt attacked. You did it in self-defense, pushing others away hard enough to keep them away. You did it to hurt, the same as you were hurting. These actions have left terrible open wounds on people who trusted and loved you. Some of them are ready to give up on not just this congregation but on the church as a whole.

Some of you have hurt others unintentionally by not being careful in your selection of words, or by small things that you did in trying to avoid the conflict. In avoiding the conflict, the message that you gave to those actively involved was that neither they nor their issues were important enough for you to intervene and help them find their way through this unfamiliar forest.

Some of you tried to play both sides by being encouraging to both, but not listening carefully as they not only described the conflict but showed you their discomfort and distress. It hurts when people won't listen and sends a message of uncaring.

This congregation can die. This congregation can also live, and not only live, but thrive as well. The choice is yours. You have the power to kill this congregation or bring it to new and vibrant life. Even though this conflict has hurt you all so badly and deeply that you might think about leaving, the simple fact that you are here today, sitting next to your friends and adversaries alike, tells us that you have hope, even if that hope is disguised in what some of you may describe as just seeing what this is all about. You would not be here if you did not have hope, and you would not commit yourselves to finding peace if you did not have hope.

Hang on to that hope. The story is told of a man named Bill who one day fell into a very deep hole while walking. He cried for help, and finally a famous preacher walked by. The preacher looked down at Bill, raised his eyes towards heaven, and prayed, "Lord, please send this man someone to assist him. Amen." With that, the preacher rushed off.

Later, a physician heard the cries and peered down into the hole. He asked Bill if he was hurt. Bill answered, "Not really. I have some scrapes and bruises, but nothing really serious." The physician nodded wisely, pulled out a pad, wrote a prescription, and threw it down to Bill. "Call me if these don't work," the physician said. With that, he left.

By now, Bill was hurting, tired, and scared. Then, a friendly voice came from above. "Hey, Bill, what are you doing down there?" Bill looked up and saw the smiling face of his best friend, Jim.

What can I say?" said Bill. "I wasn't paying attention to what was going on around me and here I am. Get me out, will you?"

With that, Jim dangled his feet over the edge of the hole and slid down to the bottom, smiling all the way.

"Jim," cried Bill. "What are you doing? Now we're both down in the hole!"

"I know," said Jim, "But I've been in this hole before. I know the way out."

"I'm now going to ask you to do something that every fiber of your being will resist: trust me/us. You have been through so much and shared so much pain together that it is difficult to trust, but that is exactly what we ask each of you to do. We have been in this hole before, and we know the way out. We will not hurt you, and we know how to help you find the light of morning.

The narrative may be longer or shorter, but it must be truthful and without accusations. The second level of turning is seamless and without any break.

> In just a few moments, we are going to have you start the healing process. Actually, the process has already begun. You know the truth of what we have said. You know that you have already looked at the wrongs of others for too long and must now turn inward if you are to find healing.
>
> Each of you has a piece of paper and a pen or pencil. Whether you see Jesus as God, a prophet, or simply a very wise man, he was right when he demanded that we examine ourselves for logs in our eyes before we start picking at the dust flakes in the eyes of others.
>
> I remember the people who have hurt me. It is more difficult to think of the people I have hurt. I don't want to see myself that way, but that is the way I am, and that is a truth about myself that I must face. All of us are this way, even though we may try to deny it; it is just the way we are made. We are weak, and in our weakness, we strike out at others. Though we are focused on our own pain, fear, or anger, the truth is that in striking out we cut and bruise each other.
>
> We are now entering a time of silent contemplation. For the next five minutes we are asking each of you closely to examine what you have done that may have made things worse. Forget for the moment those who hurt you and concentrate on what you did that may have hurt others. We ask you to think of whom you may have hurt and finally, to examine truthfully your intentions: were you defending yourself by pushing them away? Did you want them to experience the pain you experienced? Were you afraid and acting out of fear? Take five minutes to examine these questions and write down your findings. Please do this is a spirit of silence and godly contemplation. You may get up and move about, but please do not talk with each other.

16

Forgiveness: Remembering

Those who do not remember the past are condemned to repeat it.

~Attributed to George Santayana

HEALING MEMORIES

Turning is an invisible step off the land and into a small boat and sailing in the safety of the harbor. However, we cannot enter a new harbor without risking the open sea. In a situation of conflict, writing down things people did that may have been hurtful turned your boats into the channel between the harbor and the sea. Remembering will take them through.

Remembering requires turning from personal victimhood towards recognizing and acknowledging our wrongdoing. As much as I may not want to, I must remember, confront, claim ownership of, and confess my wrongdoing. This is the highest barrier to forgiveness and reconciliation. It must be approached gently and from the side.

The participants have already accepted their common woundedness under the mantle of victimhood and have begun to consider the probability that they have also wounded others.

Once again, we are helping empathy transform into compassion to produce repentance. The target of repentance is individual ownership of harmful actions and behaviors.

- Turning helps us own the truth of what we have done by recalling specific aggressive (and passive) acts that hurt others or contributed to the conflict in other ways.
- Repentance turns the participants from denial of doing something that hurt another to acceptance that they did.
- Remembering needs outward ownership and acknowledgment, commonly called "confession."

ONLY CONFESS

Confession is simply a statement of truth, nothing more or nothing less. As used here, confessing is telling the truth about what one did and taking ownership of anything that caused emotional pain. The effect is interesting: it tells the injured that what happened was real, not something they imagined.

Having the reality of the offense confirmed by the person who did it makes it easier to understand, which also makes it easier to forgive. Confession requires dropping my defensive barriers by owning what I did—it is an admission against my interests. Confession is problematic because it requires me to abandon the mask of anonymity or self-righteousness that covers my sin.

Denying responsibility preserves my reputation and misdirects the anger of the victim.

Confessing reverses this by embracing the victim's anger and tarnishing my reputation. Not only is it a role reversal, but it is also a step into vulnerability. Once admitted, ownership cannot be denied.

A simple confession ("I did it, and it was wrong") is sufficient for some to forgive. Confessing requires the offender to come out of hiding but serves as a pressure-release valve for the soul. It purges bodies and souls of residual fear and anger that inhabit our minds long after the conflict is over. In this way, confession has a positive effect on the victim and the confessing offender.

Overcoming Barriers

Conflict victimizes everyone, and we are quick to claim the mighty mantle of victimhood. We know this role is powerful because others gather around us in a protective shield. The purpose of remembering is to discard that veil.

Guilt is not easy to see or admit. We believe that we are victims and justified in reacting in the same way we are attacked. We are hurt, and in our anger, we want them to suffer as we suffer—and a little bit more as a warning that we are not to be trifled with. The transformation from victim to offender lies in the desire to inflict more pain than was received. The escalation, which we defend as self-defense, transforms the victim into an offender.

Claiming victimhood shifts responsibility away from oneself to another, thus blaming someone else for what we did. It tries to spotlight them, leaving the actual offender cloaked in shadow.

The key to changing this deceit is not head-on assault but a subtle shift in perspective. It is found in recovering the whole truth from the warped memories of conflict and then confessing our anger, resentment, and desire for revenge as motivation for our actions.

Placing the truth of our wrongdoing before others loosens its grip on us and eventually releases us entirely. Knowing the truth, however, is often unsettling. As I wrote earlier, the truth will set you free, but first, it tends to make you miserable.

Knowing the truth allows us to make sense of confusing events but also strips away self-deceit. It also gives perspective where perspective was lacking, encouraging empathy to continue growing.

The emotional dynamics of conflict distort our memories, so one challenge is in recovering and relating true and right memories. The benefits to victims and offenders alike can be enormous. As we begin to know and understand the bigger picture than what is in our heads, it changes in form and character to something that no longer overwhelms us with anger, fear, sorrow, or remorse. It is transformed into something redemptive by restoring the hope of forgiveness and renewed relationships.

Remembering is often resisted out of fear of re-experiencing the pain and confusion of the events. Helping participants in the conflict understand that it is in the past and cannot harm them again is like the emotions felt in an intense dream: they may feel real but are not real and cannot cause further harm. What happened is in the past. It cannot be changed, but it also cannot harm.

What happened cannot be changed, but what was threatening can be transformed into something redemptive; what injured now heals. It tells us what and whom we are forgiving or being forgiven by. Denying the past clamps a lid on anger and lights a roaring fire underneath. As the pressure builds, there comes the eventual certainty of an explosion. Remembering dampens the fire and brings relief. Confessing partially forces people out of victimhood by restoring their sense of control.

The responsibility for action shifts from the offender to the offended, and it is common to see confusion mixed with confirmation. Though the offender is now clearly identified, the offended must acknowledge the confession for what it is: a self-sacrificing truth statement.

Let's be honest. We like it when the good guys and the bad guys are clearly shown, and there is no contradictory crossover between them. But life isn't etched in pure black and pure white. Instead, it is etched in ever-changing nuances of gray. This means that we must consider the possibility that the conflict is also etched in shades of gray rather than stark black and white.

It means we might be wrong in assessing the other, which requires change. As Richard Rohr puts it, "The journey to happiness involves finding the courage to go down into ourselves and to take responsibility for what's there. All of it. This means looking at the self without flinching, owning up to whatever wreckage we find, while also acknowledging that there are some promises and some energy there . . ."[1]

Each side is likely partially correct. By being only partially right and partially wrong, neither side is forced into a corner where the ego will strike back.

GUILT ENOUGH TO GO AROUND

I was invited to a Christian peacemaking conference in Ohio a few years ago. The program was full of workshops, but one piqued my interest as it was on interest-based mediation. This win-win collaborative approach to conflict resolution was new to the sponsoring organization but was widely used nationwide. Having used it for many years in secular situations such as divorce settlements, I was pleased to see that two respected professors were presenting it as a means of meeting actual needs and addressing emotional wounds instead of focusing solely on property distribution. Towards the end, a Christian mediator sitting in front of me became agitated and asked the presenters, "Where's the sin? How do I know who sinned and needs to repent?" She needed to "pin the sin"

1. Rohr, *Quest for the Grail*, 57.

on someone, which is the opposite of what needs to happen to heal the wounds of conflict. She did not seem to grasp that everyone involved carried part of the sin burden, regardless of their side. She seemed to see these conflicts as clear demarcations between victims and offenders, and she was there to convict the offenders. She forgot the warning in 1 John 1:8—"If we say we have no sin, we deceive ourselves, and the truth is not in us."

Solid research from Harvard University shows that everyone involved in a conflict contributes to making the conflict worse, which would be considered a "sin."[2]

The good news is that everyone then also has the power to make things better. Below is a short list of how people unintentionally contribute to the problem:

- They might have repeated something negative they were told about someone.
- They might have repeated or embellished gossip.
- They might have planned an attack strategy.
- They might have just sat by and watched.

All of these constitute participation, but many believe that being a spectator makes them innocent. Not so. In Matthew 25, Jesus condemned the Pharisees who decorated old graves but did nothing for the living while excusing themselves with, "We never would have joined them in killing the prophets." In other words, given the opportunity, they would have stood by and done nothing to stop the killing. Jesus saved some of his strongest language for those who lead outwardly righteous lives but who would rather watch the trenches fill with blood than get their hands dirty by trying to stop the bloodshed: "Snakes! Sons of vipers!" He then asked a terrifying question: "How will you escape the judgment of hell?" Jesus was trying to shake them from their hypocrisy.

Refusing to see our guilt by focusing on the foibles and warts of others forms a barrier to self-examination and keeps us from seeing ourselves as we are. Jesus was emphatic that his followers needed to look at their actions first, not as a response to what someone else did.

We must also repent from our victimhood to recognize and acknowledge our wrongdoing, confronting the truth of our motivations

2. Dansie, "Multigroup Analysis."

and actions. Can I be honest? We are all hypocrites when it comes to this. We desperately want to be innocent victims who unfeeling, uncaring ogres have wronged. We yearn for the protection and sympathy of victimhood. We don't want to examine our actions and don't want anyone else to examine them either, so we try to divert attention by blaming the other person. We don't want to look at the "oppressor" and see ourselves, but, as Dietrich Bonhoeffer wrote, "Silence in the face of evil is itself evil: God will not hold us guiltless. Not to speak is to speak. Not to act is to act."[3]

Communal Confession

Confession is the Judaic and Christian norm for corporate forgiveness, whether by an individual on behalf of the congregation (Neh 1:6,14; Dan 9: 4–19) or by the congregation itself (Ezek 10:1, 16; Neh 9). Some may argue for more, but they will have a difficult time. Leviticus 26:40–42 states that a simple confession of sins will restore God's covenant with Jacob, Isaac, and Abraham. Then there is Jeremiah 3. Like a spurned suitor, God cries out for unfaithful Israel's return, promising mercy and abated anger on a straightforward condition: "Only acknowledge your guilt—you have rebelled against the LORD your God." "Only" excludes all other requirements; otherwise, it would have no meaning.

Some may argue that these promises are Old Testament and no longer valid. James 5:16 brings the concept into modern Christianity: "Therefore confess your sins to each other and pray for each other so that you may be healed. The prayer of a righteous person is powerful and effective."

The importance of confession is recognized in the Christian Scriptures as well.

- The most explicit statement of the power of simple confession is found in 1 John 1:8–9: "If we claim we have no sin, we deceive ourselves, and the truth is not in us. If we confess our sins, he is faithful and just and will forgive us our sins and purify us from all unrighteousness."
- Confession, forgiveness, purification. Though many will want to add more requirements for God's forgiveness or perhaps change their sequence, doing so requires adding meaning that is not there.

3. Attributed to Dietrich Bonhoeffer but not found in his published writings.

Confessions generally fall into one of three categories: self-serving, shame-based, or sacrificial. Self-serving confessions usually attempt to grab the spotlight and proclaim one's innocence. Shame-based confessions tend to claim victimhood or cast blame on others. Sacrificial confessions acknowledge ownership of something harmful and express guilt and repentance.

To Whom Is Confession Made?

Who was the sin against? If it was against God, we must confess to God. To seek forgiveness from those we have harmed, we must confess to those we have harmed. This is face-to-face communication. Intermediaries cannot carry out this direct, face-to-face communication. It is difficult and humiliating, but do not underestimate its power.

As noted earlier, Jesus saw this as so important that he told his followers to abandon their offerings near the altar and reconcile face-to-face with the brother or sister "who has something against you" before returning to the altar with the offering (Matt 5:24–25). We must note that "something" means anything, whether or not we believe it to be justified!

Group conflicts provide "act anonymity," while confession gives a name and a face to what was done and who did it. Confessions declare, "I am here, and I did this." Once admitted, it cannot be retracted. It also results in a powerful, voluntary role reversal as the victim regains validation and power, which the one confessing has relinquished. You may see visible relief from the injured when this happens. They begin to sit up a little straighter as their injuries are confirmed, and it becomes clear that the fault is not (entirely) theirs. In a true story of murder, forgiveness, and reconciliation, Katy Hutchison says that hearing someone's name links the unfamiliar and the familiar, the unknown to the known. It creates a sense of recognition and subtle unease, even if we've never met the person. In essence, speaking their name makes them real.[4]

Though public confession is more uncomfortable than private confession, it holds us accountable to others. It is easier to change once we take ownership of what we have done in front of others.

So, when and to whom should confession be made?

Confession should be made to those affected by the action, ensuring it does not create further harm. If the entire group was affected, the

4. Hutchison, *Walking After Midnight.*

confession should be addressed to the group; if only one person was targeted, it should be directed solely to them. The level of disclosure should match the act's visibility—public actions require public confessions, while private matters should remain private.

Confession should be clear but not excessively detailed to avoid causing additional harm. It should focus on what was done, not why, as explanations at this stage often do more damage than good.

The most effective confession should acknowledge the actions taken and any underlying emotions, such as anger toward another person or feelings of despair. While some may see this as making excuses, it highlights our shared humanity.

Example: "I purposely hid the financial reports where you could not find them. I was so scared that I had made a terrible mistake that I just wanted to hide."

Though this approach gives reasons, it is different in that it focuses on John's fears and insecurities. Had he gone on to say that he had hidden the financial reports because John thought Tom was being a jerk, an obvious rabbit trail for Tom to follow would be the defensive retort, "I was being a jerk? What about you?" Feelings are universal, but reasons are personal.

Pontius Pilate: "*What is truth?*"
John 18:37

"TRUTHINESS" AND TRUTH

The next problem lies in finding an agreeable "truth." Too many of us rely on what comedian Stephen Colbert has termed "truthiness," which is the quality by which a person claims to know something intuitively, instinctively, or "from the gut" without regard to evidence, logic, intellectual examination, or even facts.

We believe our "truthiness" because it is what we remember. Unfortunately, what we remember is often distorted to reflect well on us and ill on others.

In conflict, we become stuck on what we believe to be the truth. Still, proclamations of factual truth can be frustratingly fragile. Self-serving bias warps the senses, and emotion interprets events in distorted ways with the result that we remember in self-serving ways.[5] Even though we

5. Brainerd and Bookbinder, "Semantics of Emotion."

may both have a niggling understanding that we are slanting things in our favor, we justify it by claiming victimhood. Unfortunately, science has proven that memory is an amalgam of fact and interpretation.

- If I have done something to you, I will likely remember and emphasize details that minimize my actions and maximize my justification.
- You are likely to exaggerate the memory of what I did and its impact on you.
- If my justification is so self-serving and warped that you cannot see something to grab onto as truth, you will see me as lying, which adds insult to injury.
- Telling the truth and accepting it as truth are the most essential factors in confession.
- There is little chance of mutual forgiveness and reconciliation if the truth remains so distorted it cannot be agreed to.
- Though knowing the truth and truth-telling do not imply a promise of forgiveness, they give it better context and meaning. The act becomes understandable, though not acceptable.

We cannot order or otherwise require anyone to confess. Approached wrongly, it can have disastrous effects.

Peacemaker: "It's time to confess what you have done."

They (collectively!): "Confess? Confess what? We were just defending ourselves! It's their fault!" Everyone points fingers at each other and storms out the door—end of process. Go home. Do not collect your fee.

The simplest way to help them confess is to have them describe precisely what they did in a plain and simple acknowledgment and nothing more:

Debbie: "Tom, I wrote the letter."

Now, Tom has a name and face attached to the letter that attacked his competency. As contrary as this may seem, it is now easier for Debbie to seek forgiveness, and Tom to grant it. Curiosity increases as people begin to accept ownership for actions that others have not associated with them, making it easier for the peacemaker to interject questions that lead to even greater curiosity, such as, "What was going through your mind when you wrote it?"

Exploring the thoughts behind the actions often reveals the fears and frustrations that were driving them, thus allowing them to speak to these foundational and universal fears. Since having these fears is a shared experience, compassion is increased.

Again, do not have them describe why they did it as this introduces justifications that will usually be self-serving and counterproductive. Instead, describing what you see and asking clarifying questions will usually produce a much better result. Since this is face-to-face, the other party will hear and benefit from the responses.

Peacemaker: "I can tell that what Diane did is really upsetting you. You also seem very sad."

Mary: "I just want to cry. I can't stand to be near her anymore. We were so close before all this."

Peacemaker: "I can see that it was a close relationship, and that you miss it deeply. Do you suppose that Diane misses the relationship? Does she seem sad?"

Mary: "She might. I don't know. She seems angry."

Peacemaker: "How do you interact with her?"

Mary: "Now when I see her coming, I just turn around and walk away."

Peacemaker: "How does it feel to you when someone you care about turns around and walks away when she sees you?"

Mary: "It hurts."

Peacemaker: "Do you suppose that walking away from Diane hurts her?"

Mary: "I guess so."

Peacemaker: "Do you think that walking away, with its message of rejection, makes things better or worse in your relationship?"

Mary: "Worse."

Peacemaker: "What in your power can you do to stop making things worse?"

We have done two things: We have helped Mary see how she is actively part of the conflict and making things worse and helped her see that she has the power to make things better. In helping her find her power, she can gain confidence that the problem can be resolved. We have helped restore hope while also helping her find the "log in her eye."

Another example:

Peacemaker: "What were you feeling when you wrote the letter, and what did you hope to accomplish?"

Bob: "I was angry and hurt that some of them had said that our minister, Jerry, was not doing his job. It felt like an attack on me, since I was the one who recruited him. I know him better than any of them and he's doing what we hired him to do. I wanted them to give him a chance."

Peacemaker: "So you felt personally attacked?"

Bob: "Yeah. In talking about him, they're talking about me. It doesn't feel good."

Fred (interjecting): "Bob, I had no idea you felt that way. It's not your fault. You introduced us to Jerry, but hiring him was a group decision. I'm sorry that you feel we were after you. We weren't."

Knowing the thinking and reasoning behind an act removes much of the sting, as it is not senseless but a reaction to something else.

When "truths" collide in any conflict, it is normal to see one's own memory as factual and truthful and the opponent's memory as untruthful and deceptive, particularly in group conflicts, where collective memories often supersede personal stories. The tellers hold their own story up as truth. The receivers hold the same story up as distortions or lies.

Do not try to figure out which story is accurate, for neither story is objective truth. The peacemaker's job is to help them find their collective truth, which they will shape and form.

Collective memory has several characteristics. It:

1) is shared by the group and seen as an accurate depiction of the past;
2) tends to be biased, selective, and distorted;
3) is a unique, distinct, and exclusive telling of the group's past;
4) is used to justify social actions in the past, present, and future; and
5) serves to form, maintain, and strengthen group identity. [6]

In changing collective memory, the groups critically examine and revise the past so that it synchronizes, and a new truth narrative emerges from the common themes in their stories.

Untangling the Wreckage

Start with small things.

- Finding parallels in hopes and dreams for the future identifies commonalities that positively change how they see and understand each other. What are their dreams for children and grandchildren?

6. Beim, "Cognitive Aspects."

- Begin by working on small and inconsequential issues. As they become more used to being with each other again, they can tackle more important issues.
- Small successes breed larger successes, allowing trust to increase.
- As trust increases, so does acceptance of truth statements.
- They don't have to agree completely—competing narratives can begin to coexist as long as they have a common core that both sides see as truthful, which in turn becomes a commonly held center, a "master story."

Identifying and stating the master story of the conflict allows those within it to process a whole made of many parts, and a new truth emerges that enables them to accept the past and see a new future together.[7]

THE REMEMBERING NARRATIVE

> Thank you for your trust and patience. I know that what I just had you do was difficult. I asked you to look deep inside of yourselves and to see beyond what others have done to what you have done. I noticed some of you reacting strongly to the task. Some of you started out looking hard and angry, but you softened. Some of you were crying as you recalled both what others did to you and what you did to them.
>
> We cannot confront the past without remembering it. We cannot lessen the pain without remembering what it was. We cannot leave it behind without remembering what it is that we leave. Some might argue that we should forgive and forget, but only God seems able to forget. We must forgive, but forgiveness requires remembering what we did and what was done to us; otherwise, there is nothing to forgive.
>
> The good news is that in remembering and re-experiencing the emotions of the moment, we begin to take back the power it has held over us.
>
> Jesus told us to love and pray for our enemies. While we may not see ourselves as enemies in this room, we act as enemies when we hurt each other through our actions and inactions. These are the sins of commission and omission that you confronted a few moments ago.

7. Broome, "Reaching Across the Divide."

> Think now: who are you most angry with, feel most betrayed by? Who is it that you once trusted and now trust no longer? I will ask you to do something you may not wish to do. I am asking you to take two minutes to pray for those people you thought of when I asked who you are most angry with or whom you feel betrayed your trust. As you pray for them, visualize their faces as wounded sinners who need God's love and your love. Please pray that God will bless them beyond anything you can think of and heal them. Please do that right now.

After two minutes:

> Please look around and ask yourselves this question: "Who prayed for me?" That's right, someone in this room, perhaps several, just prayed that you would be healed, and that God would bless you beyond all measure. Do you know who it is? Is he or she sitting across the room or right next to you? The fact is that everyone in this room, and those who could not be here today, has had multiple people praying for them in the last few moments.
>
> It is humbling to realize that someone has just prayed for us because we have hurt them, and they have seen us as their enemy. It's not a place where we wish to be, but it is where we are. Our goal today is to move out of anger and recrimination and into a place of safety and restoration, and you have just taken the first steps. Congratulations!
>
> We all know what it feels like to be hurt by someone we trust. We all know what it feels like to feel betrayed by a friend. You have already thought of those who have hurt you, and now I am asking you to think of those you may have hurt. You know who they are.
>
> Several years ago, I was having a bad day: my plane was late, the car rental contract was wrong, and the hotel lost my reservation. As I checked into my meeting, the receptionist honestly said, "It really stinks to be you today, doesn't it?" Her words stopped me dead in my tracks, for she had tuned in to my feelings with the precision of a diamond cutter. She helped me change my focus from my personal "pity party" to how I had reacted and how that reaction was now affecting others. In doing so, I was unexpectedly ashamed of myself for reacting and behaving in the way I did. Though I could rationalize it, I could not justify it. Living in my own frustration, I had unfairly justified hurting others. It was wrong, and I now needed forgiveness.

Why did someone pray for you? What did you do that hurt people? What did you do that contributed to the conflict, even if your intentions were not to hurt others but to defend yourself? Did you cut someone off in mid-sentence, dismissing him or her like a foolish child? Did you repeat a rumor about someone? Did you twist the facts "just a little bit" to make yourself look better and them worse? Did you respond in anger instead of listening? Did you lie about something? Did you cut someone down behind his or her back?

It is true that there are a lot of thorns on the roses, but the reverse is just as true: thorns have roses. I have been shifting your way of looking at the conflict ever since we started. Many of you have now changed how you see the conflict and each other. You are beginning to see that the damage was not isolated but universal. You have begun to confront your own guilt. In your guilt, there is hope.

What are you willing to risk by healing yourselves and your relationships? What is it worth to have your friends back and to restore your relationships? We have now come to another difficult juncture. The Bible has a command for Christians that we would rather ignore. We find this very specific command in the New Testament book of James: "Therefore, confess your sins to each other and pray for each other so that you may be healed. The prayer of a righteous man is powerful and effective" (Jas 5:16). It's a two-part command: confess and pray for healing. It recognizes the universal woundedness that permeates this room. It says that confession opens the doorway for the Spirit of God to begin healing us from the past and strengthening us for the future.

In our self-righteousness during the conflict, we have lost true righteousness. We have left the high path of holy living for the low road of contention. We need to reclaim the power of our prayers through a return to the path of the Lord. The gateway to that path is clearly stated. It is a confession.

You have already prayed for each other and most likely been prayed for, and now I am asking you to take the most significant risk of all: to come out of hiding and confess something you did that may have hurt and made things worse, even though it may have been well-intentioned. A confession is nothing more than a statement of truth. No excuses. No reasons why you did it. Just what you did. It need not be fancy or elaborate, but it needs to be the truth.

I am asking that no one judge anyone who confesses, for there is a very strong statement in the Lord's Prayer that we skip through as quickly as we can, and that is this: we ask the Lord to forgive us in the same manner as we forgive others. Worse, Jesus clearly said that God does not forgive us if we do not forgive others. Even worse, the Bible says that whatever standards we use to judge others will be used against us. God sees it as what we have said and done and calls it sin.

Remember this: you shall know the truth, and the truth will set you free (John 8:31, 32).

Please join me in prayer for a moment. *Holy One, you are the comforter. You bring us the power to do things that we cannot do, and right now, we need that power, for we are afraid. You want us to step out and leave the boat of our comfort, but the water is dark, deep, and cold. We are afraid, Holy Spirit. The storm batters our small boat, and the waves threaten to sink us. We are afraid, Holy Spirit. Change the wind that powers the mighty waves of our fear. Then give us the courage to step over the side to walk on the water of your grace. Hold my hand as I step over the rail and onto the unknown.*

This may be difficult, but we are together in our need of forgiveness. Who will walk on the water of grace with me through their confession? Remember, it's just a simple statement of ownership, of "I did this." This is not a time to say you are happy or sorry that you did it, but only a time to claim what we have done and rid ourselves of all deception. Amen.

By prior agreement, the congregation leaders now confess their own negative thoughts and actions before the congregation. The peacemaker must be ready to intervene instantly if someone begins an attack on the one confessing. The peacemaker controls the process by enforcing the ground rules that they made earlier. No one is allowed to challenge, e.g., "That's not all you did!"

The confessions will become more spontaneous as the people see that this is now a consecrated and holy place where the Lord is healing his people.

Peacemaker: "This is not the time to express remorse, but some will do so. Simply let them know that we will explore the dynamics of remorse shortly."

Once confessions are completed, there should be a ten- to fifteen-minute decompression break.

Refreshments should be available.

However, it is important to continue the forward momentum, so the break should not be any longer.

17

Forgiveness: Understanding

The good thing about crying, I'd realized, was the catharsis you felt when everything finally came out. It was as though I'd cried tears of poison; poison that didn't have to be inside me anymore.

~JEREMY JENKINS

FROM ENEMY TO PARTNER

ON A BITTERLY COLD late December night, two physicians, a man and a woman, sat with me. They had co-founded a successful medical practice now in danger of collapse due to their present conflict. We had been working for a little over two hours when everything changed. He had just described how he came from a boisterous family where everything was exaggerated, where invading personal space was how one showed conviction, and angry yelling was the norm. He was a big man, about 6'4" and 250 pounds, and seemed quite pleased with having leaned over his partner's desk while yelling at her full force while waving his arms. I then asked her, at 5'2" and 100 pounds, "What happens when you get yelled at?" A tiny, four-year-old's voice answered, "You get hit." Silence. I will never forget the look on his face. It was as if a horse had kicked him in the gut. His shoulders slumped, and his face collapsed in utter devastation. He had no inkling of how she had responded to his "normal" conflict behavior. He couldn't even speak for several seconds and finally managed to sputter, "Oh, no, I had no idea, I'm so . . . I would never . . . oh, please, I'm so sorry."

He finally understood what he had done and was horrified at how he had hurt her and left her terrified. Understanding often marks the turning point for those who choose to drop their final objections and forgive.[1]

On reconvening, the peacemaker invites participants to describe an act that they found hurtful and how it hurt them, but without identifying who did it or claiming to know why it was done.

It is simply, "This is what you did, and this is how it hurt/affected me." It may describe how the conflict has wounded them rather than something done by a specific person, but it will probably contain both. Once we understand how we are wounded and how we have hurt others, we naturally begin to feel remorse mixed in with our anger. The deeper we understand, the more profound our remorse will be. Genuine remorse fuels an outpouring of grief that dissipates pent-up anger and reaches out to the ones we have hurt.

When our remorse is finally more potent than our anger and fear, we will express it in an apology. It is the heart of healing because it heals the heart.

A simple apology is nothing more than the confession of an act that injured another followed by an expression of remorse, of "being sorry." That's all. Where confession says, "I did it," apology says, "I did it, and I'm sorry."

Apology takes the initial outward layer of confession and adds a layer of sorrow. Neither is that powerful by itself, yet they become more significant than the sum of their combined parts.

THE SECRET LIFE OF APOLOGY

While confession is usually verbal, an apology may also be verbal or expressed in several ways. It only requires genuine sorrow for one's actions and their hurtful impact.

People tend to be imprecise in what they mean when demanding an apology and assume that their understanding of what constitutes a "proper" or "full" apology is shared. It isn't.

1. Puls, *Road Home*.

- Some see an apology as just confession and remorse.
- Others expect changed behaviors and offers of compensation.
- A simple apology made to a person who requires more will fail, which is one of the reasons this process is layered—it eventually reaches almost everyone's level of need.
- The apologizer seeks something that only the victim can produce: forgiveness.
- The success or failure of an apology depends partially on the reality of the expressed sorrow and partially on the acceptance or rejection of the apology by the injured, with acceptance or rejection of the sorrow's reality determining the outcome.

To apologize requires humility in the truest sense:

- It reduces your stature in your own eyes and in the eyes of everyone who knows about it.
- It says that you did something that you regret because it was wrong—it is a moral indictment one places against oneself.
- An apology is offered in the hope, not certainty, of forgiveness.
- It is a huge risk with no guarantee of benefit.
- If it works, the benefits can be enormous.

Apology changes the very substance of what one has done from unforgivable to forgivable and changes the apologizer from uncaring brute to penitent sinner.

Confession requires "redemptive memory," and apology requires genuine expressions of sorrow and can be classified as "redemptive speech." It is a layering of sorrow on truth.

The apostle Paul said about such sorrow, "Godly sorrow brings repentance that leads to salvation and leaves no regret, but worldly sorrow brings death" (2 Cor 7:10).

Making It Real

The reality of sorrow, not eloquence, is the heart and soul of successful apologies. Ineloquent apologies from the bottom of the soul can break through the final barriers to forgiveness. Elegant but insincere apologies make things worse!

Apologizing shifts how others perceive us by revealing our vulnerability and remorse, while seeking from them what we cannot achieve on our own. Apology closes the door behind us that we walked through in confession, cutting off our only avenue of retreat. Even the most heinous crimes may be transformed into something forgivable if true confession and sorrow are expressed.

Raymond Helmick and Rodney Petersen rightly argue, "Far from being weak or masochistic, this is the power seen in Christ that breaks the cycle of violence. What makes forgiveness more than conflict management or a program for negotiation is that it draws us to the center of what we believe to be the nature of things."[2] In other words, apology exists within a language of atonement that restores a wounded image by admitting that one's behavior has injured another human being and by taking responsibility for both behavior and damage. It purges feelings of sorrow and animosity and offers redemption to the offender, healing the relationship.[3]

In other words, if there is wrongdoing, there must also be a place for "right-doing." Apology is about "right-doing" through rebalancing moral scales and opening to relational repair, whether between two people, hundreds of people, or nations. To put it differently, shame condemns us for who we are, while guilt condemns what we have done. One can be changed, while the other cannot. Disapproving what was done while not disapproving of the person who did it helps the offender acknowledge ownership and take responsibility for it. The result is a rebalancing of the moral scales, encouraging the offender to "make things right."

Taking Off the Mask.

An apology seeks reconciliation and requires at least the offender and the offended. However, apologizing is often resisted or even refused even though it is the most powerful factor under the apologizers' control in seeking forgiveness and repairing relationships. It benefits victims by allowing them to fully process their emotions about the trauma. Once

2. Helmick and Petersen, eds., *Forgiveness and Reconciliation*, 15.

3. Koesten and Rowland, "Rhetoric of Atonement."

processed, those emotions are less threatening, allowing barriers to forgiving to be lowered.

But . . . apologizing carries with it a paradox: Honor is restored through the act of relinquishing it, of "doing the right thing." It requires our masks to be dropped and our defenses to be abandoned. We must "own" what we did and make it ours forever.

We earlier discussed the concept of "face." The senses of honor and "face" are inseparable. How can losing face through apologizing result in restored face? That is the paradox, but it has a solution: Everyone knows what it is like to be humiliated, so the voluntary humiliation of apologizing shows courage, and seeing someone who has voluntarily harmed you without a defensive face pulls empathy to the surface from deep within us. We feel humiliated with them. In their burning faces and stuttering speech, we see ourselves.

Accepting the apology restores face and honor to both.

A warning: trying to save face not only negates the apology but also creates a different conundrum—the act of trying to save face by partially denying either personal responsibility or the reality of the damage done results in a more profound loss of face than if no defense were mounted in the first place, and with an additional loss of empathy towards the offender. Saving face is a lose/lose strategy.

The most effective apology renounces all defenses and admits that the act was wrong, placing the apologizer at the victim's mercy. It figuratively leaves us standing naked and defenseless in the courts of human opinion and godly judgment, saying in effect, "It was not your fault; it was mine, and it was wrong of me to do it."[4]

How Before Why

How I say or show that I am sorry makes all the difference. Though it may be disguised, harming another is always about gaining power over that person. Showing honest remorse for the act and its damage returns the power one took. The apology indicates clearly that the victim did not deserve what was done, elevating the victim while at the same time lowering the offender—in effect, it rebalances the relational scales. Apology seeks to reestablish a relationship of mutual respect that power grabs throw out of balance.

4. Gobodo-Madikazela, *Human Being Died*, 21.

The apology is the place where the offender should most appropriately explain, but only at the victim's clear invitation.

- Some victims need to know "why" before they can forgive. This knowledge helps them to place the incident into a more understandable—though not acceptable—framework.
- "Why" requests generally mean that the victim suspects a more significant context into which it fits and seeks to place the act within that context to understand and forgive.
- Asking to know "why" also seeks orderly dialogue rather than one-sided monologue, and this two-way conversation re-establishes broken communication.
- Once "why" is asked, a humble answer can break down the final barriers to forgiving.

If an explanation is requested,

- Limit the scope to why they committed a clearly defined offense, e.g., "I wrote the letter because I was angry, and I wanted to get back at you."
- If the scope is too broad, the explanation may be received as a blanket excuse by shifting blame to another person or the larger group.
- Do everything you can to help the participants avoid spontaneous explanations, as they will likely be seen as excuses.
- Even bad reasons are acceptable, but excuses are not.

Slow Dancing

Apology is not one-sided, as the victim also plays an integral role.

To bear witness is to tell the truth about what one has experienced and knows firsthand. Witnessing is gut-wrenchingly real, with no rounded, fuzzy edges allowing factual embellishment. The rawness of victims witnessing blunts embellishment, which increases trust and intimacy between victim and offender.

There is something cathartic about telling a story of pain and suffering to a sympathetic audience. As anyone who has ever seen victims testify in court can attest, such witnessing is painful and profoundly intimate.

As the stories play out, their emotions flicker and change until both join in the dejection of sorrow. The dance is now deeply intimate as they act on each other; the victim becomes strong, and the offender becomes weak with sorrow. Seeing this sorrow, the victim now reaches out to raise the offender by accepting the apology or seeking more information. The power of the interaction arises from this seemingly paradoxical blend of the intimate and the public.[5]

Telling stories of pain intentionally inflicted, sorrow, anger, and confusion at the outset of this stage triggers a collective sense of sadness, but it also allows a sense of relief, of a burden lifted. After witnessing what was private, grief and pain become shared. Some have even reported a sense of personal release that may make the apology easier to accept. The intimacy that can envelop offender and victim where they reach for each other in mutual dependency and vulnerability is difficult to explain, but powerful to see and experience. As anyone who has experienced this can attest, there is a sudden internal change from withholding to yielding, of a dam breaking. It is powerful, and the public nature of the apology gives validation that it is real.[6]

Witnessing within a carefully defined construct allows victims to restore face and dignity. After hearing the misery one has caused as a simple fact statement and without accusations, the offender, standing defenseless before his victim, offers an unadorned statement of sorrow and remorse.

It is a simple but powerful gift.

SIMPLE GIFTS

A good apology is simple and looks like this:

"I lied to you. I broke the vase. I am sorry that I lied to you, and I'm sorry that I broke the vase. Will you please forgive me?"

Body language and voice inflection must be congruent with the words: somber and without defensiveness.

Witnessing in this case might look like this if it comes after the apology:

5. Lazare, *On Apology*.
6. Davis, "Mystery of a Genuine Apology."

"Thank you for being honest. I was pretty sure that you did it, and it hurt when you lied about it. I can replace the vase, but I cannot replace our friendship. I forgive you."

Why Apologies Fail

Have you ever been baffled after your apology failed? I have! If we are to help make effective apologies, we also need to know why they fail.

Bitter Gifts

Failed apologies usually have most of the same ingredients as successful apologies, except that one of the critical elements of confession and regret is missing or just not quite all there. It's like trying to eat an omelet cooked in a hot steel pan with no oil—burned and inedible.

Apologies will fail if:

- The centerpiece of regret is seen as false or self-serving.
- There is stiffness in delivering the apology, which is the refusal to show humility.
- Apologizing with a harsh tone and angry demeanor pushes people further away.
- This is a cynical attempt to manipulate one's way out of consequences. Cynicism is usually spotted quickly as the words, voice inflection, facial expression, and body language are crooked and incongruent.
- Pride is the highest barrier between the destructive act and one's sense of guilt for violating a social norm, allowing for a false apology. Pride insists, "I wasn't entirely right, but neither were you." It blames the victim for being victimized. This is the "I did it, but you deserved it" strategy.

Almost every religion recognizes the destructiveness of pride. The ancient Judaic text of Job says that, in his suffering and humiliation, "Job sat down on a dunghill" (Job 2:8). Sitting on a dunghill was considered the lowest and most degrading position in ancient times, representing the depths of Job's misery and loss.

Pride tells us we can "fake it" and get away with it. Pride says that apologizing is just a formality. Pride says, "I don't mean it, and you're a sucker if you fall for this." Pride makes light of the offense, in effect saying, "Hey, it wasn't so bad. There's nothing to be upset about. Get over it!"

The non-apology fails to identify what was done, who did it, or omits any real expression of regret, or says "we apologize" rather than "We are sorry for what we did." Unsolicited explanations are deadly as they may diminish the seriousness of the offense ("It was just a little bomb"), diminish the seriousness of the damage ("He was up and about in only three days"), and even diminish the humanity of the victim ("He was a felon").

Some will seek redemption in offering compensation ("I paid his medical bills"), but all of these will fail if genuine remorse is not shown. Add to this blame-shifting through self-redeeming disclaimers that blame the victim, e.g., "I would not have done that if you had/had not . . ." In other words, "You made me hit you!" Or, minimizing the value of the person: "I'm sorry your sister was killed. Please understand that I was fighting to end the oppression of my people." This translates as "A lot of people died. Big deal." It is also a shame-based tactic to deflect blame towards the victim.

The goal of understanding is to help them understand and feel the pain they have caused in others. Sorrow lies just below the surface; we only need to ask it to come forth. It will form a collective lament as the Holy Spirit convicts them of wrongdoing.

THE UNDERSTANDING NARRATIVE

> You have already come far on this challenging journey. Though the road still leads upward, the climb is no longer as steep as it once was, and the ending is not far away. I can tell by looking at you that some have found your way to peace and forgiveness. It shines on your faces. Holy Spirit, please stay with us; we need you to encourage and comfort us throughout the journey.
>
> Initially, we described your physical, emotional, and spiritual experiences during the conflict. Heads nodded as I explained the various ailments that have moved through you like a wave of suffering. We then held our breath as we dove under the water to find and raise to the surface those things we had done that may have made things worse instead of better, then stepped onto the heaving sea in confession. We now shift our focus inwards once again as we find ways to heal our distress.

At this point, the peacemaker should interject a personal story showing remorse for having hurt others. For example:

> I remember a conflict I had with my wife several years ago. We had exchanged some sharp words over something, but I noticed that this argument was different from the others. Even though we usually recovered quickly from our disagreements, I saw that she had withdrawn from me. She spoke to me, but there was sadness in her eyes. She did not engage me in conversation but instead went to our bedroom to read. This continued for a few days before I finally asked her what was happening. She was slow to respond, and only when she saw that I was genuinely interested did she start talking. I don't remember the words anymore, but I do remember a growing sense of horror inside me as she described how I had said something that had cut her to her very soul. I had attacked her at her weakest, most vulnerable point, and I had done it deliberately and flippantly. She now wondered if I still loved her and if I still valued her.
>
> I was dumbstruck. My words had hurt her so deeply that she now questioned both my love and her worth as a human being. Now I understood her confusion and fear. Within a few moments, I was in tears, grieving at the damage I had caused to the person dearest to me. I was nauseated to know and understand what I had done. All I could say through my tears was how sorry I was. Within a few moments, we were weeping in each other's arms. At first, they were tears of sorrow and shared pain, but they soon changed to tears of joy and comfort as we reconnected as husband and wife.
>
> The same thing has happened here. You have hurt each other in unexpected ways and caused wounds that are open and raw. I am asking you to do two things. Look inward and go deep inside yourselves to answer this question: What hurt you most? [Pause thirty to sixty seconds.] As soon as I said that, something jumped into your mind. You each saw a picture or thought of someone and heard something someone said, saw something someone did, or read what someone wrote. Now, fix it in your mind. How did it hurt you?
>
> Please pray with me. *Holy One, we are about to let go of the boat. Hold us tight and close. Let us know that you are here because we are afraid of sinking. Give us courage. Help us to hear through your ears and to show the same compassion that you have shown us. Thank you, Holy One, for being our power. We are called to walk on the water of peace. Grant us the courage and faith to do so. Amen.*

> I will ask you to do something in two parts. In this first part, I am asking all who can to express something that has hurt them and how it has hurt them. I am not looking for your anger, for your anger is the result of the hurt, not the cause. Nor are we looking for blame, as blaming gives away your power to the one who hurt you. No, I am asking you to keep your power by simply stating something that hurt you and how it affected you.
>
> It could sound like this: "I was devastated when Brad introduced a motion to the board to remove me from the treasurer's position without any warning or discussion. When it was obvious that people had already discussed it without my knowledge and then voted me out, I was so shocked I could barely breathe. I still don't know what I did to be shoved out. I feel like I was thrown away like yesterday's newspaper."
>
> These are simple statements of truth about what hurt you and how you were affected. We do not seek to accuse and blame anyone, but we need to know whom we have hurt.
>
> A caution before we begin: these statements will not be easy to make or hear, but we must make and hear them. We cannot move to heal if we do not know who needs our healing. Please make your statements in a spirit of reconciliation, not further battle. My job is to help and coach if you need it. There will be opportunities to respond.
>
> Who will begin?

Once again, the various leaders make their first statements in a spirit of reconciliation with each other. This section must be done in a prayerful and conciliatory manner, as we are dealing with deep emotional injuries that are tied to explosive anger. However, the strongest emotions will probably be grief and remorse. Expect tears, for we are now deep inside the grieving process. In addition, this is where the Holy Spirit will work at the deepest level to convict people of their wrongdoing. Some may try to express their remorse but try to have them hold off by assuring them that the next section is the right place.

Once the statements taper off, the peacemaker reinserts himself into the process by reassuring them of how far they have come.

> I am amazed and humbled by your presence. You have stepped out of the boat and walked across the water of the most frightening part of our journey together. Through your simple statements, you have addressed your woundedness in front of everyone here.

We know what it is like to be hurt by someone we trust, but we have just been reminded of the power we have used to hurt our brothers and sisters. We have betrayed their trust. We are now reminded of what it feels like to know that we hurt someone far more than we realized. Tears of remorse are welling up in some, while others feel sickened to know the extent of the harm they have caused. We have succeeded in confronting ourselves. We now know the truth of the statement, "We have met the enemy, and he is us."

There is an old South African hymn of lament that describes our predicament. The primary word in the hymn is "Senzenina." It means, "What have we done?" We cannot undo the past, but we can confront it, hoping to heal for the future. We have told painful truths because silence kills. We have admitted to ourselves, to others, and to God what we have done. We have expressed our woundedness, and now we confront ourselves fully and squarely—what have we done? It is a congregation-wide lament.

In a moment, I will ask you, as people of God, to express your regret and sorrow for what has happened here and your part in it. If you have someone that you must address, please do so. The Scriptures say that God will not reject a broken and contrite heart, and the time has come to express our contrition.

Once again, it need not be an elaborate statement. Sincere simplicity works best. However, I will add a request in the form of a caution: Please do not go beyond expressing your sorrow or explaining why you did something unless you are specifically asked why. If you are asked, respond by telling what was going on in your mind when you did it, such as anger, fear, or the desire to hurt as you felt you were injured. Again, this is not about blaming; it is about confronting ourselves with who we are as sinners needing forgiveness.

Please join me again in a short prayer. *Holy One, we thank you for the courage to walk on the water of our fear and express in godly and loving words how we have wounded and been wounded by each other. By confronting ourselves, we know that we stand accused and guilty. Thank you for convicting us, Holy One, for without that conviction, we will not move to healing. Thank you for loving us, warts and all. Be with us now as we express our sorrow for our actions. Holy One, you know us better than we know ourselves. You have snatched us from the death of forgetfulness, knowing that life is found in remembering. Our beginning is complete, but we are not yet home. Once again, walk among us*

and give us the courage to step farther away from the safety of our small boat. Thank you, O Lord most high. Amen.
Who will begin?

The leaders again make the first statements, but others may jump in—their internal dams have burst, and they can no longer hold back. They have re-experienced their pain and vicariously experienced the pain they caused. Their experience is no longer isolated but shared. In realizing a shared experience perceived by others as isolated, barriers they erected for their safety begin to be quickly dismantled.

Here, the question of "why" will be most frequent. This is also where it will be most effectively answered.

Strong emotion is probable in this final segment before the last major break. As regrets are expressed, I expect people to begin moving towards each other in tearful embrace. There will be combinations of tears and laughter in the catharsis of the moment. It is in this segment that many people will forgive and be forgiven.

Working with people in conflict is never entirely predictable, of course. Peacemakers must be flexible in allowing people to talk and express themselves, but they must sometimes intervene when their means of expressing themselves are overly hostile or unintentionally harmful. Even so, I caution you not to interfere too quickly, as the anger expressed shows the distress they have experienced, printing a more indelible image on the mind of the other.

Caution: There will be a natural tendency to believe that this completes the process, but it does not. Many have forgiven, but some have not. The final two segments will be easier and faster to move through and will help the remaining skeptics to forgive and build the foundations for reconciliation.

The group will begin to move about, so this is a natural place to break for forty-five to sixty minutes. This would be a good time to serve lunch. Expect the process to continue throughout the break as people seek out those they have hurt and apologize for their actions. The mood will be highly charged and positive, though there will still be those who must see transformed behaviors and receive offers of justice to forgive.

From the Inside Out

Expressing how the experience has changed us commits us to new behaviors in front of witnesses.

The language of transformation says, "I have learned from this experience, and I am committed to changing my life." The message it sends is, "You no longer need fear me. You are safe with me. I value you enough to change."

This latest change of mind and direction says to the victim and the larger assembly that

- We, the offenders, can live in harmony within the community; and
- We are open to becoming holy people as we shuck off the layers of accumulated sin.
- We are requesting readmission to the holiness of fellowship.
- Confession says, "I hurt you, and it was deliberate." It is short, unadorned, and utterly repentant.
- Apology says, "What I did was wrong, and I am sorry."
- Transformed behavior more endearingly says, "I learned. I changed. Never again."

CHANGING THE WIND

A revealing story is so vital that it is repeated in all four Gospels: Luke 8:22–25; Matthew 8:23–27; Mark 4:36–41; and John 6:16–21.

The crowds around Jesus were unrelenting, demanding that he teach and heal them. Seeking peace and rest, Jesus said to the disciples (my paraphrase), "Hey, guys, let's take the boat and go over to the other side of the lake." Everyone that could fit piled into the boat, and off they sailed. Within a few minutes, Jesus was sound asleep.

Ferocious squalls can come out of nowhere off the hills around a lake like Galilee. One minute, the water is calm, and the next, there is wind and rain and spray in such a mix that you can't see where you are, where you were, or where you are going. Steep, choppy waves come at you from every direction at once. These squalls can be unpredictable, chaotic—and terrifying.

The wind was howling as the sharp and confused waves started coming over the sides and into the boat. The disciples were bailing, but the water was coming in faster than they could throw it out. Jesus was so exhausted that he slept through the tumult. As the water in the boat rose, the small vessel rolled deeper and deeper into the wave troughs, which allowed even more water to come in over the sides. They were in danger of sinking.

Finally, one of them shook Jesus awake, crying, "Master, Master, we're going to drown!"

Jesus looked at the frightened faces of his young followers, then at the raging lake. He got up and told the wind to be still and the sea to be calm. Within a few moments, the wind was gone, and the waves were back to standard size. Jesus did not take away their fear; he changed the wind, taking away the cause of their fear.

Transformed behavior shows that the wind that drives us has changed. The change is plain for all to see and proclaims, "I am different than I was. I am no longer a threat. I am transformed into something better and trustworthy." The winds of anger drive our small boat towards the rocks without mercy, no matter what we do to try to control it. Repentance turns us from our anger. Remembering relieves internal pressure by confessing what we have done. Understanding our mutual woundedness causes us to cry out in sorrow. Turning our lives over to the One who changes the wind transforms and frees us to live redeemed lives.

It is impossible to embrace fully without risking everything in trust.

The Return

The challenge for the peacemaker in this stage is to create a safety zone strong enough to allow for such transparency without creating an expectation where people feel forced. Genuine openness is always voluntary and can only happen when people feel vulnerable.

Transparency requires rigorous honesty in ourselves as we examine our lives for sin and deception and allow the grace of God to flood us. To get there, we must make a searching and fearless moral inventory of ourselves, for this is more than confessing what we have done—it goes deep into who we are. It finds the hollow places in our lives and seeks to fill them. It roots out the hidden places where we squirrel away anger and resentment and seeks to remove them. It is a process of emptying and draining off the poisons that have supplied our energy during the fight. It is the opposite of blaming, for it is about owning not just what we have done but who we are and giving it all up to the changing power of God.

Transformation goes beyond the temporariness of conflict to permanent changes in who we are. While some may find it difficult to forgive those who remain unrepentant, such undeserved forgiveness is the scriptural norm. Forgive anyway.

Reconciliation—or Not?

If we are to forgive all wrongs, does that mean we must repair all relationships? Paul supplies part of the answer in Romans 12:18, in which he writes, "If it is possible, as far as it depends on you, live at peace with everyone." Paul recognized that the only person under your control is you. There is no requirement to go back into a harmful relationship.

Changed behaviors must always accompany reconciliation. Otherwise, we will return to our old habits. Failing to intentionally, willfully, and prayerfully change is an invitation to disaster.

Though forgiving opens the door to possible reconciliation, reconciling is still a choice. We can forgive and reconcile or forgive and leave.

Congregations, however, are called to be reconciled communities. This means that those in the church must forgive and find the path to reconciliation if the congregation is to remain whole. Failure to reconcile can only result in more trouble and pain. Everyone in the conflict is guilty, but I can only redeem my own wrongdoing. Therefore, mutual repentance is required, not for forgiveness, but for transformed behaviors that rebuild communal trust and reconciliation.

The forgiving church is a *teshuvah* (return to the path of the Lord) church, freeing itself from sin through mutual repentance, confession, godly sorrow, and changing ways.[7]

The roles of victims and offenders in church conflicts are often interchangeable. Once again, we must repent. While we may be legitimate victims, we must also understand that elevating victimhood is a reason to remain where we are.

Transformed behavior results from an internal change in orientation away from the self and towards the other, exactly paralleling biblical

7. Miyirsky, "Teshuvah in Judaism."

teaching. When transformation becomes real, a sense of mutual absolution often leads to reconciliation.

Transformed behaviors are visible and noticeable, creating an upward spiral of mutual benefit by adding on to the power of the previous levels, adding observable proof that the emotions of confession and apology are real. Genuine behavioral changes show not only a reformed offender but also one who acknowledges their wrongdoing and desires to heal the victim. The peacemaker's role is to help the offender express his or her commitment to changing the offending behaviors and in helping create a mutually supportive system that gently but firmly restores the offender.

To thrive rather than simply survive, the congregation must establish a new set of expectations and accountability standards. Otherwise, the behaviors that created the conflict are likely to reappear.

Turning, remembering, and understanding were about the past. Transformation and healing are about the future. They move us away from what was towards what can be.

Where the peacemaker was previously quiet and comforting, he or she should now show positive energy, congratulating them on their work and encouraging them for the work ahead. He or she describes the next section as one of the lessons learned and how they have changed because of that learning. It is a time for commitment to transformation by word and deed.

THE TRANSFORMATION NARRATIVE

> Welcome back! It is so good to see so many people filled with hope! You have made tremendous strides. Some steps may have seemed small, while others probably seemed huge. I'm sure there were times when some of you looked at what you were asked to do as a huge hole that we were urging you to jump across. But you jumped, and you made it across.
>
> Some of you are wondering why we are still here. We are still here because we need to do two things. First, we must commit to changing how we will act in the future when disagreements arise. My life's most deeply impressed lessons have usually been the most painful ones. They have often come through the painful acknowledgment that my behaviors failed to help the situation and hurt the people closest to me. They resulted in the

loss of trust. To rebuild trust, we must be trustworthy. And so, we must change.

If we do not change, what has happened here will happen again. It may be more destructive or less, but it will be damaging, as we will repeat the behaviors that made this conflict destructive in the first place. Though what we did made sense at the time and may have seemed rational, we have now heard and seen the results. To continue without changing and expecting a better outcome is a type of insanity. To counteract this tendency, we will examine the lessons we have learned and commit to acting in new and better ways as a result of those lessons.

The final thing we must do is make things right with each other. I will speak more of this when we reach that point.

Let us pray. *Once again, Holy One, we ask you to convict us so we can change. We seek your blessing and power, for we know who we are, but only you know who we can be. Transform us from gold ore to gold so that in becoming purer and holier, we may bring your church from where it was to where it should be, a lighthouse shining a powerful beacon across the restless sea. Amen.*

Once again, go deep inside yourselves. For the next few minutes, focus on what you did that backfired, was misconstrued, contributed to the conflict in general, or hurt someone. For each instance, determine what you will commit to doing next time. Once again, we will speak these things aloud before the entire audience. Why? Because saying it in front of others eliminates our tendency to back away from change. It commits us to doing it, as everyone will know it and watch for it. Yes, I am creating pressure on you, but this entire process is about the heat and pressure of what the Bible calls the refiner's fire. Without heat and pressure, we cannot become purified and refined.

Note: I have found over the years that the more clearly I state my intentions, the less resistance there will be. Transparency in the peacemaker smooths the process, for it shows both humility and integrity. Understanding the reasoning behind the crucible makes it easier to endure, as they know the intended outcome and that it has a purpose much higher than simple discomfort.

The work at this stage will be done more quickly. They have been thinking about what to do differently for some time, and many will be able to answer these questions without further thought. For many, committing publicly to change their ways will be sufficient for forgiveness. Others may struggle.

Reconvene them after three to five minutes. If the leaders have previously negotiated new communication protocols, this is the time to announce what they are. Once again, it is important that they be seen as leaders; their legitimacy is reaffirmed through their willingness to admit their need for change and their commitment to follow through. Their leadership is reaffirmed by showing their willingness to stand before the assembly with their agreements.

The final part of this stage is still managed, but less tightly than before. The statements may have a prelude of apology to the group and specific individuals. They may be short statements of how they will act in the future. The important part is that the statements are made as a commitment to change, meaning they are clear statements with a clear commitment, e.g., "This is what I did, and this is what I will do." The peacemaker should ask clarifying questions if the commitment is less than clear, such as in the following sequence:

Bob: "I guess I kind of overreacted a couple of times. I'll try not to do that."

Peacemaker: "Bob, what are you committing to here?"

Bob: "I said I'll try."

Peacemaker: "Are you saying that you won't do something the same way next time, or that you might do the same thing?"

Bob: "Well, I guess I might try and fail, so I'm saying I'll try."

Peacemaker: "Are you saying that you might try once or twice and then not try again?"

Bob: "No, I'm just saying that I might not always be able to do it. I might slip up."

Peacemaker: "Are you willing to give people the right to help you?"

Bob: "What do you mean?"

Peacemaker: "If you slip up, are you giving them permission to gently let you know that you are slipping?"

Bob: "Well, yeah, I guess."

Peacemaker: "And can they tell you how they would prefer that you act, as long as it is done in a caring way?"

Bob: "Yeah, I can do that. I'm just afraid I'll slip up and they will jump all over me."

Peacemaker: "That's fair. Everyone here, how many of you are afraid that you will slip up?"

If they are honest, every hand in the room will raise, expressing similar concerns and reassuring Bob that he is normal.

One of the ideas behind this part of the process is that myriad individual commitments equate to group commitments for change and permission to offer and accept help. If the group knows that it has not just the right but also the responsibility to remind each other gently of their commitment to change when they start behaving in old ways, then they also have given each other permission to ask for help in doing so. This begins the process of becoming a restorational congregation.

Once the change statements have stopped, take a short break.

On return, affirm the group. "You have come an amazing distance. This morning, many of you had little hope that anything positive would happen here today, and now most of you are filled with hope and energy. You have walked on the water. Now it is time to dance on it!"

18

Forgiveness: Healing

The point of justice and mercy anyway is not "they deserve it" but "this is the way God's world should be," and we are called to do those things that truly anticipate the way God's world *will* be.

~N. T. Wright

THE KISS OF MERCIFUL JUSTICE

As each level builds on the work of the earlier level, it becomes less specific and more interactive and interpretive. The confession is specific: a simple verbal statement acknowledging ownership of a damaging act. Apology adds expressions of remorse that can be verbal or not. Changed behavior is still more obscure as it is deeply individualized, yet it describes the entire congregation as it changes to create a shared future.

The Justice/Mercy Continuum

We have arrived at the final, most fluid, and creative level: Healing.

It is common to talk about justice with euphemisms such as "Justice was served." But if asked what that means, most people will only respond vaguely. Many will cite the ancient biblical principle of "an eye for an eye."

But have you ever actually read it? It is found in Exodus 21:12–27 (NIV):

> Anyone who strikes a person with a fatal blow is to be put to death. However, if it is not done intentionally, but God lets it happen, they are to flee to a place I will designate. But if anyone schemes and kills someone deliberately, that person is to be taken from my altar and put to death. Anyone who attacks their father or mother is to be put to death. Anyone who kidnaps someone is to be put to death, whether the victim has been sold or is still in the kidnapper's possession. Anyone who curses their father or mother is to be put to death. If people quarrel and one person hits another with a stone or with their fist and the victim does not die but is confined to bed, the one who struck the blow will not be held liable if the other can get up and walk around outside with a staff; however, the guilty party must pay the injured person for any loss of time and see that the victim is completely healed. Anyone who beats their male or female slave with a rod must be punished if the slave dies as a direct result, but they are not to be punished if the slave recovers after a day or two, since the slave is their property. If people are fighting and hit a pregnant woman and she gives birth prematurely but there is no serious injury, the offender must be fined whatever the woman's husband demands and the court allows. But if there is serious injury, you are to take life for life, eye for eye, tooth for tooth, hand for hand, foot for foot, burn for burn, wound for wound, bruise for bruise.
>
> An owner who hits a male or female slave in the eye and destroys it must let the slave go free to compensate for the eye. And an owner who knocks out the tooth of a male or female slave must let the slave go free to compensate for the tooth.

Most do not know that these laws were made to limit revenge, not codify it.

Later prophets added mercy to the formula:

- "He has shown you, O mortal, what is good. And what does the LORD require of you? To act justly and to love mercy and to walk humbly with your God." Mic 6:8
- "This is what the LORD Almighty said: 'Administer true justice; show mercy and compassion to one another.'" Zech 7:9
- "The LORD, the LORD God, merciful and gracious, longsuffering, and abounding in goodness and truth, keeping mercy for thousands, forgiving iniquity and transgression and sin . . ." Exod 34:6–7

- "Therefore know that the LORD your God, He is God, the faithful God who keeps covenant and mercy for a thousand generations with those who love Him and keep His commandments . . ." Deut 7:9
- "With the merciful You will show Yourself merciful . . ." 2 Sam 22:26
- "All the paths of the LORD are mercy and truth, to such as keep His covenant and His testimonies." Ps 25:10
- "But You, O LORD, are a God full of compassion, and gracious, long-suffering and abundant in mercy and truth." Ps 86:15
- "Righteousness and justice are the foundation of Your throne; mercy and truth go before Your face." Ps 89:14
- "The LORD is gracious and full of compassion, slow to anger and great in mercy. The Lord is good to all, and His tender mercies are over all His works." Ps 145:8–9
- "Through the LORD's mercies we are not consumed, because His compassions fail not. They are new every morning; great is Your faithfulness." Lam 3:22–23
- "Who is a God like You, pardoning iniquity and passing over the transgression of the remnant of His heritage? He does not retain His anger forever, because He delights in mercy. He will again have compassion on us, and will subdue our iniquities. You will cast all our sins into the depths of the sea." Mic 7:18–19
- "For God so loved the world that He gave His only begotten Son, that whoever believes in Him should not perish but have everlasting life." John 3:16
- "But God, who is rich in mercy, because of His great love with which He loved us, even when we were dead in trespasses, made us alive together with Christ (by grace you have been saved) . . ." Eph 2:4–5
- "And Jesus, when He came out, saw a great multitude and was moved with compassion for them, because they were like sheep not having a shepherd. So He began to teach them many things." Mark 6:34
- "Therefore, in all things He had to be made like His brethren, that He might be a merciful and faithful High Priest in things pertaining to God, to make propitiation for the sins of the people. For in that

He Himself has suffered, being tempted, He is able to aid those who are tempted." Heb 2:17–18

- "Seeing then that we have a great High Priest who has passed through the heavens, Jesus the Son of God, let us hold fast our confession. For we do not have a High Priest who cannot sympathize with our weaknesses, but was in all points tempted as we are, yet without sin. Let us therefore come boldly to the throne of grace, that we may obtain mercy and find grace to help in time of need." Heb 4:14–16
- "Therefore, be merciful, just as your Father also is merciful." Luke 6:36
- "Thus says the LORD of hosts: 'Execute true justice, show mercy and compassion everyone to his brother. Do not oppress the widow or the fatherless, the alien or the poor. Let none of you plan evil in his heart against his brother.'" Zech 7:8–10.
- "Blessed are the merciful, for they shall obtain mercy." Matt 5:7
- "Blessed be the God and Father of our Lord Jesus Christ, the Father of mercies and God of all comfort, who comforts us in all our tribulation, that we may be able to comfort those who are in any trouble, with the comfort with which we ourselves are comforted by God." 2 Cor 1:3–4

What, then, is biblical justice?

Just as the layers have become increasingly fluid and difficult to define, so too is justice. The dictionary is of little help as it defines justice as the act of being just. Ask ten people what that means, and you will get ten different answers. In other words, your definition of justice depends entirely on how you conceive it.

Most people and our society equate justice to proportional punishment. "An eye for an eye" fits one's anger and justifies it, claiming the right to inflict damage on the offender at least equal to the offense inflicted.

Exodus codifies punishment and limits revenge, breaking the escalation cycle.

It is perversely pleasurable to bystanders (and ourselves) to punish those we see as "deserving it." Just look at all the "instant karma" videos on YouTube!

Sometimes, we may feel a sense of angry finality when the punishment is carried out, such as when a murderer is executed.

However, had Jesus demanded strict justice, Paul would never have become the leading apostle of the church he was persecuting. Justice under the law condemned the woman caught in adultery to death by stoning, but Jesus ignored the law and challenged those who had not sinned to throw the first rock at her (John 8:1–11). They turned and walked away.

She would have been killed on the spot if Jesus had followed the Laws of Moses. Instead, justice was both affirmed and transcended through grace. There would be little hope if justice were administered without the intervention of mercy.

In refusing mercy, we place ourselves above God. We idolize ourselves, placing our self-righteous judgment above what God commands.

We call the phenomenon of godly justice "grace." It means this: "Inscribed on the very heart of God's grace is the rule that we can be its recipients only if we do not resist being made into its agents; what happens to us must be done by us. Having been embraced by God, we must make space in ourselves for others and invite them in—even our enemies."[1]

I cannot pray for enemies' well-being, health, and prosperity without developing empathy for them. Forgiving breaks the cycle of revenge through a solemn act of great power that says, "I will put a spoke in the wheel of revenge and stop it dead in its path. The cycle is broken."

Why Justice Fails to Satisfy

"Justice is satisfied" is an empty statement. Justice fails to satisfy and cannot bring "closure," however we define it. We expect more than justice can deliver. Strict justice creates a paradox where, in attempting to make one whole, the original loss is compounded by demanding that even more be lost, often through the trauma of testifying in court.

"I thought we would be happy, but we're not. It's a sad time" (anonymous).

Justice cannot restore intangibles. Even if something stolen is returned, justice cannot restore the time it was gone.

Justice takes by force what might be freely offered if the offender sees a chance for redemption.

Anger demands punishment and pain. However, honest confession requires telling the truth, even this painful truth. To deny a desire for

1. Volf, *Exclusion and Embrace*, 129.

revenge is a self-deceiving lie that offers an empty shell of love that leads to repressed bitterness and hatred.

In ancient Scriptures, justice holds one accountable while at the same time showing mercy and compassion. The prophet Micah writes, "What does the LORD require? To act justly, to love mercy, and to walk humbly with your God" (Mic 6:8). The prophet Isaiah says, "Wash and make yourselves clean. Take your evil deeds out of my sight; stop doing wrong. Learn to do right; seek justice. Defend the oppressed. Take up the cause of the fatherless; plead the case of the widow" (Isa 1:17). Psalm 85:10 paints a beautiful picture with simple words: "Mercy and truth are met together; righteousness and peace have kissed each other" (KJV).

This changes the rule from the either/or of justice or pardons to the yes/and of justice and mercy. We call it restorative justice, for it is both justice and restoration.

The World Turned Upside Down

During the Revolutionary War, when the British army surrendered to the American forces at Yorktown, their band played a tune called "The World Turned Upside Down." Surely, the British Empire reeled at the thought of being defeated by such rabble as common farmers. To forgive effectively turns the world upside down as well, but in a positive way!

For mercy to displace revenge requires the believer to acknowledge God as God, not the idol of revenge. God requires us to sacrifice the right of anger and revenge to the healing power of mercy. Forgiving, then, is a form of sacrificial worship.

Punishment without mercy reduces rather than increases compliance, increasing the likelihood that the offense will be repeated and other offenses will be committed.

True justice, then, is both just and merciful. It restores!

Love changes justice through mercy, moving away from lock-step rules of penalties and punishments and into the fluid and ever-changing realm of restoration. Justice says, "I must punish you in equal measure to what you did." Mercy says, "I value you above what I have lost; I value our relationship above what you took from me. Let us restore what we had." Thus, justice and mercy are no longer separate but combined into an intimate relationship, the final act in this ever more intimate dance of guilt, sorrow, forgiveness, and redemption.

The Kiss of Mercy

Justice without mercy is a return to the law of revenge, and mercy without justice ignores accountability. Mercy combined with justice opens one to amazing and healing nuances and opens the doors to reconciliation.

God's righteousness requires justice because he cannot ignore sin, but his mercy tips the scales of justice to bring them into balance, correcting what was wrong and returning the offender to a full relationship with God and people.

That same tension carries over into what God expects of his people when Micah states that the Lord requires them to "act justly and to love mercy and to walk humbly with your God" (Mic 6:8).

Summoning Mercy

Just how much justice does there need to be?

I don't know, and neither do you! Only the former opponents know what needs to happen to cement their reconciliation—and they most likely need some help sorting it out. Even a tacit affirmation of justice can trigger the decision to forgive. Most researchers agree that justice is a necessary component of reconciliation but also agree that how they are intermixed is without borders. It may be that the forgiver sees the pain and humiliation written large on the offender and decides that justice has already been served.

The Healing Narrative

This narrative is the shortest and may be done by either the peacemaker or the senior resident clergy. I recommend the senior clergy as a way of transferring power back to people formerly in conflict.

> Justice finds all of us guilty and requires us to make things right again. We cannot take back the pain we have given or the pain we have received. We face two choices, one stark and one that heals: walk away or make things right. This is commonly known as justice, but it has become fluid and soft-edged throughout this day.
>
> Some of us are tempted to demand all manner of penalties for those we believe have attacked and hurt us, but we have already seen that we are all wounded here. We are injured enough.

Justice declares us guilty, but mercy has a counterclaim, and says, "I forgive you." If justice requires that we must change, then mercy offers forgiveness as the reward.

Our focus now shifts to our future as brothers and sisters, and as a congregation. We have one last task. We ask that everyone seek out those we have harbored anger or resentment against, those we have hurt in thought and deed, and seek to make things right again. We now drop all remaining defenses and come to each other just as we are, without any claim to innocence. If you need to confess and apologize to someone, this is the time. We bear the same wounds, and the healing is also the same.

Many in this room have already forgiven, and many have been forgiven, but there remains the final question that we must ask that leaves us open to justice and mercy: What must I do to make things right again between us?

Let us pray. *Holy One, you have ended our beginnings, and we ask you to complete our ending now as we seek to heal each other in the mutual embrace of our love and yours. Make us open to justice, in whatever shapes it may take, and let us find bountiful mercy. Be with us as we begin to dance on the water in the joy of reconciliation. We thank you for being our guide and comforter, for we have needed both. In the name of the amazing God who demands mercy above sacrifice, whose name is Jesus, amen.*

Seek out your brothers and sisters and find healing!

19

Ending with a New Beginning

The visionary starts with a clean sheet of paper and reimagines the world.

~Malcolm Gladwell

I always ask permission to follow up with the congregation a few months after I leave and grant permission to contact me at any time to assist with problems.

This process is imperfect but works and can permanently change people's lives. The two physicians I mentioned kept their practice together for another fifteen years and only closed it when he joined a local hospital as a supervising physician, and she accepted the position of intern supervisor for a medical school. Perhaps most important is the comment she made to me about the mediation process and the cathartic moment that broke the logjam. She said, "Darrell, it's amazing what happens when God gives you new eyes to see with." That comment still brings tears to my eyes as I type this more than twenty-six years later.

Sometimes, it seems as if nothing is happening when working through the process, but working through traumatic memories cannot be rushed, so silence is your friend.

It was very late one Saturday night in a middle-sized suburban church. We had been working for hours, were tired, and had reached a stalemate. There were eighteen men in the room, including the pastors. I had been pushing gently but persistently for honest communication when everything stopped. No one said anything. I had done all I could and silently prayed for the Holy Spirit to fill the room. The silence seemed to deepen, and the tension was almost electric. Finally, an elder stood up and looked at the deacon sitting across from him. His voice choked as he said, "Brother, I have sinned against you. I hurt you, it was deliberate, and it was wrong. Please, forgive me." They regarded each other, and tears began to flow. Within seconds, they embraced. Within a few moments, everyone in the room was engaging with others in seeking and granting forgiveness. The dam had broken, and healing had begun.

Peacemaking is a full-contact proposition and is not for the fainthearted. Through this intervention, forgiveness, and reconciliation process, we attempt to change the very nature of faith communities. I wish it was a panacea and could cure every congregational illness, but it cannot. Even Jesus' prayer for unity in the church has not (yet) been achieved. I pray that those using this process can refine it and take it into venues where hate reigns supreme.

Forgiving cannot be forced. Certainly, none of us can command it from someone else. The only person I can control is me, which, as I have said, is a challenge in itself. However, there is an ancient road map to healing that clinical science has affirmed: seeking and granting forgiveness whether we see ourselves as being at fault or not. We must go deep within ourselves, find those attitudes and memories that cause us to point outward, and reverse them, not to wallow in guilt but to correct it. Forgiveness is reciprocal, and the predicament of reciprocity is real—if we do not forgive, we are not forgiven (Matt 6: 14–15).

Jesus said we must put away our old ways and become as teachable, open, and innocent as children, no matter what happens. It says that we will know the truth and that the truth will not just be something nice to know but will blow the doors to our prison cells off their hinges and call us out into a new, brightly lit world where the kingdom of God is not a dream—it is here.

Some religious communities have always practiced forgiveness and reconciliation, but most seem to have lost their way. What I have offered here is not new but is simply a restatement of those principles we already knew, supported by three decades of careful research.

This process is not limited to faith communities. It can be used by any group that has gone through conflict and wishes to rebuild relational closeness. It can also be used in any situation where emotional and spiritual wounding has occurred, such as a congregation reeling from its minister's moral failures.

Standing in the gap as a peacemaker is not easy, nor is standing between angry people much fun. It isn't for everyone. A close friend once said standing in the middle means getting hit from both directions, and there is truth in that statement. However, I have also come to agree with Augustine of Hippo, that the Beatitudes show a progression of stages. First, we must learn to seek forgiveness, then to forgive, and finally, we may become peacemakers. We must become poor enough in spirit to turn inward, away from those we wish to blame, to find and recognize our guilt. Within that recognition appears the memory of what we have done and the damage it caused, plunging us into mourning and godly sorrow. In the grieving cry of "what have we done?," we are humbled and meek, for we know without reservation that we are both victims and oppressors. We then begin to hunger and thirst after righteousness, which necessarily includes right living in all our relationships; otherwise, it becomes the hypocrisy of self-righteousness. We learn to be merciful when we realize how badly we crave mercy instead of the justice we so often deserve, even though we have no claim to mercy other than God's grace. Seeking and granting mercy in forgiveness cleanses our hearts as we *return to the Lord's path*.

As for me, part of this quest came from my inability to forgive a childhood abuser. I was trapped in my anger, confusion, and pain and almost swallowed by the black hole of depression. I was finally able to forgive when I understood that his behavior was compulsive and resulted from his own terrible emotional and spiritual wounds. I have learned much about weaknesses I knew I had and discovered new ones. With the help of God, I can help others find healing and wholeness through forgiving, by changing how I react to conflict, and by offering support and intervention when conflict erupts. We must move beyond our words, wounds, and fears to stand in the gap—we can only break the cycle by breaking the cycle.

All of it deeply wounds us, but the wounds are good, for in them, we find our weaknesses and strengths, our abilities to absorb pain and help others—and ourselves—leave it behind.

APPENDIX 1

The Tasks of the Transition Process

Adapted from C. Otto Scharmer, *Theory U.*

The healthy faith community is always in transition, but the transition I am writing of is the more formal transition process we must go through when leadership changes or a new direction is needed. We tend to resist transitional processes until we have no choice but to change or die.

Transitions cannot be forced; they are only guided. Forced transitions have a way of rearing up in resistance of such strength that it can overpower the process and leave the organization where it was—slowly dying and decaying. Successful transitions take their time, and many will become impatient ("Are we there yet?"). That is why it is about letting go (rather than casting off) and letting come (rather than grabbing on).

Transitions are always uncomfortable, and discomfort breeds resistance, which can easily become conflict. If we understand this and reassure the people that their discomfort is normal and to be expected, the likelihood of destructive conflict diminishes.

Emotions run high in the opening tasks because of the grieving process (leaving part of the past behind is to leave part of ourselves behind) and fear of the unknown. As the transition progresses, the feelings gradually cool as people come together, put aside their differences, fears, and grief at what has been lost, and focus on a shared future.

The Holy Spirit

Together, we can only do so much, but together, with the leading and gentle coaxing of the Holy Spirit, we can do much more. By accessing an open mind, heart, and will, we become ever more sensitive to the Spirit's leading. Please note that the entire process involves co-sensing, co-becoming, and co-creating, both with each other and with the guidance and active involvement of the Holy Spirit.

TASKS OF THE TRANSITION PROCESS

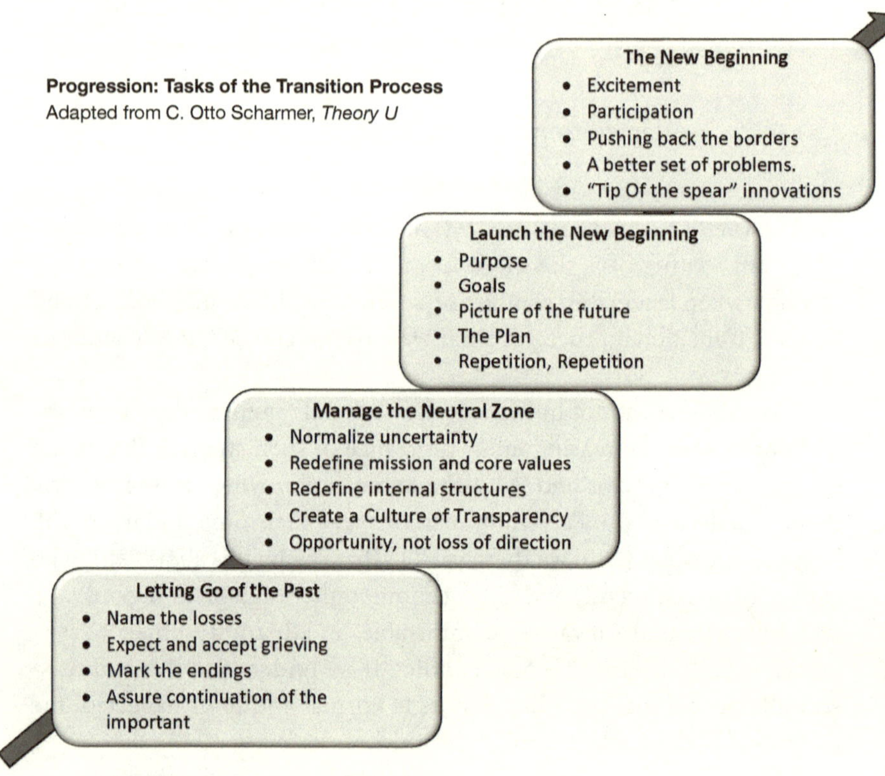

Offloading Patterns of the Past

Every church and ministry has unspoken traditions and expectations. As the church moves away from the past, it must offload the unspoken expectations of the past by identifying them (what is being lost) and grieving them. It is also necessary to identify unhealthy patterns that have developed regarding communications, expectations, and boundaries. The transitional tasks will address and instill new patterns.

Tasks

We naturally rush things, expecting this process to be accomplished quickly. Complaining about how long it takes is common, so complaining is normal. The reality, for churches at least, is that the transition process takes two to three years under normal circumstances and can last longer for the new norms and patterns to be fully ingested and part of the body. Although some will be impatient, it is the discomfort of change and a desire for the discomfort to end. Rushing the process only increases the amount of time it will take.

PART 1—LETTING GO

The Voice of Judgment. Change always brings out the voice of judgment. People will complain. People will declare why something will not work. People are uneasy and unwilling to change until the pain of staying where they are becomes greater than the fear of change. The key is simple: this is a stressful time of creativity, experimentation, grieving, and expectation. Please suspend judgment as we work together to seek our way into the next chapter of God's story. In essence, you are asking people to see with new eyes, not to be afraid of looking at old things in new ways and new things as open possibilities.

The Voice of Cynicism. Some will be cynical and express their cynicism by declaring, "That won't work!" or "We did that once, and it didn't work." Sometimes, it comes in outright challenges and attacks. Rather than react with a rebuttal, instill a spirit of curiosity in yourselves. Redirecting their negative energies is often nothing more than listening to them with sympathy and deep interest.

The goal is to become open to the Holy Spirit, sensing a new calling for the church.

The Voice of Fear. At this point, fear is almost always about the future and the unknown and how persons will fit into the new concept. Even though it may be couched in inclusive phrases or even "on behalf" of others, the voice of fear is deeply personal and must be treated with care. We must release it consciously and intentionally.

The key is gentle inquiry: "What is it that bothers you most about this?" "What needs to happen for you to be more comfortable?"

Connecting to God

This is where the process begins to change from concerns of the past to visions for the future. It relies on a very challenging question: What question lies at the heart of our work? Answering that question will take considerable time, prayer, and dialogue. It will be different for every church. Even the idea of there being a question at the heart of what you do will be a difficult concept for many, but it is something that church leaders have wrestled with since the church's earliest days.

This is also where the Holy Spirit becomes a more and more powerful, even palpable, presence. Why? The question cannot be answered without the Holy Spirit, but it is an experience that cannot be forgotten!

PART 2—LETTING COME

If we have done our work and become fully present and open to the Holy Spirit, uploading healthy practices gains speed and energy.

Voice of Hope. The voice of hope will begin to saturate those present. At this stage, it is about possibilities, not destinations. Hope restores confidence and cohesion. We are now co-creating a new vision for the future with the Holy Spirit. It is a time of possibilities and excitement.

Do not try to force it. Let it come. It will.

Voice of Passion. As energy and possibilities grow, so too does the voice of passion. This is where we crystallize the vision and the intentions of the new direction. Passion for what can be is contagious and allows you to plan out the steps ahead, and have people clamoring to be part of the process.

When this is being done, it is time to enact some of the larger changes in direction. There will be resistance, but not nearly as much as there was.

Voice of Freedom. As the church settles onto its new course, the voice of freedom emerges. It is a sense of new beginnings where mourning the past has ended. This is where we begin prototyping new "tip of the spear" ministries that both pierce and heal the community and where the turn from the old paradigm to a new vision and mission is completed.

There will still be problems, of course. During the process, you will identify issues that have gone unnoticed before, and that must be addressed for new patterns to emerge. Patience, transparency, and mutual trust can be created and maintained throughout the process, but they depend on the leaders practicing all three.

Congratulations! You should now be dealing with a better set of problems!

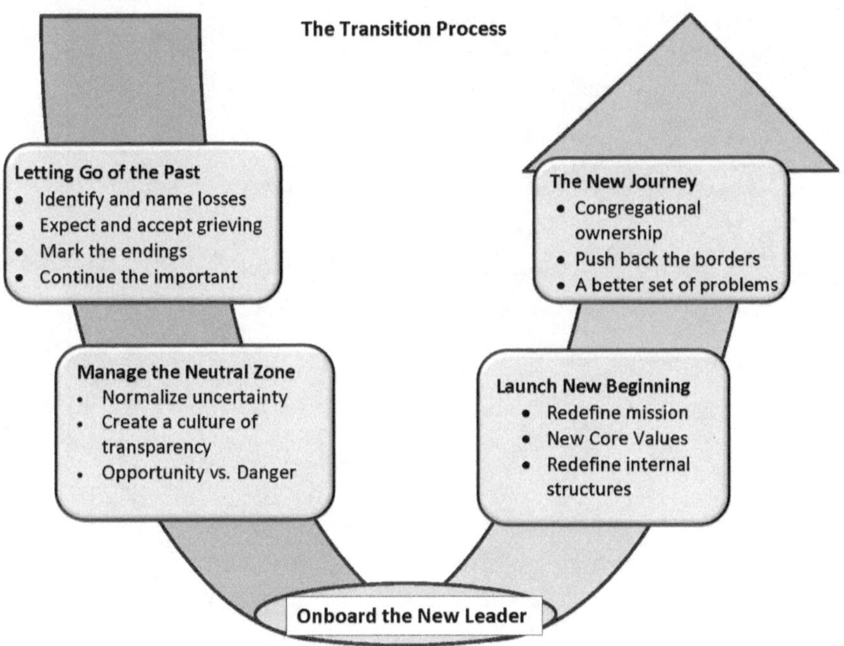

Adapted from:

C. Otto Scharmer, 2016
Theory U: Leading from the Future as it Emerges (2d Ed.)
San Francisco: Barrett - Koehler

References

"5.8 Biases and Errors in Thinking. AP Psychology. Biases." https://library.fiveable.me/ap-psych/unit-5/biases-errors-thinking/study-guide/DIq2vGGjPbRN3hEazKoV.

Adams, Christopher J., Holly Hough, Rae Jean Proeschold-Bell, Jia Yao, and Melanie Kolkin. "Clergy Burnout: A Comparison Study with Other Helping Professions." *Pastoral Psychology* 66, no. 2 (2017) 147–75.

Alcoholics Anonymous. *The 12 Steps*. New York: AA World Services, 1952.

American Psychological Association. "Anxiety." https://www.apa.org/topics/anxiety.

———. "Anxiety Disorders." 2023. https://www.psychiatry.org/patients-families/anxiety-disorders.

———. *APA Dictionary of Psychology*, 2023. Washington, DC: American Psychological Association.

———. "Personality Disorders." In *Diagnostic and Statistical Manual of Mental Disorders 5*, 645. Washington, DC: American Psychiatric Association, 2013. https://www.psychiatry.org/patients-families/personality-disorders/what-are-personality-disorders.

———. "What Are Anxiety Disorders?" January 2017. https://www.psychiatry.org/patients-families/anxiety-disorders/what-are-anxiety-disorders.

Babu, B. Ravi. "Beliefs, Values, Attitudes." https://www.scribd.com/document/595011988/beliefs-values-attitudes.

Bansal, Gaurav, and Fatemeh Mariam Zahedi. "Trust Violation and Repair: The Information Privacy Perspective." *Decision Support Systems* 71 (2015) 62–77. https://doi.org/10.1016/j.dss.2015.01.009.

Barna Research. "Pastors Share Top Reasons They've Considered Quitting Ministry in the Past Year." April 2022. https://www.barna.com/research/pastors-quitting-ministry/.

———. "What Pastors Wish They'd Been Prepared For." *Leadership*, April 2023. https://www.barna.com/research/pastors-better-prepared/.

Barnard, Laura, and John Curry. "The Relationship of Clergy Burnout to Self-Compassion and Other Personality Dimensions." *Pastoral Psychology* 61 (2012) 149–63. https://doi 10.1007/s11089-011-0377-0.

Baugh, James. *Solution Training: Overcoming Blocks in Problem Solving*. New York: Firebird, 1999.

Bayer, Y. M. "Memory and Belonging: The Social Construction of a Collective Memory During The Intercultural Transition Of Immigrants From Argentina In Israel." *Journal of Multidisciplinary Research* 8, no. 1 (2016) 25–46. https://www.proquest.

com/scholarly-journals/memory-belonging-social-construction-collective/docview/1804901817/se-2.

Beim, Aaron. "The Cognitive Aspects of Collective Memory." *Symbolic Interaction* 30, no. 1 (2007) 7–26. https://doi.org/10.1525/si.2007.30.1.7.

Belz, Emily. "Deep in the Heart of Megachurch Country, Dallas Mourns a Summer of Pastor Scandals." *Christianity Today*, September 23, 2024. https://www.christianitytoday.com/2024/09/megachurch-dallas-mourns-pastor-scandals/.

Black, Samantha. "Ancient and Modern Ritual: A Creative Approach to Working with Grief, Loss, and Change." *Embodied Philosophy*, May 25, 2023. https://www.embodiedphilosophy.com/ancient-and-modern-ritual-a-creative-approach-to-working-with-grief-loss-and-change/.

Blair, Leonardo. "Founding Pastors Resign from Cross Timbers Church After Josiah Anthony Scandal." *Christian Post*, August 22, 2024.

Block, Peter. *The Answer to How Is Yes*. San Francisco: Barrett-Kohler, 2003.

Bonhoeffer, Dietrich. *Letters and Papers from Prison*. Chicago: Touchstone, 2011.

———. *Life Together: The Classic Exploration of Christians in Community*. New York: HarperOne, 1978.

Boyles, Brian. "5 Steps for Leading Your Church Through Change." *Insights: Church Life & Ministry*, 2022. https://research.lifeway.com/2022/05/17/5-steps-for-leading-your-church-through-change/.

Bowen Center for The Study of The Family. "Introduction to the Eight Concepts." https://www.thebowencenter.org/introduction-eight-concepts.

Brainerd, C. J., and S. H. Bookbinder. "The Semantics of Emotion in False Memory." *Emotion* 19, no. 1 (2019) 146–59. https://doi.org/10.1037/emo0000431.

Brent, James. "Augustine of Hippo. The Beatitudes: Stages of Christian Development." Catholic Exchange. https://catholicexchange.com/the-beatitudes-stages-of-christian-development/.

Bridges, William. *Managing Transitions: Making the Most of Change*. 25th anniversary ed. Boston: DaCapo Lifelong, 2017.

Briller, Sherylyn, and Andrea Sankar. "The Changing Roles of Ritual in Later Life." *Generations* 35, no. 3 (2011) 6–10.

Broome, Benjamin J. "Reaching Across the Dividing Line: Building a Collective Vision for Peace in Cyprus." *Journal of Peace Research* 41, no. 2 (March 2004) 191–209.

Brubaker, David. *Promise and Peril: Understanding and Managing Change and Conflict in Congregations*. Herndon, VA: Alban, 2009.

Buber, Martin. *I and Thou*. Chicago: Touchstone, 1971.

Buchanan, Mark. *Your God is Too Safe: Rediscovering the Wonder of a God You Can't Control*. Sisters, OR: Multnomah, 2001.

Burrow, Anthony L., and Patrick L. Hill. "Flying the Unfriendly Skies? The Role of Forgiveness and Race in the Experience of Racial Microaggressions." *The Journal of Social Psychology* 152, no. 5 (2012) 639–53. https://doi:10.1080/00224545.2012.686461.

Burton, Tara Isabelle. "A Megachurch Pastor Resigns After Sexual Misconduct Allegations. The Larger Problem Remains." Vox.com, April 13, 2018. https://www.vox.com/identities/2018/4/13/17234606/bill-hybels-willow-creek-resignation-megachurch-pastor-scandal.

Cameron, Kim, and Robert Quinn. *Diagnosing and Changing Organizational Culture*. 3rd ed. San Francisco: Jossey Bass, 2011.

Canadian Medical Association. "What Is Compassion Fatigue?" 2020. https://www.cma.ca/physician-wellness-hub/content/compassion-fatigue-signs-symptoms-and-how-cope.

Capretto, Peter. "Empathy and Silence in Pastoral Care for Traumatic Grief and Loss." *Journal of Religion and Health* 54, no. 1 (June 2015) 339–57. DOI: 10.1007/s10943-014-9904-5.

Carroll, Lewis. *Through the Looking Glass.* Philadelphia: Henry Altemus, 1897.

Carter, Sherrie Bourg. "The Tell-Tale Signs of Burnout . . . Do You Have Them?" *Psychology Today,* 2013. https://www.psychologytoday.com/blog/high-octane-women/201311/the-tell-tale-signs-burnout-do-you-have-them.

———. "Where Do You Fall on the Burnout Continuum?" *Psychology Today,* May 2009. https://www.psychologytoday.com/us/blog/high-octane-women/201205/where-do-you-fall-on-the-burnout-continuum.

Cherry, Kendra. "What Is Transformational Leadership?" Very Well Mind, 2022. https://www.verywellmind.com/what-is-transformational-leadership-2795313.

Churchill, Winston. "We Shall Fight on the Beaches." America's National Churchill Museum. https://www.nationalchurchillmuseum.org/we-shall-fight-on-the-beaches.html.

Ciampa, Dan. "After the Handshake—Succession Doesn't End When A New CEO Is Hired." *Harvard Business Review*, December 2016. https://hbr.org/2016/12/after-the-handshake.

Choi, H. "Feeling One Thing and Doing Another: How Expressions of Guilt and Shame Influence Hypocrisy Judgment." *Behavioral Sciences* 12, no. 12 (2012) 504. https://doi.org/10.3390/bs12120504.

Commodity Futures Trading Commission. "CFTC Charges Washington State Pastor with Fraud, Misappropriation in Multilevel Marketing Scheme Targeting Hispanic Americans." December 10, 2024. https://www.cftc.gov/PressRoom/PressReleases/9015-24.

Cooke, Philip. "The Top Six Risky Habits of Pastors in Trouble." Ministry Watch, 2024. https://ministrywatch.com/the-top-six-risky-habits-of-pastors-in-trouble/.

Cox, William T. L., and Patricia G. Devine. "Stereotyping to Infer Group Membership Creates Plausible Deniability for Prejudice-Based Aggression." *Psychological Science* 25, no. 2 (2013) 340–48. https://doi.org/10.1177/0956797613501171.

CP Staff. "Dallas Pastor Steve Lawson Removed from Ministry over 'Inappropriate Relationship with a Woman,'" *Christian Post,* September 20, 2024. https://www.christianpost.com/news/dallas-pastor-steve-lawson-removed-from-ministry.html.

Crisp-Han, Holly, Glen Gabbard, and Melissa Martinez. "Professional Boundary Violations and Mentalizing in the Clergy." *Journal of Pastoral Care Counselling.* 65, nos. 3–4. (Fall-Winter 2011) 1–11. https://10.1177/154230501106500307. PMID: 22452146.

Daley, Antony E., Jr. "Succession Planning in Organizations: Understanding Organizational Survival Patterns in Nonprofit Organizations." PhD diss., Regent University, 2020.

Dansie, E. J. "A Multigroup Analysis of Reintegrative Shaming Theory: An Application to Drunk Driving Offenses." PhD diss., Utah State University, 2011. 854464331. https://www.proquest.com/dissertations-theses/multigroup-analysis-reintegrative-shaming-theory/docview/854464331/se-2.

Davidson, M. Meghan, Nicole Lozano, Brian Cole, and Sarah Gervais. "Associations Between Women's Experiences of Sexual Violence and Forgiveness." *Violence and Victims* 28, no. 6, 2011. https://doi:10.1891/0886-6708.VV-D-12-00075.

Davis, Joseph. "The Mystery of a Genuine Apology." *Psychology Today*, June 2024. https://www.psychologytoday.com/us/blog/our-new-discontents/202406/the-mystery-of-a-genuine-apology.

Department of Justice. "Former Tri-Cities Pastor Indicted for Multi-Million Dollar Cryptocurrency Scam." January 9, 2025. https://www.justice.gov/usao-edwa/pr/former-tri-cities-pastor-indicted-multi-million-dollar-cryptocurrency-scam.

Diagnostic and Statistical Manual of Mental Disorders 5. Washington, DC: American Psychiatric Association, 2013.

Duckett, Michaela L. "Clergy More Likely to Suffer Depression, Anxiety." *The Charlotte Post*, August 28, 2023.

Dudley, Carl. "Conflict: Synonym for Congregation." *Faith Communities Today*, 2011. https://faithcommunitiestoday.org/conflict-synonym-for-congregation/.

Dudley, Carl, and Nancy Ammerman. *Congregations in Transition: A Guide for Analyzing, Assessing, and Adapting in Changing Communities*. San Francisco: Jossey Bass, 2002.

Elliott, Barbara. "Forgiveness Therapy: A Clinical Intervention for Chronic Disease." *Journal of Religion and Health* 50, no. 2 (June 2011) 240–47.

Enright, Robert. *Forgiveness Is a Choice: A Step-by-Step Process for Resolving Anger and Restoring Hope*. Washington, DC: APA LifeTools, 2011.

Eturralde, Jessica. "Steven Lawson Removed from Mininstry for 'Inappropriate Relationship.'" Ministry Watch, 2024. https://ministrywatch.com/steven-lawson-removed-from-ministry-for-inappropriate-relationship.

Every, K. "Growing Scar Tissue Around the Memory of 'That Day': Sites of Gendered Violence and Suffering in Contemporary South African Literature." *Journal of International Women›s Studies* 17, no. 2 (2016) 30–42. https://www.proquest.com/scholarly-journals/growing-scar-tissue-around-memory-that-day-sites/docview/1777749439/se-2.

Filippova, Elena V., and Tatyana Pivnenko. "Psychological Boundaries Of 'I' In the Role Play of Peer-Unaccepted Children." *Psychology in Russia; Moscow* 7, no. 1 (2014) 62–72. http://psychologyinrussia.com/volumes/pdf/2014_1/2014_1_62-72.Pdf.

Fisher, Roger, and William Ury. *Getting to Yes: Getting to Agreement Without Giving In*. New York: Penguin, 2011.

Flanelly, Kevin, Stephen Roberts, and Andrew Weaver. "Correlates of Compassion Fatigue and Clergy Burnout in Chaplains and Other Clergy Who Responded to the September 11th Attacks in New York City." *Journal of Pastoral Care & Counseling* 59, no. 3 (2005) 213–24.

Gallemard, Jeremy. "The Basics of Knowledge Transfer: A Beginner's Guide." *Smart Tribune*. https://blog.smart-tribune.com/en/knowledge-transfer#one.

Gino, Francesca, and Michael Norton. "Why Rituals Work." *Scientific American*, May 2013. https://www.scientificamerican.com/article/why-rituals-work/.

Glasl, Friedrich. *Confronting Conflict*. Stroud, Gloucestershire, UK: Hawthorn 1998.

Global Leaders Institute for Arts Innovation. "Unlocking Leadership Potential: The Promise of Theory U." https://www.globalleadersinstitute.org/blog-post/unlocking-leadership-potential-the-promise-of-theory-u/.

Gobodo-Madikazela, Pumla. *A Human Being Died That Night: A South African Woman Confronts the Legacy of Apartheid*. Boston: Mariner Books Classics, 2004.

Goffman, Erving. "On Face-Work: An Analysis of Ritual Elements in Social Interaction." *Omran For Social Sciences* 30 (2017) 213–31.

Graves, M., and E. Rechniewski. "From Collective Memory to Transcultural Remembrance." *Portal* 7, no. 1 (2010). https://doi.org/10.5130/portal.v7i1.1534.

Graves-Fitzsimmons, Guthrie, and Maggie Siddiqi. "Christian Nationalism Is 'Single Biggest Threat' to America's Religious Freedom." Center for American Progress, 2022. https://www.americanprogress.org/article/christian-nationalism-is-single-biggest-threat-to-americas-religious-freedom.

Hannon, P. A., J. Finkel, M. Kumashiro, and C. E. Rusbult. "The Soothing Effects of Forgiveness on Victims' and Perpetrators' Blood Pressure." *Personal Relationships* 19, no. 2 (2012) 279–89. https://doi.org/2012. 10.1111/j.1475-6811.2011.01356.x.

Harcek, T. D. "Apology Not Accepted: The Impact of Executive Rhetoric, Communication Strategies, Media Coverage and Time on Crisis Management and Public Perception During Major Oil Spills." PhD diss., Western Michigan University, 2018. https://www.proquest.com/dissertations-theses/apology-not-accepted-impact-executive-rhetoric/docview/2085933471/se-2.

Hartford Institute. "American Congregations 2015: Thriving and Surviving." https://faithcommunitiestoday.org/wp-content/uploads/2019/01/American-Congregations-2015.pdf.

Harvard University. "What Is Integrative Negotiation?" https://www.pon.harvard.edu/tag/integrative-negotiation/.

Hastings, Deborah. "Texas Megachurch Pastor Tony Cammarota Fired After Confessing to 'Moral Failure,' Church Says." *Inside Edition*, July 19, 2024.

Helmick, Raymond, and Rodney Petersen, eds. *Forgiveness and Reconciliation: Religion, Public Policy, and Conflict Transformation*. Philadelphia: Templeton Foundation, 2001.

Hendricks, Thomas. "Shame and Aggression: A Dangerous Combination." *Psychology Today*, April 1, 2022. https://www.psychologytoday.com/us/blog/the-pathways-experience/202204/shame-and-aggression-dangerous-combination.

Henley, William Ernest. "Invictus." 1875. https://worldview.unc.edu/news-article/invictus/.

Hicks, Boniface. "Benedictine Spirituality III, The Ear of Your Heart." 2020. https://www.fatherboniface.org/wordpresshome/spiritual-reflections/benedictine-spirituality-iii-the-ear-of-your-heart/.

Huprich, Steven K., and Sharon Nelson. "Malignant Self-Regard: Accounting for Commonalities in Vulnerably Narcissistic, Depressive, Self-Defeating, And Masochistic Personality Disorders." *Comprehensive Psychiatry* 55, no. 4 (May 2024) 989–98. https://doi:10.1016/j.comppsych.2013.09.017.

Hutchison, Katy. *Walking After Midnight: One Woman's Journey Through Murder, Justice, and Forgiveness*. Oakland, CA: New Harbinger, 2006.

Isaacs, William. *Dialogue and the Art of Thinking Together*. New York: Currency Doubleday, 1999.

Isakov, Alexander; Amelia Holcomb, Luke Glowacki, and Nicholas Christakis. "Modeling the Role of Networks and Individual Differences in Inter-Group Violence." *PLoS One; San Francisco* 11, no. 2 (February 2016) https://journals.plos.org/plosone/article?id=10.1371/journal.pone.0148314.

Jaworski, Joseph, and Claus Otto Scharmer. "Leadership in the New Economy: Sensing and Actualizing Emerging Futures." *The Leadership Laboratory for Competing in the New Economy,* Society for Organizational Learning, 2000. https://www.researchgate.net/figure/Four-Modes-of-Dialogue-from-Scharmer-2000_fig2_241885603.

Jiménez, Marisela. "Leadership Style, Organizational Performance, and Change Through the Lens of Emotional Intelligence." *Foundations of Management* (2018) 237–50. https://doi:10.2478/fman-2018-0018 237.

Johns Hopkins Medicine. "Forgiveness: Your Health Depends on It." https://www.hopkinsmedicine.org/health/wellness-and-prevention/forgiveness-your-health-depends-on-it.

Johnson, Barry. *Polarity Management: Identifying and Managing Unsolvable Problems.* Amherst, MA: HRD, 2014.

Kahler, T. "Drivers: The Key to the Process of Scripts." *Transactional Analysis Bulletin* 5, no. 3 (1975) 280–84. https://doi.org/10.1177/036215377500500318.

Karpmann, Stephen B. "The New Drama Triangles." USATAA/ITAA Conference Lecture, 2007. https://karpmandramatriangle.com/pdf/thenewdramatriangles.pdf.

Kellogg, Carolyn. "Pastor Mark Driscoll's Books Withdrawn from 180 Christian Stores." *Los Angeles Times,* August 13, 2014.

Khaw, Khai Wah, et al. "Reactions Towards Organizational Change: A Systematic Literature Review." *Current Psychology*, April 2022, 1–24. https://link.springer.com/article/10.1007/s12144-022-03070-6.

Koenig, Harold G. "Religion, Spirituality, and Health: The Research and Clinical Implications." 2012. *ISRN Psychiatry*: 278730. //https://onlinelibrary.wiley.com/doi/10.5402/2012/278730.

Koesler, John. "Yes, Charisma Has a Place in the Pulpit." *Christianity Today* 68, no. 24 (May 2024). https://www.christianitytoday.com/magazine/2024/may-june/.

Koesten, Jay, and Robert C. Rowland. "The Rhetoric of Atonement." *Communication Studies* 55, no. 1 (2004) 68–87. https://www.tandfonline.com/doi/abs/10.1080/10510970409388606.

Krause, N., and C. G. Ellison. "Forgiveness by God, Forgiveness of Others, and Psychological Well-Being in Late Life." *Journal for the Scientific Study of Religion* 42, no. 1 (2003) 77–93. https://pubmed.ncbi.nlm.nih.gov/21373377/.

Krejcir, Richard. "Statistics in the Ministry 2025." Pastoral Care, Inc., 2025. https://www.pastoralcareinc.com/statistics/.

Krell, Eric. "Weighing Internal vs. External Hires." *HR Magazine,* January 2015. https://www.shrm.org/hr-today/news/hr-magazine/pages/010215-hiring.aspx.

Lang, K. "Helping Churches Respond to Their Members in Grief by Providing a Grief Recovery Seminar." DMin diss., Biola University, 2012. https://www.proquest.com/dissertations-theses/helping-churches-respond-their-members-grief/docview/1335198783/se-2.

Larcher, David, Charles O'Reilly, Brian Tayan, and Anastasia Zakolyukina. "Are Narcissistic CEO's All That Bad?" Rock Center for Corporate Governance, 2021. https://papers.ssrn.com/sol3/papers.cfm?abstract_id=3937526.

Larcher, David, Stephen A. Miles, and Brian Tayan. "Outgoing CEOs Shouldn't Pick Their Replacements." *CEO Performance & Compensation,* 2018. https://work.boardspan.com/library/articles/outgoing-ceos-shouldn-t-pick-their-replacements?article_id=441.

Lawler, K. A., J. W. Younger, R. L. Piferi, et al. "The Unique Effects of Forgiveness on Health: An Exploration of Pathways." *Journal of Behavioral Medicine* 28 (2005) 157–67. https://pubmed.ncbi.nlm.nih.gov/15957571/.

Lazare, Aaron. *On Apology*. New York: Oxford University Press, 2005.

Lee, S., V. C. Ramenzoni and P. Holme. "Emergence of Collective Memories." *PLoS One* 5, no. 9, 2010. https://journals.plos.org/plosone/article?id=10.1371/journal.pone.0012522.

Lifeway Research. "Greatest Needs of Pastors." January 11, 2022. https://research.lifeway.com/2022/01/11/u-s-pastors-identify-their-greatest-needs/.

———. "Pastors Have Congregational and, for Some, Personal Experience with Mental Illness." 2023. https://research.lifeway.com/2022/08/02/pastors-have-congregational-and-for-some-personal-experience-with-mental-illness/.

Lin, W. F., D. Mack, R. D. Enright, D. Krahn, and T. Baskin. "Effects of Forgiveness Therapy on Anger, Mood, and Vulnerability to Substance Use Among Inpatient Substance-Dependent Clients." *Journal of Consulting and Clinical Psychology* 72, no. 6 (2004) 1114–21. https://doi.org/10.1037/0022-006X.72.6.1114.

López, J. J., M. I. Serrano, I. Giménez, and C. Noriega. "Forgiveness Interventions for Older Adults: A Review." *Journal of Clinical Medicine* 10, no. 9 (2021) 1866. https://www.mdpi.com/2077-0383/10/9/1866.

Marsh, Ann, and Greta Lorge. "How the Truth Gets Twisted." *Stanford Magazine*, 2012. https://stanfordmag.org/contents/how-the-truth-gets-twisted.

Martens, Willem H. J. "Shame and Narcissism: Therapeutic Relevance of Conflicting Dimensions of Excessive Self Esteem, Pride, and Pathological Vulnerable Self." *Annals of the American Psychotherapy Association* 8, no. 4 (Summer 2005) 10–17.

Martin, Michael. "Reinforcing the Foundation of Trust." Evangelical Council for Financial Accountability. https://www.ecfa.org/Content/Reinforcing-the-Foundation-of-Trust.

Mayo Clinic. "Depression (Major Depressive Disorder)." https://www.mayoclinic.org/diseases-conditions/depression/symptoms-causes/syc-20356007.

———. "Personality Disorders." https://www.mayoclinic.org/diseases-conditions/personality-disorders/symptoms-causes/syc-20354463.

———. "Personality Disorders: Symptoms." https://www.mayoclinic.org/diseases-conditions/personality-disorders/symptoms-causes/syc-20354463.

May, Ross W., Marcos Sanchez-Gonzalez, Kristen A. Hawkins, Wayne B. Batchelor, and Frank D. Fincham. "Effect of Anger and Trait Forgiveness on Cardiovascular Risk in Young Adult Females." *American Journal of Cardiology* 114, no. 1 (2012) 47–52. https://pubmed.ncbi.nlm.nih.gov/24819901/.

McFeely, Shane, and Ben Wigert. "This Fixable Problem Costs U.S. Businesses $1 Trillion." Gallup.com, 2019. https://www.gallup.com/workplace/247391/fixable-problem-costs-businesses-trillion.aspx.

McNeal, Reggie. *The Present Future: Six Tough Questions for the Church*. San Francisco: Jossey-Bass, 2009.

Miyirsky, Yehudah. "Teshuvah in Judaism: A Guide to Repentance." Brandeis University, 2021. https://www.brandeis.edu/jewish-experience/holidays-religious-traditions/2021/september/atonement-yom-kippur-mirsky.html.

National Institute on Aging. "Coping with Grief and Loss." https://www.nia.nih.gov/health/grief-and-mourning/coping-grief-and-loss.

NBC News. "Pastor Robert Morris Resigns from Gateway Church After Child Sex Abuse Allegation." June 18, 2024. https://www.nbcnews.com/news/investigations/robert-morris-resigns-gateway-church-child-sex-abuse-allegation-rcna157806.

North, Joanna. "Wrongdoing and Forgiveness." *Philosophy* 62, no. 242 (1987) 499–508.

Nouwen, Henri. *The Wounded Healer.* New York: Image, 1979.

Organick. G. "Non-Apology in the Age of Apology." *The Denning Law Journal* 31, no. 1 (2020) 149–64. https://www.ubplj.org/index.php/dlj/article/view/1793.

Pargament, Kenneth I., and James W. Lomax. "Understanding and Addressing Religion Among People with Mental Illness." *World Psychiatry* 12, no. 1 (February 2013) 26–32. https://pubmed.ncbi.nlm.nih.gov/23471791/.

Pearson, Bethyl. "Power and Politeness in Conversation: Encoding of Face-Threatening Acts at Church Business Meetings." *Anthropological Linguistics* 30, no. 1 (1988) 68–93.

Pearson, Bethyl, and K. Samuel Lee. "Politeness Phenomena in Korean and American Church Business Meetings." *Intercultural Communication Studies* 1, no. 2 (1991) 149–62.

Peck, M. Scott. *The Different Drum: Community Making and Peace.* 2nd ed. New York: Touchstone, 1998.

Postell, Marissa. "Stress Tops Mental Challenges Pastors Face." Lifeway Research, April 26, 2022. https://research.lifeway.com/2022/04/26/stress-tops-mental-challenges-pastors-face/.

Program on Negotiations Staff. "Four Conflict Negotiation Strategies for Resolving Value-Based Disputes." Harvard Negotiations Project, Harvard University. https://www.pon.harvard.edu/daily/dispute-resolution/four-negotiation-strategies-for-resolving-values-based-disputes/.

Puls, Darrell. "Leadership Transitions and Faith Community Conflicts: An Unexplored Territory." *ACResolution Magazine.* Association for Conflict Resolution, April 2018, 21–23.

———. *Let Us Prey: The Plague of Narcissist Pastors and What We Can Do About It.* Rev. ed. Eugene, OR: Cascade, 2020.

———."Narcissistic Pastors and the Making of Narcissistic Churches." *Great Commission Research Journal* 12, no. 1 (2020) 87–112.

———. *The Road Home: A Guided Journey to Church Forgiveness and Reconciliation* Eugene, OR: Cascade, 2013.

———. "Should We Negotiate with Terrorists—A Counterpoint." Mediate.com. https://mediate.com/should-we-negotiate-with-terrorists-a-counterpoint.

Rainer, Sam. "How to Handle a Church Staff Person's Moral Failure." https://churchanswers.com/podcasts/rainer-on-leadership/how-to-handle-a-church-staff-persons-moral-failure/.

Ramani, Subha, Karen D. Könings, Karen V. Mann, Emily E. Pisarski, and Cees P. M. van der Vleuten. "About Politeness, Face, and Feedback: Exploring Resident and Faculty Perceptions of How Institutional Feedback Culture Influences Feedback Practices." *Acad Med* 93, no. 9 (September 2018) 1348–58. https://pubmed.ncbi.nlm.nih.gov/29517523/.

Regina Star. "Justin Bieber's Former Hillsong Pastor Fired For 'Moral Failures.'" https://www.iheart.com/content/2020-11-05-justin-biebers-former-hillsong-pastor-fired-for-moral-failures/.

Rhodes, Kevin. "Why Preachers Fail Morally." Convictions of Honor, January 11, 2024. https://convictionsofhonor.org/why-preachers-fail-morally/.

Ricciardi, Emiliano, Guiseppina Rota, Lorenzo Sani, Claudio Gentili, Ana Gaglianese, Mario Guazzelli, and Pietro Pietrini. "How The Brain Heals Emotional Wounds: The Functional Neuroanatomy of Forgiveness." *Frontiers in Human Neuroscience* 7, no. 839 (2013). https://www.frontiersin.org/journals/human-neuroscience/articles/10.3389/fnhum.2013.00839/full.

Riordan, S. L. "There's No Playbook for This: Exploring Employee Experiences and Emotions During Digital Transformation." PhD diss., The George Washington University, 2023. https://www.proquest.com/dissertations-theses/theres-no-playbook-this-exploring-employee/docview/2730343039/se-2/.

Rohr, Richard. "2022 Daily Meditations: Nothing Stands Alone." Center for Action and Contemplation. https://cac.org/daily-meditations/2022-daily-meditations/.

———. *Everything Belongs: The Gift of Contemplative Prayer.* Chestnut Ridge, PA: Crossroad, 2003.

———. *Falling Upward: A Spirituality for the Two Halves of Life.* San Francisco: Jossey-Bass, 2004.

———. *Quest for the Grail.* Spring Valley, NY: Crossroad, 1994.

Russell, Luke. *Real Forgiveness.* New York: Oxford University Press, 2023.

Salmond, Susan W. "Managing the Human Side of Change." *Orthopaedic Nursing* 17, no. 5 (Sep/Oct) 38–51.

Saiya, N., and S. Manchanda. "Christian Nationalism and Violence Against Religious Minorities in the United States: A Quantitative Analysis." *Journal for the Scientific Study of Religion* 64, no. 1 (2025) 3–18.

Sawchuk, Craig. "What Is Depression? A Mayo Clinic Expert Explains." Mayo Clinic, 2022. https://www.mayoclinic.org/diseases-conditions/depression/symptoms-causes/syc-20356007.har.

Scazerro, Peter. "Pastoral Burnout and Self-Compassion." Emotionally Healthy Discipleship. https://www.emotionallyhealthy.org/author/pete-scazzero/page/79/.

Scharmer, C. Otto. *Theory U: Leading from the Future as it Emerges.* San Francisco: Barrett-Kohler, 2009.

Scott-Kakures, Dion. "Unsettling Questions: Cognitive Dissonance in Self-Deception." *Social Theory and Practice* 35, no. 1 (2009) 73–106.

Senge, Peter, C. Otto Scharmer, Joseph Jaworski, and Betty Sue Flowers. *Presence: An Exploration into Profound Change in People, Organizations, and Society.* New York: Currency Doubleday, 2005.

Shadow, Cyndie. "An Exploration of Knowledge Transfer and Career College Executive Succession Planning." PhD diss., Walden University, 2018.

Shah, Syeda Nadia. "Relationship Between Violence, Empathy, and Aggression." *Peshawar Journal of Psychology and Behavioral Sciences* 1, no. 1 (2016) 73–84. https://doi.org/10.32879/pjpbs.2015.1.1.73-84.

Shellnut, Kate. "Former Mars Hill Elders: Mark Driscoll Is Still 'Unrepentant,' Unfit to Pastor." *Christianity Today,* July 21, 2021. https://www.christianitytoday.com/2021/07/mars-hill-elders-letter-mark-driscoll-pastor-resign-trinity/.

Shonk, Katie. "3 Types of Conflict and How to Address Them." Harvard Law School Program on Negotiation, *Conflict Resolution,* 2023. https://www.pon.harvard.edu/daily/conflict-resolution/types-conflict/.

Simonson, Helen. *Major Pettigrew's Last Stand.* New York: Random House, 2010.

Slocum-Gori, Suzanne, David Hemsworth, Winnie W. Y. Chan, Anna Carson, and Arminee Kazanjian. "Understanding Compassion Satisfaction, Compassion Fatigue and Burnout: A Survey of the Hospice Palliative Care Workforce." *Palliative Medicine* 27, no. 2 (2011) 172–78. https://doi:10.1177/0269216311431311.

St. Cyr, Sylvia. "ECFA Adds New Integrity Standard to Respond to Moral Failings in Ministry." *The Roys Report*, May 27, 2024. https://julieroys.com/ecfa-adds-new-integrity-standard-respond-moral-failings-ministry/.

Staff. "Founder of Harvest Bible Chapel Fired for Misconduct And 'Highly Inappropriate Comments.'" CBS News, 2019. https://www.cbsnews.com/chicago/news/harvest-bible-chapel-pastor-founder-fired-james-macdonald/.

Stone, Douglas, Bruce Patton, and Sheila Heen. *Difficult Conversations: How to Discuss What Matters Most*. New York: Penguin, 2010.

Synergy Services. "What Does Synergy Mean to You?" https://www.synergyservices.org/blog/what-does-synergy-mean-to-you/.

Tavuchis, Nicholas. *Mea Culpa: A Sociology of Apology and Reconciliation*. Redwood City, CA: Stanford University Press, 1993.

Ten Elshof, Greg. *I Told Me So: Self-Deception and the Christian Life*. Grand Rapids: Eerdmans, 2009.

Thomas, Kenneth, and Ralph Kilmann. "Thomas-Kilmann Conflict Mode Instrument." 2009, 2023. https://kilmanndiagnostics.com/overview-thomas-kilmann-conflict-mode-instrument-tki/.

Thompson, Curt. *The Soul of Shame: Retelling the Stories We Tell About Ourselves* Downers Grove, IL: InterVarsity, 2015.

Toussaint, Loren L., Amy D. Owen, and Alyssa Cheadle. "Forgive to Live: Forgiveness, Health, and Longevity." *Journal of Behavioral Medicine* 35, no. 4 (2012) 375–86. https://pubmed.ncbi.nlm.nih.gov/21706213/.

Treasury Board of Canada Secretariat. "Succession Planning and Management: The Five-Step Process." https://www.tbs-sct.canada.ca/gui/spgr/spg-gpgr-02-eng.asp?for=hrps.

Tunajek, Sandra. "Compassion Fatigue: Dealing with an Occupational Hazard." *AANA Journal* 60, no. 1 (2006) 24–26.

Turner, Mason. "The Health Benefits of Forgiveness." https://wa-health.kaiserpermanente.org/forgiveness-health-benefits/.

Tutu, Desmond. *No Future Without Forgiveness*. New York: Image, 2000.

UC Berkeley ExecEd. "The Impacts of Poor Mental Health in Business." https://executive.berkeley.edu/thought-leadership/blog/impacts-poor-mental-health-business.

University of Reading. "Values, Beliefs and Attitudes." https://www.futurelearn.com/info/courses/supporting-learning-secondary/0/steps/58621.

Vasudev, P. M. "Beyond Shareholder Value—A Framework for Stakeholder Governance." Ottawa Faculty of Law Working Paper No. 2021-03, 2020. https://papers.ssrn.com/sol3/papers.cfm?abstract_id=3717968.

Verhezen, Peter. "Giving Voice in a Culture of Silence. From a Culture of Compliance to a Culture of Integrity." *Journal of Business* 96 (2010) 187–206. https://link.springer.com/article/10.1007/s10551-010-0458-5.

Volf, Miroslav. *Exclusion and Embrace: A Theological Exploration of Identity, Otherness, and Reconciliation*. Nashville: Abingdon, 1996.

Walk, Marlene, and Femida Handy. "Job Crafting as Reaction to Organizational Change." *The Journal of Applied Behavioral Science* 54, no. 3 (2018) 349–70. https://journals.sagepub.com/doi/10.1177/0021886318777227.

Walters, Chino L. "Exploring the Absence of Pastors Implementing Effective Succession Strategies in Black Pentecostal Churches." PhD diss., Columbia International University, 2021.

Wasberg, Gregory D. "Differentiation of Self and Leadership Effectiveness in Christian Clergy: A Mixed Methods Study." PhD diss., Capella University, 2013.

Weisbord, Marvin, and Sandra Janoff. *The Future Search: An Action Guide to Finding Common Ground in Organizations & Communities.* San Francisco: Barrett-Koehler, 2000.

White, John, Jr. "Theology of Control: Christian Nationalist Violence and Hostility." *The Journal of the NPS Center for Homeland Defense and Security,* Homeland Security Digital Library. https://www.hsaj.org/articles/22898.

Whited, Matthew C., Amanda L. Wheat, and Kevin T. Larkin. "The Influence of Forgiveness and Apology on Cardiovascular Reactivity and Recovery in Response to Mental Stress." *Journal of Behavioral Medicine* 33, no. 4 (August 2010) 293–304. https://pubmed.ncbi.nlm.nih.gov/20364307/.

William Bridges Associates. "Bridges Transition Model." https://wmbridges.com/about/what-is-transition/.

Witvliet, C. V., K. A. Phipps, M. E. Feldman, and J. C. Beckham. "Posttraumatic Mental and Physical Health Correlates of Forgiveness and Religious Coping in Military Veterans." *Journal of Trauma Stress* 17, no. 3 (June 2004) 269–73. https://pubmed.ncbi.nlm.nih.gov/15253099/.

Wohl, M. J. A., L. DeShea, and R. L. Wahkinney. "Looking Within: Measuring State Self-Forgiveness and Its Relationship to Psychological Well-Being." *Canadian Journal of Behavioral Science* 40, no. 1 (2008) 1–10. https://doi.org/10.1037/0008-400x.40.1.1.1.

Worthington, Everett L., Jr., Charlotte Van Oyen Witvliet, Pietro Pietrini, and Andrea J. Miller. "Forgiveness, Health, and Well-Being: A Review of Evidence for Emotional Versus Decisional Forgiveness, Dispositional Forgivingness, and Reduced Unforgiveness." *Journal of Behavioral Medicine* 30 (2007) 291–302. https://doi.org/10.1007/s10865-007-9105-8.

Yankelovich, Daniel. *The Magic of Dialogue: Transforming Conflict into Cooperation.* New York: Touchstone, 1999.

Young, Joel. "Burnout: What It Is and Why It Matters." *Psychology Today*, December 2022. https://www.psychologytoday.com/us/blog/when-your-adult-child-breaks-your-heart/202212/burnout-what-it-is-and-why-it-matters.

Zhou, Ningning, Yicheng Wei, Clare Killikelly, Xin Xu, Eva M. Stelzer, Andreas Maercker, Juzhe Xi, and Kirsten V. Smith. "The Relationship Between Social Acknowledgment and Prolonged Grief Symptoms: A Multiple Mediation Effect of Beliefs About the Goodness and Controllability of Grief-Related Emotions." *European Journal of Psychotraumatology* 14, no. 2, 2023. https://doi.org/10.1080/20008066.2023.2220633.

Zimmerman, Mark. "Overview of Personality Disorders." *Merck Manual Professional Version,*2023.https://www.merckmanuals.com/professional/psychiatric-disorders/personality-disorders/overview-of-personality-disorders.

www.ingramcontent.com/pod-product-compliance
Lightning Source LLC
LaVergne TN
LVHW100526110826
845146LV00002B/796

* 9 7 9 8 3 8 5 2 4 6 1 1 3 *